Japanese multinationals

Japanese multinationals

Strategies and management in the global kaisha

Edited by
Nigel Campbell and Fred Burton

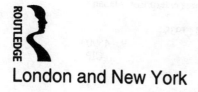

London and New York

First published in 1994
by Routledge
11 New Fetter Lane, London EC4P 4EE

Simultaneously published in the USA and Canada
by Routledge
29 West 35th Street, New York, NY 10001

© 1994 Nigel Campbell and Fred Burton

Typeset in Times by
NWL Editorial Services, Langport, Somerset

Printed and bound in Great Britain by
Mackays of Chatham PLC, Chatham, Kent

British Library Cataloguing in Publication Data

A catalogue record for this book is available from the British
Library

Library of Congress Cataloging in Publication Data
Japanese multinationals: strategies and management in the global
   kaisha / edited by Nigel Campbell and Fred Burton.
       p. cm.
     1. Industrial management – Japan.   2. Strategic alliances
(Business) – Japan.   3. Corporations, Japanese –
Management.   4. International business enterprises – Japan –
Management.
   I. Campbell, Nigel.   II. Burton, Fred., 1938– .
   HD70.J3J3943 1994   93–45900
   338.8′8952 – dc20   CIP

ISBN 0–415–09607–3

Contents

Figures

Tables

Contributors

Schon Beechler is Assistant Professor of Management and International Management at the Graduate School of Business, Columbia University. Dr Beechler received her Ph.D. in Business Administration and Sociology from the University of Michigan and her B.A. in Sociology and Anthropology from Oberlin College. Dr Beechler was the recipient of the Fulbright Research Fellowship in Tokyo, Japan, from 1986 to 1988. She has conducted research on the management and strategies of Japanese affiliates in South-east Asia and Europe and is currently researching management practices at Japanese, other Asian and American affiliates in Mexico and in eight countries in South-east and East Asia.

M. Bensaou is Assistant Professor at INSEAD, Fontainebleau, France. He holds graduate degrees in civil and mechanical engineering from France's 'Grandes Ecoles', an M.A. in Management Science from Hitotsubashi University, Tokyo, and a Ph.D. in Management from the Massachusetts Institute of Technology. His current research interests, in the area of networks of organizations, focus on the management of interfirm relationships, information exchange and the role/impact of information technology within networks. He addresses these issues from an international perspective, with a regional focus on Japan. Professor Bensaou's current work focuses on buyer–supplier co-ordination strategies in the US and Japanese automotive industries.

Allan Bird is Assistant Professor of Management and International Business at the Stern School of Business, New York University, and Visiting Professor at the Graduate School of Business, Columbia University. Dr Bird received his Ph.D. in Organizational Studies from the University of Oregon. He received his B.A. in Asian Studies from California State University, Fresno, and his M.A. in Comparative Studies from Sophia University in Tokyo, Japan. Dr Bird was the recipient of a Fulbright Research Fellowship in 1987 and an NEC Faculty Fellowship in 1990. His research interests include Japanese human resource management practices in foreign affiliates and Japanese top management.

Fred Burton is Senior Lecturer in International Business in the School of Management, University of Manchester Institute of Science and Technology (UMIST). He has acted as consultant to multinational companies and international organizations, including the United Nations Development Programme and the European Foundation for Management Development. He has published widely in international management and economics journals.

David Cairncross is a lecturer at Imperial College of Science, Technology and Medicine, London, where since 1989 he has been associate director of the Japan-Europe Industry Research Centre and is now a member of the Management School. From 1986 to 1989 he was on the staff of the Science University of Tokyo; prior to that he was for ten years an officer of the House of Commons, where he worked on the staffs of the parliamentary committees on foreign affairs and science and technology.

Nigel Campbell is the Director of the Greater Manchester Centre for Japanese Studies and a Senior Lecturer at Manchester Business School.

Vagelis (Evagelos) Dedoussis is a graduate of the University of Athens (Greece), Waseda University (Japan), Asia University (Japan) and Griffith University (Australia). He has worked for a number of foreign and Japanese companies during his long stay in Japan. He also spent several years in Australia researching management practices in Japanese subsidiaries. He has contributed articles on Japanese management to both Japanese and English language journals. Currently he is Assistant Professor at the Department of Management and Marketing, King Fahd University, Saudi Arabia.

Daniel Dirks received a degree (Dipl. oec.) in Economics and Business Administration from Witten/Herdecke University, Germany's first private university. He currently holds a position at the Takeda Institute for Organizational Theory and Organizational Development at Witten/Herdecke; he is a member of the founding committee for a Japanese–German university in Yamagata prefecture. His research interests include international management, Japanese management systems, organizational development and management education.

Ronald Dore, Professor in the Centre for Economic Performance, London School of Economics, has made a lifetime study of Japanese society. He has taught at London University (LSE and SOAS), Sussex, British Columbia, Harvard and the Massachusetts Institute of Technology. His books include *British Factory, Japanese Factory* (California University Press, 1973 and 1991); *Flexible Rigidities* (Athlone and Stanford University Press, 1987) and *Taking Japan Seriously* (Athlone and Stanford University Press, 1988).

Hiroyuki Itami is Professor of Management in the Department of Commerce of Hitosubashi University. His current research interests are in corporate strategy, the economic analysis of internal organization and management control. He is the author of *Mobilizing Invisible Assets*, published by Harvard University Press in 1987, and numerous articles in English and Japanese. He has also worked as a consultant for Matsushita, the Ford Foundation, Nomura Securities and other international firms.

Naoto Iwasaki is an Assistant Professor of International Management at Obirin University, Kanagawa-Prefecture. Currently he is directing comparative studies of innovation and corporate networking behaviour. He has published articles on this topic in several academic journals and looks forward to other international experiences.

Tadao Kagono is Professor of Business Administration at the School of Business Administration, University of Kobe. He has written extensively on Japanese multinationals and consults actively with many international companies.

Corrado Molteni is teaching Comparative Economic Systems (Japanese Economy) at Bocconi University in Milan. He is responsible for the Japanese Section of the Institute of Economic and Social Studies for East Asia, Bocconi University. He studied at the Graduate School of Hitotsubashi University, where he obtained a Ph.D. in Social Studies in 1986.

Vladimir Pucik is Associate Professor at The Center of Advanced Human Resource Studies at the Industrial and Labour Relations School, Cornell University. He was born in Prague, Czechoslovakia, where he studied international economics, law and political science. Later, he received a master's degree in international affairs – specializing in East Asia – and a Ph.D. in business administration from Columbia University. Before joining Cornell University, Dr Pucik was a faculty member at the School of Business, University of Michigan, and spent three years as a visiting scholar at Keio and Hitotsubashi University in Tokyo. His research interests include management practices in global firms, transnational human resource policies, strategic alliance strategies and comparative management with an emphasis on Japan. He has published extensively in academic and professional journals, as well as contributing to a number of books and monographs in the area of international business and personnel management.

Frank-Juergen Richter is an Assistant Researcher of the Graduate School of Systems Management, Tsukuba University, Tokyo. He studied mechanical engineering and business administration in Germany, his native country, as well as in Mexico and France. In his doctoral thesis which he is currently about to complete he analyses strategic alliances between European and Japanese firms.

Freddy Saelens has an engineering degree from the University of Louvain and a masters and a doctorate from the School of Management, University of Manchester Institute of Science and Technology (UMIST). He has worked for a number of years in the corporate planning and strategy department of a major multinational and has published widely on Japanese business. He is Visiting Professor at the Brussels Campus of the University of Boston.

Roger Strange is Senior Lecturer in Economics and Head of the Management Centre at King's College London, University of London. He has been Visiting Professor at the Institute of Social and Economic Studies, Osaka University, Japan and at the Department of International Economics, Nankai University, China. He is the author of *Japanese Manufacturing Investment in Europe: its Impact on the UK Economy* (1993) and co-author of *British Manufacturing Investment Overseas* (1985) and *Statistical Sources of the United Kingdom: the Food Industries* (1992).

Noriya Sumihara is currently an Assistant Professor of Anthropology at Tenri University, Nara, Japan. He graduated from Kobe University, Japan, in 1981, and received his M.A. in Anthropology at New York

University in 1984. He received his Master of Philosophy in 1987 and Ph.D. in Anthropology at New York University in 1992. He specializes in urban anthropology and the anthropology of work.

Tohru Takai is a Doctoral Candidate of International Management at Waseda University, Tokyo. He is an expert in the areas of international strategy and management, formation and implementation of strategic alliances and strategies for corporate planning processes. He has written and advised widely in these subject areas.

Sully Taylor is Assistant Professor of International Management at the School of Business Administration, Portland State University. Dr Taylor received her Ph.D. in Business Administration from the University of Washington, and her B.A. in Latin-American History from Southern Methodist University. Dr Taylor conducted her dissertation research on research and development management in Japan as a Fulbright Research Fellow in 1988. She has conducted research on international human resource management systems in multinational corporations operating in Mexico, Europe and the USA, and also conducts research on the transfer of Japanese management abroad.

Yoshiya Teramoto is Professor at the Graduate School of Systems Management, Tsukuba University, Tokyo. His current research interests are in interfirm relationships, organizational learning and industrial evolution. He also works on consulting programmes for huge Japanese companies. He has held several university and research institute positions in Japan as well as in England.

Yukihiro Wakuta is a Doctoral Candidate of Business Administration at Keio University, Tokyo. He has done research on the organization and management of industrial enterprises, information technology industries and corporate networks. He has taken part in international comparisons covering the subjects mentioned, with specific respect to the utilization of new technology.

Chapter 1

Introduction

Nigel Campbell

Little space is needed in this introduction for another litany of the achievements of Japanese multinationals. Rather, it is as well to remember that the international expansion of Japanese companies is still very recent. Despite well-known successes in the automobile and electronic industries, in many other manufacturing industries (aerospace, apparel, furniture, pharmaceuticals etc.) and in services Japanese companies do not hold many leading positions. Even in motor vehicles and parts, and restricting the analysis to companies in the *Fortune* 500, Japanese companies account for only 31 per cent of the sales.[1] The importance of Japanese multinationals is not only in their emerging position in the global economy, but also in the fact that they come from a country with a different business system.

The opening chapter by Professor Ronald Dore takes up this theme by asking whether Japanese or Anglo-Saxon capitalism will win out in the long run. In Anglo-Saxon economies prevailing norms and institutions encourage individuals and organizations to keep their options open. By contrast, commitment is preferred in Japan and this encourages long-term investment and leads to a different pattern of employee motivation.

Keeping options open is the heritage of the Anglo-Saxon fascination with the ability of well-functioning markets to allocate resources efficiently. Unfortunately this focus on market mechanisms frequently limits understanding of other important kinds of efficiencies, which are especially well-developed in Japan. These are concerned with the co-ordination and co-operation necessary to produce and develop reliable products quickly.

Co-ordination between economic actors in the two systems is different – one tends to favour an arm's-length relationship, while the other is more based on trust and mutual obligation. This is what makes the study of Japanese multinationals particularly interesting. As they expand out of their home base how do Japanese multinationals reconcile the conflicting pressures to introduce the systems they use at home or to adjust to local requirements? This management task is a subset of the general problem of reconciling the demands of global integration with local responsiveness. However, much of the literature in this area has been concerned with the extent to which production and product development should be centralized or dispersed.

The papers in this volume are more concerned with what happens when Japanese multinationals have to manage a Western workforce. To what extent can Western firms transfer and apply Japanese practices? What happens in joint ventures and strategic alliances, when the two approaches interact closely? Most of the papers are based on recent empirical work which has not been reported elsewhere. This overview of the volume starts with a forecast of great expansion in Japan's overseas business, derived from the papers by Itami and Strange. The next section discusses the role of alliances with Western firms in the strategies of Japanese multinationals. The papers by Burton and Saelens, Teramoto *et al.*, and Molteni lead to the conclusion that Japanese partners are skilful at gaining benefits from their alliances and that Western partners need to do more to avoid being left in weaker competitive positions. Partnerships between Japanese multinationals and university research departments are now also emerging as explained in the paper by Cairncross. This is also leading to anxiety about the loss of scientific talent. The final section covers the papers by Beechler and Bird, Beechler and Taylor, Dedoussis, Pucik, Sumihara, Dirks and Bensaou. It describes the practices being used by Japanese multinationals overseas and the problems which result.

FUTURE GROWTH IN JAPAN'S OVERSEAS BUSINESS

The clash between Japanese and Anglo-Saxon capitalism has already led to trade friction and has raised fears of Japanese domination on both sides of the Atlantic. As the paper by Itami points out this is despite Japan's low ratio of overseas to domestic production. At only 5 per cent, compared with Germany's non-EC ratio of 10 per cent and America's 15 per cent, Japan's ratio could increase greatly. Japan's overseas production could even double in the next decade, causing overseas employment to grow from 1 million to 2 million. This could lead to further trade friction and more active lobbying by threatened businessmen.

Despite the friction which Japanese trade and investment has produced it seems unlikely that Western governments will restrict Japanese inward investment. The analysis by Strange leads to the conclusion that Japanese investment has had a major impact on the UK economy, which has gained employment and output (especially exports). Further gains, which his analysis does not take account of, arise from the diffusion of Japanese management methods into other parts of the economy.

STRATEGIC ALLIANCES AND THE TRANSFER OF TECHNOLOGY

Several papers explore the issue of strategic alliances between Japanese and Western firms. Historically, Japan acquired Western technology through licensing and through strategic alliances, such as those between Toshiba and Western Electric, Siemens and Fuji Electric, and Hitachi and RCA. These early joint ventures focused on the import of technology.

The paper by Burton and Saelens, based on a database of over 200 Japanese strategic alliances in the electronics industry, finds that the import of technology remains an important strategic objective for many Japanese alliance partners. Frequently, the Japanese side also uses the alliance to penetrate an overseas market. In general, Burton and Saelens find that Japanese companies give a higher priority to strategic alliances than Western partners and they foresee continued domination of the alliances by the Japanese side to the detriment of the Western partner.

Teramoto *et al.* are also concerned, in their paper, about the unbalanced nature of strategic alliances between Japanese and Western partners. They ascribe this to Japanese partners having a better understanding of how to internalize knowledge gained from an alliance partner, diffuse it throughout the organization and finally use it to create new knowledge. They would like to see Japanese companies demonstrating more concern for a mutual exchange of knowledge rather than the present one-way extraction.

The benefits of a mutual exchange of knowledge are illustrated in the paper by Molteni which reports research on Japanese joint ventures in Italy. The successful ones are where each partner makes a contribution to the acquisition and development of complementary resources.

A similar concern about the exploitation of Western science was found by Cairncross in his research on Japanese research and development (R&D) centres in the UK. One reason why Japanese companies establish independent R&D centres in the UK is in order to get close to the science base and benefit from the creativity of British scientists. Some observers feel concerned that, if the resulting discoveries are then put into production outside Britain, the UK loses, as compared with the same scientists being employed by a British firm.

ORGANIZATION STRUCTURE

The paper by Kagono and Campbell makes the paradoxical claim that, despite the obligational nature of relationships, Japanese multinationals in the electronics sector make more use of market mechanisms to co-ordinate between sister units than Western firms. This arises because of the Japanese preference for keeping production and sales divisions as separate profit centres.

Production divisions are usually organized around technologies or products, whereas sales divisions handle a range of products suitable for a particular customer group. In Japan domestic sales divisions frequently work through regional sales branches. Overseas there is usually a sales company in each country. Relationships between production and sales are handled by negotiation.

Formal negotiations take place twice a year when sales and production divisions meet to agree quantities and prices for the next six-month period. These negotiations take place in Japan in Japanese and hence few non-Japanese can participate.

MANAGEMENT PRACTICE OVERSEAS

Japanese management is of interest because of the belief, widely held by academics and managers, that Japanese practices are a superior way of management and work organization. Many Western corporations have begun to adopt systems and practices associated with Japanese management. Hence there is a considerable interest in the transfer and application of Japanese management to other countries. It is fortunate that in this volume there are several empirical papers which bear directly on these issues.

Dedoussis has carried out research with eight Japanese manufacturing subsidiaries in Australia. His work provides an important new perspective for research on the human resources management (HRM) practices of Japanese overseas subsidiaries. First he points out the differences between the conditions which apply to core employees in the large firms in Japan and the conditions which apply to overseas employees. Core workers in Japan have security of employment, seniority-based remuneration, structured career paths, large biannual bonuses, substantial welfare benefits and involvement in decision making. In most overseas subsidiaries such conditions do not apply.

Second, although we do find group work, job rotation, internal training, loose demarcations and a limited amount of company welfare in overseas subsidiaries these tend to be in the larger subsidiaries and where there are a substantial number of blue-collar workers. In other words size and industry sector have an importance influence on the adoption of Japanese practices. Small units frequently cannot afford to introduce certain approaches, and in many service businesses, like banks and trading companies, locals are hired to perform specific jobs and would not benefit from practices designed for generalists.

Thus, much of the research concerned with the extent to which the practices that apply to core workers in large Japanese corporations are replicated for local employees overseas, is misplaced. Dedoussis believes that a comparison between the treatment of core workers in Japan and the treatment of local workers overseas is inappropriate. Rather, the treatment of local workers overseas is similar to the treatment of peripheral workers (non-core employees in the main company and employees in subsidiaries, affiliates and subcontractors) in Japan.

What he found in Australia was that local workers overseas are treated differently from the expatriates – they are not subject to the same recruitment, training, appraisal, promotion, development and reward schemes. In other words the dichotomy between core and peripheral workers in Japan extends overseas. Expatriates seconded overseas are core workers, while everyone else is in the peripheral category. This view of the overseas operations of Japanese multinationals fits in well with the concept of the Japanese firm as dually controlled, i.e. controlled by owners and employees.

Beechler and her colleagues are also interested in understanding how Japanese multinationals are managing their local workforces. Like Dedoussis they do not believe that Japanese companies follow a single common approach. The paper by Beechler and Bird demonstrates this via a survey of the HRM practices of 64 American subsidiaries (both manufacturing and service) of Japanese multinationals. The authors use a framework which distinguishes between three HRM strategies. An Accumulator strategy is based on maximum employee involvement and skilled execution of tasks; a Facilitator strategy recruits self-motivated personnel and encourages and supports them to develop, on their own, the skills and knowledge which they believe are important; finally, a Utilizer strategy is predicated on minimal employee commitment and high skill utilization. The Accumulator strategy exhibits strong parallels with accepted conceptions of Japanese HRM practices.

Of the 64 subsidiaries surveyed only nine were pursuing a Utilizer strategy compared with 28 using an Accumulator strategy and 27 using a Facilitator strategy. Thus it is clear that Japanese multinationals do not all use the same policies. A substantial number of companies recognize the importance of retaining and developing employees by providing incentives which allow for more individual freedom. The research also points to the adoption of a number of HRM practices simply because of the need to conform to government regulations.

The extent to which HRM practices conform to the demands of the external environment was also researched by Beechler and Taylor in their work on Mexican maquiladoras (in-bond assembly plants located inside Mexico). They collected data from four American and four Japanese firms and found that the Japanese firms were more likely to try to impose their parent company HRM practices. This was particularly true when the Japanese thought that their HRM practice represented a significant competitive advantage. Even after 11 years one Japanese maquiladora was still trying to implement Japanese policies and practices.

The most successful maquiladora was a Japanese firm which had developed a hybrid approach combining elements of the parent company's system with elements of a purely local nature. Sumihara's paper gives a detailed account of the development of a hybrid compensation system in the New York sales subsidiary of a Japanese company. Whereas Dedoussis implies a rather top-down approach to the choice of local practices, Sumihara proposes that they evolve as a result of interaction between the Japanese and the local culture.

The paper by Bensaou also deals with the evolution of a hybrid system, but in this case it is a hybrid evolving as a result of the attempt by American car manufacturers to introduce the Japanese system of supplier relations. Based on empirical findings from a cross-sectional study of supplier relationships in Japan and America, Bensaou found that the American car companies had adopted some of the Japanese co-ordination mechanisms but had not convinced their suppliers that the relationship was now one of trust and mutual obligation.

A more comprehensive assessment of the relationship between localization and performance is reported in the paper by Pucik. His study was based on extensive field interviews and a survey of the top local executives in 32 Japanese subsidiaries in the USA. The results show that key performance measures (market share, profitability and satisfaction of executives) are strongly associated with giving more authority to local managers. Local managers like to be involved in key decisions and where they are involved the performance of the subsidiary is likely to be better.

These results lead Pucik to conclude that Japanese multinationals need to take steps to make their local managers part of the global decision making. Using the terminology of Dedoussis local managers need to become core employees. They need to be given careers rather than just jobs. They will need to spend time at head office and learn the Japanese language. This will be a formidable task and will require substantial investments in training and development.

One way to start the education process will be to improve communication and understanding between Japanese and local managers in overseas subsidiaries. Dirks' paper suggests that integration requires tackling cultural differences between Japanese and local managers by enhancing the role of 'interfaces' and by using problem-solving approaches to tackle the differences.

In short, there is great variety in the management practices used by Japanese multinationals overseas. They vary depending on the size of the subsidiary and the nature of its workforce (all white-collar as in banks and trading houses or preponderantly blue-collar as in manufacturing companies). However, most subsidiaries, and especially manufacturing ones, contain some elements from Japanese practice. According to Dedoussis these will be chosen in a top-down fashion to yield cost and efficiency benefits and preserve the privileges of the core employees. While this may be true in some cases in others the observed practices will result from a complex series of interactions between head office, the expatriates and local managers.

CONCLUSION

The evidence from this volume is that Japanese multinationals are still at an early stage in evolving their management strategies. Most are still finding out how to manage overseas workers. If Dedoussis is right, the core Japanese employees will resist incorporating locals into the core group and therefore fundamental changes will take place very slowly. On the other hand, Pucik's evidence is that improved performance comes from giving locals a greater say in key decisions. He suggests that Japanese multinationals will be forced to accept non-Japanese as core employees if they are to continue to compete successfully. To do this they may have to change their cherished domestic systems and modify them to fit better the needs of non-Japanese.

Different companies will adopt different solutions as is already evident from the empirical research on management practices overseas. Some will preserve the dichotomy between Japanese and local managers, while others will reduce the distinctions and seek ways to modify head office so that non-Japanese can more easily participate in its deliberations.

The pace of change will be slow. Japanese capitalism will continue to flourish in Japan. Outside Japan management systems with hybrid characteristics are emerging, both in Japanese subsidiaries and in Western firms. So far these hybrid characteristics are restricted to management approaches and work organization. A wider dispersion of such hybrid systems can be expected in the future. In time the success of these hybrid systems could influence other areas, such as the institutional mechanisms for financing industry and the values extolled by the education system. A debate has started and the future could be a hybrid of Japanese and Anglo-Saxon capitalism rather than the domination of one system.

NOTE

1 *Fortune* 500, 27 February 1992: pp. 51–198.

Chapter 2

Japanese capitalism, Anglo-Saxon capitalism
How will the Darwinian contest turn out?

Ronald Dore

ABSTRACT

Economic organization and economic behaviour in Japan – notably the employment relation, trading relations between business firms and the financing of industrial enterprise – are sufficiently different from prevailing patterns in the UK and the USA for it to be reasonable to speak of different *types* of capitalism. If it is assumed that globalization will lead to institutional convergence in the long run, which type will predominate in the resultant world form? The Anglo-Saxon one which conforms to the prescriptions of neoclassical economics and maximizes factor mobility, or the Japanese one which apparently prospers by ignoring neoclassical recipes for allocative efficiency and concentrates, instead, on other kinds of efficiency? This paper suggests some factors which have to be taken into account in searching for an answer, but hesitates to give one.

INTRODUCTION

Perhaps I should begin by apologizing for the rather sensational title. The only merit it has is to encapsulate my two main – and perhaps somewhat controversial – assertions and my consequent question. The first assertion is that Japanese capitalism differs sufficiently from the world's current dominant form of capitalism – American capitalism – in ways which are sufficiently important for one to talk of different *types* of capitalism. The second is that the integration of the world economy and the globalization of markets seem to be proceeding at such a pace that the harmonization of hitherto differing domestic economic institutions would seem to be inevitable in the long run. The question, then, is: which set of institutions – the Japanese or the American – is going to be the more influential in determining the shape of the eventual world model?

CAPITALISM IS CAPITALISM IS CAPITALISM?

Different kinds of capitalism? From both ends of the ideological spectrum Marxists and neoclassical economists would reject the idea out of hand. Marxists allow for certain *stages* in the development of capitalism – industrial capitalism, finance capitalism etc. – and would acknowledge that different countries could well differ, having reached different stages in their evolution, but that evolution unfolds according to *universal* laws. Neoclassical economists also have universal laws – they are interested in showing how an economy with a given endowment of resources would tend towards its one unique efficiency-maximizing equilibrium if only people were rational and markets perfectly competitive. Real economies, in so far as they are interested in them, are seen as differing from each other in a single dimension – how perfectly or imperfectly they approximate that theoretical ideal.

But practical men who deal with the real world and its problems have begun in recent years for the first time to talk of different kinds of capitalism. The rapid growth of Japan's and the decline of America's share in world markets is a major reason. Words like 'national competitiveness', 'national economic performance', words which were hardly heard a couple of decades ago, have come to replace 'full employment' or 'demand stimulation' in the policy debates. The USA–Japan bilateral trade gap, the bitterness of trade frictions, have led Americans in particular to seek explanations of the two countries' relative performance in arguments that 'Japan is different'. This has caused alarm in Japan because the people who have made the running in these debates are the so-called 'revisionists'. They challenge what they like to refer to as the Chrysanthemum Club view of Japan; the sister liberal democracy across the Pacific, linked to the USA by indissoluble bonds of friendship and common interest; 'the most important bilateral relationship in the world, bar none'.[1] Their argument – sometimes implicit, sometimes explicit – is that Japan as a society is organized on different value principles from the USA; there is no way that fair competition betweeen them is possible, and protectionism against Japan would therefore be justified.

It is the prevalence of such arguments, and the alarm they cause in Japan, which explains why one will nowhere find such stout defenders of the view that capitalism is one and indivisible than among Japanese neoclassical economists.

But in Europe, multiple capitalisms theory – let us call it MCT – stems from rather different roots. There have long since been attempts to chart empirically the differences in economic structures among European economies; a notable landmark being the publication of Shonfield's *Modern Capitalism* (note the singular) in 1965. Most such discussions have 'placed' economies within that spectrum of difference which has dominated the central ideological debate (reflecting, in turn, the central USA–USSR power struggle) of the second half of the twentieth century – that summed up in the 'plan versus market' dichotomy. The debates in the 1980s concerning 'industrial policy' have also largely been framed within that context, producing the paradox that it has been the left (predisposed to give a greater role to the state) which has been most nationalist, and the right which has produced the proponents of free trade internationalism.

Still, by and large, 'plan versus market' is the only dimension in which national differences are counted. National differences – see all the debate about Russia and Eastern Europe – are still habitually summarized in terms of *real* (i.e. market) capitalism and not-capitalism.

But the perception that there are other dimensions of difference has grown in the last five years – and has been enhanced, on the one hand by the problems of integration in Europe, and on the other by the structural impediments initiative – the last desperate effort of American trade negotiators, having run through all the tariff arguments and the non-tariff-barrier arguments, to find some new ground (this time, fundamental differences in economic structure and behaviour) for arguing that the Japanese were getting their trade surplus by unfair, or at least unvirtuous, means. One central theme, spelt out by Zysman in the early 1980s, has been the importance of differences in the way industry is financed (Zysman 1983).

Recently, in Europe at least, a new fillip has been given to the debate by a book published by Michel Albert, a former French planner, now President of a major French insurance company (Albert 1991). He describes the contrast – and, indeed, conflict – between what he calls Anglo-Saxon capitalism, most purely exemplified in the USA, and 'Rhenish capitalism'. The latter is most purely exemplified in German 'social market' capitalism associated not with the old Prussia but with the Rhine towns of Bonn and Bad Godesburg – the town in which the German SPD proclaimed its acceptance of capitalism as the system to work within. Sometimes he also calls it 'Alpine capitalism' – embracing Switzerland and, somehow (mountainous, after all), Sweden, with occasional references to Japan (Mount Fuji being the end of the Alpine range!). The Japan connection leads to yet another name for the non-Anglo-Saxon alternative; 'capitalisme germano-nippone'.

The two major dimensions on which he differentiates the two models are as follows. First, the operation of financial markets, the way industry is financed and the implications the chosen mechanisms have for the relative dominance in the economy of financial and industrial interests. And second, the extent to which economic institutions permit and encourage the free play of individual profit-maximizing behaviour, or alternatively curb the pursuit of profit in order to share benefits more evenly between the able and the not so able, the lucky and the unlucky.

A DIFFERENT FORM OF CAPITALISM?

I shall be concerned with a somewhat narrower range – not of issues, but of international comparison – in this paper; specifically with Japan on the one hand and what I am happy to follow Michel Albert in calling 'Anglo-Saxon capitalism' on the other. All too often, Japanese, reacting to assertions that Japanese capitalism is 'different', take the USA as their comparator, and in doing so *assume* that the USA is representative of the rest of the world. 'Different', they take it, means 'different from the rest of the world'. But by no means. One can even argue that on a world scale it is the Anglo-Saxons who are the outliers. The 'world standards = USA standards' assumption simply reflects the fact that the Anglo-Saxon economies are – ideologically, if not in terms of purchasing power – the dominant ones.

So my first task is to explain what I mean when I say that Japanese capitalism is significantly different from Anglo-Saxon capitalism, as it is exemplified in Britain and the USA.

To be sure, an astute Martian, trying to reconstruct the nature of our societies after they became extinct and having only the books of legal statutes to go on, might conclude that any differences between Japan and the USA were quite marginal. The laws of property and contract, corporation law, bankruptcy provisions and labour law are all quite similar.

Very similar, but not identical. There are, to begin with, subtle differences in the laws themselves; e.g. anti-trust provisions, the relative priority claims of employees and other creditors in bankruptcy proceedings and so on. But more important are the differences in what the law does *not* prescribe: *how* people go about making contracts; what are considered the social preconditions for doing business with people; what you decide to spell out in contracts and what you do not, how far you have recourse to legal proceedings to enforce contracts and so on. Or, to take another area of difference – the actual distribution of ownership rights and the conventions established in society governing the relative power of owners and managers; the sources of finance; the distribution in practice between labour and capital – or rather the distribution as among wages for employees, interest and dividends for the providers of capital and investment in the future of the firm.

Let me enlarge on these differences under five headings.

1 Personnel practices, as management experts would put it; 'the nature of the labour market' in economists' terms; 'the nature of the implicit labour contract' in the jargon of the lawyer.
2 The social perception of the enterprise.
3 The character of interfirm transactions.
4 Inter-competitor co-operation/collusion.
5 The role of government as creative umpire.

EMPLOYMENT PRACTICES

There are several general ways of characterizing the general character of the Japanese system – that it is organization oriented rather than market oriented; that it extends to all workers conditions of service enjoyed only by privileged managerial workers in the American or British system; and that it extends to private businesses patterns of employment which, even for managerial workers, are found only in the civil service, the police and the army. In practice this means the following.

The convention of lifetime employment

All firms prefer to recruit, and the large firms succeed in recruiting, the majority of their workers – and especially that 30 per cent of the labour force who are university graduate workers – right at the beginning of their careers and to keep them for the rest of their working life. People are sought, not for their trained ability to do certain jobs, but for their general ability – their likely capacity to learn to do a variety of jobs over the course of a working lifetime.

The emergence of a unique ability-grading educational system

Precisely because employers are looking for 'general ability' and because most personnel managers consider the intellectual dimension of that general ability to be reasonably well measured by school achievement, the educational system has become an ability-labelling system to a degree of refinement rarely found elsewhere. This is not simply a rough elite/non-elite grading of institutions as is found in Britain. University faculties are graded according to the difficulty of their entrance examinations as measured by a common scale (a scale evolved by the commercial manufacturers of practice mock tests). This strongly reinforces the lifetime employment system. It means that the top corporations can be sure they are getting the top people. It also means that the graduate of a fourth-rate university is likely to stay with a fourth-rate firm, because he is unlikely to better himself by moving; if he could not, with his record, make it into a third-rate firm at the start of his career, he is even less likely to do so later.

Employee management

Boards of directors are the top employees in a bureaucratic hierarchy. Appointment to the board is the last stage of the career of the high-flyer manager who has moved slightly ahead of his entry cohort at each previous stage. It occurs only within a fairly narrow age span; usually the early fifties. There is only minimal importation of outsiders onto boards, and they are usually appointed to represent the interests not so much of shareholders in general as of, say, the company's lead bank, its major supplier or distributor, a company with whom the firm has a major joint venture etc.

A highly predictable promotion pattern

As is just suggested, apropos directors, promotion up the corporate hierarchy for (generalist) managers (and, similarly, up the supervisory ranks for manual workers) occurs within relatively predictable seniority constraints. It is work performance which determines who gets ahead fastest, but the margin of advantage is limited by seniority. Typically it might be, for example, that of an intake aged 22–24, only the most able 10 per cent get promoted to the rank of section chief by the age of 33. Then, at the next level, perhaps only 5 per cent become a division chief at the age of 44, and only one of them, if any, becomes a director seven or eight years later.

The pattern is familiar to anyone who knows a British-type civil service. It has the very great advantage that it keeps inter-personal competition to a minimum. The best strategy for a good career is hard and co-operative work for the company; there is little chance of manoeuvring into your boss's job.

Person-related rather than job-related wages

I said 'organization oriented rather than market oriented'. With the lifetime commitment people are not often in the market. In a system of internal promotion they are not being compared, as candidates for particular jobs, with competitors coming in from the outside market. Likewise, pay is not determined by the price, determined by the forces of supply and demand, that a particular skill commands in the market. People are not paid 'the rate for the job'. They are paid according to their position on an incremental scale. *Which* scale they are on is determined by educational level/worker grade; their position on it, by age, seniority and performance assessment.

Enterprise trade unions

Given these other characteristics, it would be surprising if the labour unions were market oriented, if they were, as typically in Anglo-Saxon capitalism, unions which unite people in the same craft or profession; people who are selling the same skill in the market and have a common interest in keeping up the price at which that skill is sold. Instead unions unite all the people who have sunk their futures in the same firm and have a common concern with how that particular firm treats its workers, with how it settles the proportion of its revenues it pays in wages, the proportion going to investment etc.

Training

In an American-type market-oriented system, training enhances the skills an individual has to sell in the market. It is reasonable that he/she – or the state, acting collectively on behalf of individuals – should bear a large part of the costs. In the Japanese organization-oriented system with pay scales which are not closely tied to job-functions or skills, it is reasonable that the enterprise invests in the training of its lifelong members.

Welfare

Lifelong membership in the organization produces a parallel difference in the organization of social security, housing and leisure facilities. State and local government provides less, and the enterprise provides more, in Japan than in the American model (though the difference is not so marked as in the contrast with Britain, the other major exemplar of the

Anglo-Saxon model. In Britain, the state has many of the functions left, more individualistically, to private insurance in the USA.)

Self-definitions; the bases of social status

In market-oriented societies people asked to identify themselves by their work role (rather than their family or leisure or political role) do so primarily in terms of their occupation or profession; in organization-oriented societies they do so by their organizational membership – 'I work for Mitsubishi' rather than 'I'm a plumber, an architect, a choreographer, a rodent operative'. This dimension of conscious self-perception in turn helps to reinforce the other features – the lifetime commitment, the enterprise unions structure – listed above.

Blurring of internal stratification

Many of the features listed above apply partially to elite managerial workers in Anglo-Saxon firms – IBM is a notably 'Japanese' firm in this regard, so are some of the British elite firms like Unilever, BP etc. In the Japanese firm it applies to everyone enrolled as a 'regular' or 'permanent' worker, blue-collar workers included. Stratal divisions are only the divisions between people on different pay-scales, which the system tends to de-emphasize by minimizing any other symbolic status divisions – length of annual holidays, work times, social security provisions, access to dining facilities etc. This enhances the sense that the firm is a community of people.

SOCIAL PERCEPTION OF THE FIRM

Why are there hardly ever hostile takeovers in Japan – when it is perfectly possible to buy shares in the stock market, gain a controlling interest and turn out the existing management in Japan as in other countries? The answer lies not in the legal but in the *social* constraints on such action. As one Japanese writer remarked: 'taking over a firm simply by the power of money seems too "dry" (*dorai*) to us Japanese.'

What he was getting at is that to the average Japanese businessman, a firm is primarily a *community of people* rather than a *piece of property* that its owners can do what they like with. The contrast is an important one, recently borrowed by the Pope in his restatement of Catholic social doctrine (*Centesimus Annus* 1991).

How that came to be the dominant perception is a very interesting historical question. Of more practical import is the 'functionalist' question of what sustains that perception today. Two things stand out. The first is the employment system described above. Getting a 'regular' job in a Japanese firm *is* very much more like joining a community than entering into a temporary contractual arrangement.

The second is the way Japanese firms are financed. First, they use a lot of debt. That portion of their finance depends on the relations managers have, not with anonymous shareholders, but with bank managers – people like themselves. But much the same applies to their equity too. Most firms have got a very substantial portion of their shares locked up in the safes of *other* firms – the firms they do business with, many of whose shares they themselves hold. These 'mutual stable cross-holdings' are never traded in the market without consultation with the firm whose shares they are. With a half to three-quarters of their shares locked up in this way, managers can afford to be relatively indifferent to what speculators, trading their remaining 'floating shares', are doing to their share-price in the stock market.

INTERFIRM TRANSACTIONS

A lot of American labour economics is written as if the labour market were like the sugar market; you buy as much of it as you need at the time you need it at a price determined by supply and demand at the time. No labour market is just like that, but a lot of managers, hankering after free hire and fire, think that that is they way it ought to be. But obviously not in Japan. The Japanese labour market, as described above, is about as far from that paradigm as one can imagine any labour market being.

Very much the same difference applies in business dealings between supplier and customer firms. The way an automobile company buys its windscreens and doorhandles and carburettors in Japan is a long way from the 'draw up specifications, put out to tender among competing suppliers, choose the best buy' sort of recipe which has long dominated the rational-business-methods textbooks. Relations tend to be long term and stable, involving a lot of technical co-operation – frequently engineering co-operation – on a project long before the price the supplier will get has been bargained out. Japanese businessmen tend to divide their world into business partners with whom they have a mutual-trust relationship of this sort, and strangers with whom they deal at arm's length. Members of the latter category can graduate to the former over time. When a Japanese firm is buying from a non-Japanese firm the time required may be a good deal longer.

INTER-COMPETITOR CO-OPERATION

Japanese economists speaking to American audiences are apt to portray Japan as a fiercely competitive economy whose success is to be attributed to the entrepreneurial vigour and healthy lust for profits of Japanese private enterprise managers – never to anything so unfair as 'Japan Inc.' type government direction or government subsidies.

The competitive spirit is certainly there. Competition there certainly is. The major electronics companies work their engineers to nervous breakdowns trying to get some new hyper-gimmicked video recorder on the market a few weeks ahead of the competition, thereby gaining two or three percentage points of market share.

But this picture of fierce market competition needs some qualification. First, in general, Japanese firms are very good at perceiving, agreeing and more-or-less honestly sticking to agreements, where enlightened self-interest dictates that the line can best be drawn between competition and co-operation. Second, a good deal of the co-operation would, in a society as suspiciously anti-trust as the USA, be counted as anti-competitive and anti-social collusion. Third, agreements to co-operate are frequently based on an acceptance of hierarchy. Since the economy settled down to its post-war pattern in the 1960s small firms have rarely harboured ambitions to displace big firms, but big firms, likewise, are hesitant about trying to drive small competitiors out of business.

Taking the first point about 'cultural capacity': why should it be greater than in other capitalist countries? A greater preference for friendly rather than more hostile rivalrous relations? A higher level of the kind of rationality which calculates the probable consequences of alternative courses of action more finely over longer future time periods? Because of the proximity in time of the elaborate guild organizations which were crucial to the organization of the Tokugawa economy only 120 years ago?

All of these things perhaps, but whatever the roots the effects are apparent. In expanding markets, particularly consumer goods markets, competition can be fierce. In stagnant or contracting markets, particularly producer goods markets, 'excessive competition' is avoided. Sometimes collusive price fixing is clearly at the expense of the consumer, clearly illegal and sometimes investigated and punished by the Fair Trade Commission. Very often, however, it is recognized as having some 'public interest' justification and is blessed by the Ministry of Trade and Industry in a formal 'regulated cartel' arrangement. Investment co-ordination cartels in the process industries, temporary production cut-back recession cartels and permanent capacity reduction agreements are examples. When the refinery industry fell on hard times because of over-capacity, slower economic growth and efficient energy-saving, it was allowed to operate an informal ban on gasoline imports in return for maintaining a price structure – cheaper kerosene and dearer gasoline – than the market would otherwise have produced, a deal which was deemed to be in the public interest.

Another manifestation of the capacity for co-operation can be seen in the strength of industry associations which perform a wide range of technical and marketing services and, especially, information-gathering services.

As for the hierarchy point, the stability of market share structures is remarkable. List the top ten firms in almost any industry in 1980 and much the same ten, with only minor variations in order, are likely to be on the list in 1990. Creeping up on the firm ahead, increasing market share a percentage point or two at a time, is what competition is about. Fierce battles for dominance – as in the 1970s 'war' between Suzuki and Yamaha, the two motorbike manufacturers from the same town – are both rare and spoken of with distaste by the average Japanese businessman; excessive and mutually self-destructive competition.

GOVERNMENT AS CREATIVE UMPIRE

The way a government can best promote growth, according to the neoclassical economists, is by keeping out of the way of its creative entrepreneurs. It should limit itself to upholding the legal structures which ensure the security of property and the enforceability of contracts, and to providing those collective public goods like defence and information services and education which the market alone would not produce. The 'Japan Inc.' image suggests that the Japanese government has played a role far far removed from that ideal – the role of controlling strategist, directing investment, allocating tasks to business firms, enforcing co-operation here, competition there.

The truth is somewhere in between. The cartel arrangement for the refinery industry cited above is a good example. The government – especially the agency with jurisdiction over the bulk of manufacturing industry, the Ministry of International Trade and Industry (MITI) – has been *umpire* in controlling the cartel arrangements of particular industries, adjudicating between producer interests and consumer interests according to some criterion of 'national interest', in the formulation of which, it has to be said, the competitiveness of the Japanese nation in world markets (coinciding, largely, with producer interests) has held high priority. It has been *creative* in many respects. It has often taken the initiative in making such cartel arrangements. It has played a major role in promoting wide discussion of, and creating a national consensus about, the strategic directions in which the economy should be restructured. It has often used credit and fiscal policy to favour growth in the targeted directions. And it has provided the entrepreneurial initiative, organizational frameworks and a certain amount of cash subsidy for the promotion of a wide range of 'pre-competitive' industrial research and development (R&D).

SYSTEM CONSISTENCY

The list of individual institutional differences is already quite long. But it becomes more sensible to argue that these are different *types* of capitalism if one can show that the individual differences are consistent with each other in being derivable from certain higher-order differences, differences in underlying, animating principles.

One of the simplest, single-sentence attempts to comprehend all these differences centres on the word which Marx and Engels borrowed from Carlyle for the *Communist manifesto*, namely 'the cash nexus'. Those who remember that rather impressive piece of English prose will recall the passage about the demise of feudalism; how it burst asunder the ties of obligation which had bound people together in the old regime. In the new society of mid-nineteenth-century capitalism, they said, the only thing which bound man to man was the cash nexus – the impersonal arm's-length bargain in pursuit of self-interest. So one might put it this way (in principle in quantitative terms, even if the actual difficulties of measurement would be formidable):

The difference between the two types of economies is such that, in Japan, a much smaller proportion of economic transactions are of the pure cash nexus type; a much higher proportion are embedded in social relationships of trust and mutual obligation.

But note that this 'embedding' is not of the traditional type of which Polanyi wrote – embedding in ties of an 'ascriptive' type. It is embedding in social relations which are created by the repetition of economic exchange itself; relations which are *only entered into after assessment of the other party's competence*; they are, in other words, a function of 'achieved' and not 'ascribed' status.

An alternative, and in many ways more interesting, way of characterizing the differences is the following.

Anglo-Saxon economies are economies in which individuals always seek – and are encouraged by prevailing norms and institutional structures to seek – to keep their options open. By contrast, in the Japanese economy, economic actors are much more willing to enter into long-term commitments.

I work for A today, but if B offers me a better job I go to B. I sub-contract my widget-making to friend X, but if Y makes better widgets cheaper, he is my new friend. I have company C's shares today, but if there is the least likelihood of trouble coming, I reserve the right to dump them and buy into D instead. In Japan, none of these things is easy.

I said 'alternative, and in many ways more interesting' for the following reason. The ready 'Anglo-Saxon' mobility of factors is, according to orthodox economics, what makes for competitive efficiency. Recall all the talk about stagflation and Eurosclerosis in the 1980s. The more mobile a market is, the fewer rigidities it has and the more likely it is to maximize efficiency, to maximize output and therefore to maximize welfare. So Anglo-Saxon economies should presumably have higher growth rates than the Japanese.

THREE QUESTIONS: EFFICIENCY, DESIRABILITY AND SURVIVABILITY

But do they? That is the first of my final three questions. Which is the more efficient? Which is the better system? Which will win out?

Which is more efficient?

On the efficiency issue there would not seem to be much doubt. Look at growth rates. Look at the steady increase in Japan's share of world trade – look at the fact that an 80 per cent revaluation of the yen caused hardly more than a blip in the steady advance of Japan's exports. Consider the implications of the fact that Japan invests over 30 per cent of gross national product (GNP) per annum, and the USA less than 20 per cent, or of the fact that of patents granted in the USA only 4 per cent were granted to Japanese in 1970, but 21 per cent in 1988.

But that does not settle the issue. It is still sometimes argued that the strength of the Japanese economy lies in the competitive vigour of individuals and firms, the capacity for hard work, the frugality that produces high savings rates and the capacity for conscientiously fulfilling duties. All this is what makes the Japanese economy efficient, *in spite of* the irrationalities and rigidities of a system which stops markets from doing their proper work. These are just legacies of feudalism which time will eventually erode.

That the Japanese economy benefits from the work habits and savings habits of its people can hardly be denied, but that the institutional framework in which they work and save is such as to frustrate rather than promote their good habits seems improbable. The features of Japanese economic organization described above are becoming widely known; the flood of 'learn from Japan' books is having its effect on business schools. The director of one of them has written an eloquent tract whose main theme is the superior competitive efficiency of the strategic conquest firm as against the profit maximizing firm – read typical Japanese and typical American firm respectively (Thurow 1992).

In theory it is the Anglo-Saxon economies which ought to be more efficient because, as noted above, they approximate far more closely to the supposed preconditions for efficiency. And yet by all the obvious performance criteria they would seem to be less efficient. How does one resolve the apparent paradox? The answer is that market mobility contributes only to *allocative* efficiency – efficiency in making sure that resources get rapidly switched to uses in which they will achieve their highest returns. This tends to be the only kind of efficiency that economists talk about because it is the only one which lends itself easily to quantitative analysis.

But there are other equally, or more, important kinds of efficiency – production efficiency or technical efficiency, the capacity to perform jobs quickly, efficiently and co-operatively, without waste. It is in *that* dimension that the Japanese system scores. The way in which the Japanese system promotes this kind of efficiency was left largely implicit in the descriptive section above. The institutional features described there have two primarily relevant characteristics: their tendency to encourage long-term investment and the pattern of employee motivation they evoke. Both are intimately related to the fact that most employees can and do expect to continue working for their firm until retirement, and to the character of the firm as a self-governing community of people rather than as a piece of property of the shareholders. And the pattern of enterprise finance is, of course, an essential precondition for those features.

Which is better?

The Japanese system constrains consumers to spending only about 57 per cent of national income. Americans get to spending nearly 10 per cent more of theirs. On the other hand, the purchasing power of the Japanese consumer – and, indeed, the Japanese wage-earning consumer – has more than doubled since 1970. In the USA the average wage has actually fallen in real terms over that period. Also, the distribution of income in Japan remains much less unequal than in the USA.

So, except for those Americans – lawyers, business executives, doctors, brokers – who value the chance to win a half-million-dollar-a-year salary (which almost nobody can do in Japan), there is little on material grounds to tempt one to prefer an American-type economy. The crucial questions are about choice and commitment; untrammelled freedom and belonging. If you want to keep your options open, change jobs when you want to without much loss of pay and status, keep yourself to yourself at work and say no to the foreman who wants you to do overtime, dump your suppliers when somebody else offers a better deal, put your business school training to work by mounting bids for companies with juicy undervalued assets, if you want, in other words, the fullest opportunities for individual profit-maximization and individual self-expression, then America is the place to go – especially if you are above average in talent, education and chutzpah. If you value security and the sense of being trusted, can swallow the fact that the job choice you made in your twenties has tracked you for life and do not mind being constrained by community pressures in the use of your time and your money, then you may well prefer Japan.

Which will win out?

I do not mean by this question to add fuel to chauvinist sentiments. I do not mean what a recent American television film meant when its narrator called for a 'new Desert Storm' to prevent America losing its new war – the economic war against Japan. What I am talking about is not a battle between *states* but between *institutions*, between *systems of organization*.

My question assumes that the world economy continues to become more integrated, with national frontiers being less and less effective constraints on any economic actors – rather than retrogressing to protectionist trade blocs which may indeed turn the battle between systems into a battle between states. Increasing integration means increasing interaction, increasing competition and thence, increasing homogenization of system components. It is unlikely that the world of 2050 – or 2030, for that matter – will have room for more than one capitalist system. Whose will that world system resemble most? The American or the Japanese?

The way increasing competition leads to increasing homogenization of system components is, of course, through the Darwinian process of survival only of the fittest. Social Darwinism has two meanings: one is the Teddy Roosevelt/Margaret Thatcher belief that the tough and clever *ought* to be able to win power and riches and let the weak go to the wall because in the end 'the race' benefits from it all. The other has nothing to do with 'oughts' and just supposes that the way institutional forms evolve is something akin to the evolution of physical morphologies – except that whereas natural evolution proceeds primarily by displacement of one species by another, social evolution proceeds both by displacement and by imitation. In any case, the presumption is that it is the fittest – the most efficient – system which wins out. Hence, given what was said above about the efficiencies of the Japanese system, the *a priori* answer to our 'which will win?' question should be the more efficient Japanese system.

And one can find justification for adopting that answer in the events of the last decade. The Japanese system is spreading in the USA by both of the twin mechanisms of social Darwinism – displacement and imitation. Japanese firms have moved into the USA; in the automobile industry the already-announced plans of Japanese manufacturers will soon give them a 15 per cent share of the market – quite apart from the other 15 per cent or so taken by imports from Japan. At the same time, as exemplified in Ford's After Japan programme and in GM's Saturn project, Japanese competition has induced American manufacturers to make substantial changes in the way they do business. Just-in-time work organization, team work, flexible job definitions, job security, intensified worker training, worker participation in decision making and stable long-term supplier relationships are all part of the current rhetoric of American progressive management. The MIT book *The Machine that Changed the World* has become a best-seller with its advocacy of even more assiduous adoption of Japanese practices.

But might this not be just the swallow or two that do not make a summer? There are several arguments against simple extrapolation into the future of the trends just noted.

First, although, as argued above, Japanese competitive efficiency is not *just* a matter of long working hours, hard work and docility towards superiors, those undeniably are among the ingredients of success. As the Japanese grow more affluent (and get older – the average age of the workforce is rising rapidly) they will surely slow down. We saw, after all, a very similar phenomenon in the 1950s and 1960s when American firms moved rapidly into Europe – both displacing European firms and prompting them to imitate American production methods. The 'American challenge' had a lasting effect on production techniques; productivities were improved. But it was a one-shot effect. As American competitive vigour and cash resources declined disinvestment began; the takeover process was not sustained. Might it not be so also with the Japanese?

Perhaps, but don't count on it. The school and university system in Japan with its overpowering incentives for diligent application (sustained by the competition for status more than for money) will work to protect the work ethic against the ravages of affluence. For further doubts on the necessary connection between affluence and decline of the work ethic, consider recent trends in middle-class America. The yuppies on Wall Street who work all the hours God gives to buy that extra BMW they never have time to drive suggests that the motivating force of status consumption – the lust for positional goods – can be as much a motivator of hard work as the fear of falling into poverty.

Second, whatever has happened in the world of manufacturing methods (quality circles, just-in-time, total quality control (TQC) etc.), there are only the most marginal indications – occasional bursts of debate about industrial policy, marginal adjustments of the capital gains tax to encourage long-term shareholding, for example – of any amendment in the financial and control structures of American capitalism. It is still financial experts, trained in business schools in the art of maximizing shareholder value, who take the ultimate decisions – men and women who are likely to see themselves as having a moral duty (as well as doing the best thing for their stock options) to veto long-range investment plans when the net yield, after allowing for risks and uncertainties, falls below investment in treasury bonds. Japanese banks may already supply two-thirds of short-term commercial debt in California, but their role in the long-term bond and equity financing of American firms is still limited.

That *might* mean, of course, only that the Japanese system will dominate, in the end, more by displacement than imitation. Japanese practices may come to rule in the financing of American manufacturing because the bulk of that manufacturing comes to be done in firms of Japanese origin so that the American financial system shrinks with the shrinking of American-origin firms. But the trends are too incipient so far for anyone to extrapolate them with much confidence.

And it should not be forgotten that there are not only market forces at work, but political forces also. The distinction I made above between a battle between states and a battle between systems is conceptually sustainable, but as long as the American state continues to defend the interests of Americans with a stake in the American system and the Japanese state likewise, the two battles are inextricably interlinked.

To begin with, it is through national politics that decisions are taken whether to *allow* market forces to work or not. If the world does move back towards a system of trade blocs with internal free movement but severe restrictions on trade and investment across bloc boundaries, then it is not the firm-level processes of displacement and imitation which will be the important Darwinian mechanisms involved, but the struggle between power blocs.

And even if the (very strong) economic forces preventing such regional blocism prevail and an open international system is maintained, there are more things than competitive efficiency which determine an institution's survival power. Michel Albert (1991) has a fascinating chapter which addresses itself precisely to the question

> why, when German capitalism has so much more to recommend it than the Anglo-saxon – not only in efficiency but also in its power to produce a decent society – why is it that the whole world – including the Germans – seem bedazzled by the glamour of America and increasingly inclined to accept the international 'harmonization' of, e.g., financial markets, in an America-converging, rather than a Germany-converging way?

His answer is 'cultural power', as potent an evolutionary advantage as economic power.

And if the Germans are susceptible to the Americans' mesmerizing self-confidence in the total rightness and justice of their own institutions (a self-confidence, it seems, that could survive at least two more generations of Millikens and Boeskies), how much more so the Japanese, who seem far more inclined, in any case, to cultural modesty, who seem always to be apologizing ('please give us time') for the fact that they are not white Westerners and who have a 40-year post-war history of deferentially accepting American elder-brother leadership – not to mention the brain-washing of the present generation of Japanese economists in American graduate schools.

It is possible, of course, that the collapse of American self-confidence will come suddenly. It is possible that the Japanese and the Germans might find that they have, not only a coincidence of interest of the kind that led to the triple alliance in 1940, but actually some coincidence of philosophy and beliefs about individualism and society which makes it worth while to co-operate in shaping a world capitalist system to their, rather than to Anglo-Saxon, predilections. But I would not count on it.

It should not be forgotten, either, that Japan's edge in economic power is counterbalanced by American superiority in military power, international political influence and the self-confidence at the bargaining table which goes with those things. These resources have been consistently used over the last 20 years to pressure Japan into changing the legal and administrative framework of Japanese capitalism in ways that have the effect – and are often designed to have the effect – of making Japanese capitalism a bit more like American capitalism. The so-called structural impediment initiative talks of 1989–90 are a recent example of just such an effort – rather more sustained and systematic than most.

But it is in the nature of government-to-government negotiations that they can only act on legal and administrative structures – that is to say, mostly only on the 'government as creative umpire' aspects of the system; agricultural protection, the Large Retail Store Law which protects small against big retailers, government procurement practices, cartel arrangements in the construction industry, levels of public investment and so on. *Some* of the changes American negotiators pressed for would alter the incentives for 'defecting' from the norms which govern the behaviour of private actors and sustain the existing system – marginal changes in company report disclosure rules, for example, or in the regulation of takeover bids or of cross shareholdings. But these would only be minor changes, not very likely to produce enough deviant behaviour for the norms to weaken. The fact remains that the distinctive character of Japanese capitalism rests not so much on anything very distinctive in legal and administrative structures, as on a distinctive set of conventions, implicit understandings and norms of acceptable behaviour. That, for all the leverage that American negotiators can muster, and for all the support they can claim within Japan (from the cheap rice lobby, the large retail store owners, stock exchange professionals etc.), sets inevitable limits to the effects that government-to-government negotiations can have.

Perhaps the reader will have firm views on the relative survivability of the two systems. I do not.

NOTES

1 See, for example, Prestowitz (1988), Fallows (1989) and Johnson (1989).

REFERENCES

Albert, Michel (1991) *Capitalisme Contre Capitalisme*, Paris: Seuil.
Johnson, Chalmers (1989) 'Trade, revisionism and the future of Japanese–American relations', in K. Yamamura (ed.) *Japan's Economic Structure; Should it Change?*, Seattle, WA: Society for Japanese Studies.
Prestowitz, Clyde (1988) *Trading Places*, New York: Basic Books.

Fallows, James (1989) *More Like Us*, New York: Houghton Mifflin.
Shonfield, Andrew (1965) *Modern Capitalism*, Oxford: Oxford University Press.
Thurow, Lester (1992) *Head to Head*, New York: Morrow.
Zysman, John (1983) *Governments, Markets and Change*, Oxford: Robertson.

Part I

Global strategies

Chapter 3

The globalization of Japanese firms

Hiroyuki Itami

ABSTRACT

Despite the trade friction created by Japan's export penetration of Western markets and, more recently, the take-off of Japanese overseas direct investment, the dependence of Japan's industries on foreign markets is less than in the USA and Germany. Nevertheless the concentrated pattern of Japanese exports and investment in the machinery industries, in the USA and Europe, has led to trade friction. The internationalization of Japanese industry is likely to continue. Thus, Japanese companies will continue to have to cope with management problems and issues arising from trade friction.

INTRODUCTION

The globalization of Japanese firms is of concern to both government officials and managers. The pattern of Japan's exports and overseas investment has changed significantly in the last ten years. Trade friction, originally created by exports, continues to exist, and to this has been added new concerns arising from overseas investment. This paper reviews the globalization of Japanese firms and assesses future developments. In the first section the pattern of Japan's exports and overseas investments are compared with those of the USA and Germany. This is followed by a section which stresses the local as opposed to offshore nature of Japanese overseas investment.

The next section deals with the impact of 'shocks' (oil price rises and yen appreciation) on globalization trends. This is followed by a discussion of the role of the machinery industry, which dominates Japan's internationalization, in causing trade friction. The final section forecasts further growth in Japan's international business accompanied by continued difficulties in relations with other countries.

COMPARING JAPAN'S EXPORTS AND OVERSEAS INVESTMENT WITH THE USA AND GERMANY

By 1988 Japan accounted for 9.4 per cent of world exports, the third largest behind the USA and Germany (the former West Germany unless noted otherwise), each with 11.4 per cent.[1] Japan's exports represent 9.4 per cent of its gross national product (GNP), a dependence that is not particularly high when compared with other countries, e.g. 26.8 per cent in Germany and 6.6 per cent in the USA. The description 'export dependent' is clearly more applicable to Germany than it is to Japan. A major difference between the exports of Germany and Japan is their final destination. Whereas 37 per cent of Japan's exports are shipped to the USA, followed by 6 per cent to South Korea and Germany respectively, Germany's exports are more evenly distributed, the major recipients being France (12 per cent), the USA (9 per cent) and the UK (9 per cent).

The top 25 Japanese exporters are concentrated in four industries – automobiles, electronics, precision machinery, steel – and account for 52.5 per cent of Japan's total exports. These companies typically exhibit high export ratios, as shown in Table 3.1. The average percentage exported by the firms in the Ministry of International Trade and Industry (MITI) survey was 20.9 per cent of sales, and most Japanese firms continue to be greatly dependent on domestic sales.

Since the mid-1980s a sharp increase in exports to North America and Europe has occurred, so that by 1988 these regions accounted for over half of Japan's export markets – 36.3 per cent and 21.1 per cent respectively.

Despite the role of Japan as a major exporting nation, the significance of exporting in the Japanese economy should not be overstated. For example, domestic private consumption for 1988 was more than six times that of exports. Consequently, supposing exports were to fall by 20 per cent, a mere 3.5 per cent increase in domestic consumption would compensate for this. These figures approximate to events in Japan after the 1985 appreciation of the yen, since when the Japanese economy sustained high growth into the late 1980s. Predictions of a rapid decline in the Japanese economy because of the devastating effect of yen appreciation on exports did not materialize, because the magnitude of exports is small relative to Japan's GNP. On the other hand, the dominance of the USA market as an export destination and the concentration of exports in the hands of a small number of firms and industries accounts for much of the trade friction between Japan and Western trade partners.

Table 3.1 Japan's top 25 exporting companies, 1988

Rank	Company	Export sales (billion yen)	Export ratio (%)
1	Toyota Motors	2,373.5	35.5
2	Honda Motors	1,628.6	61.8
3	Nissan Motors	1,497.3	41.8
4	Matsushita (Panasonic)	1,378.4	33.8
5	Mazda Motors	1,168.5	63.0
6	Mitsubishi Motors	919.0	48.4
7	Toshiba	896.2	30.7
8	Hitachi	809.3	25.0
9	Sony	761.6	60.5
10	Nippon Steel	622.7	26.1
11	Nippon Electronic	564.6	22.2
12	Canon	496.4	73.9
13	Sharp	473.8	47.7
14	Mitsubishi Electrical Machinery	460.9	20.7
15	Isuzu Motors	449.0	43.9
16	Suzuki Motors	379.3	46.5
17	Mitsubishi Heavy Industrial	371.2	21.7
18	Fujitsu	360.2	18.0
19	NKK	344.7	27.3
20	Sanyo Electronics	317.5	32.2
21	Sumitomo Metalworks	301.5	28.6
22	Nippon Victor (JVC)	300.2	48.3
23	Fujitsu Industrial	285.6	43.1
24	Kawasaki Steel	279.5	26.6
25	Kobe Steel	275.1	23.4

Source: Introduction to the Modern-day Corporation (in Japanese),
     Nikkei Shimbunsha, 1990
Note: Excluding trading companies.

Relative to their exports the scale of overseas production by Japanese companies is even smaller. Overseas production in 1988 was about one-fourth of exports and only 5 per cent of domestic production. Of course, there are companies, like Matsushita and Sony, whose overseas production ratios are close to 30 per cent, but overseas production for the majority is very small scale. For Japan the ratio of non-domestic production to domestic production was less than 4 per cent throughout most of the 1980s compared with ratios for Germany (non-EC production) and the USA of over 10 per cent and 18 per cent respectively (Japan Export–Import Bank 1990).

The number of people working in Japanese companies abroad is also small. In 1988, of 4,689 Japanese subsidiaries abroad in manufacturing industries, 1,351 were engaged in local sales and other non-production activities and 2,862 were engaged in local manufacturing. In 1990 the total number of local employees in Japanese manufacturing subsidiaries was just 1.05 million (MITI 1991), about one-tenth of the number of domestic employees in Japanese manufacturing.

The number of employees sent from Japan to work abroad long term approximates to only four per company. Yet Japanese firms complain that there is a scarcity of international talent and that training personnel for posts overseas poses difficult problems. The small number sent abroad (0.15 per cent of the numbers employed in manufacturing companies in Japan) is concentrated in a small number of companies. The number of expatriate employees in Matsushita Electric was slightly over 1,000 in 1989 (2 per cent of domestic employees) and Toshiba has 550 employees working abroad (0.8 per cent).

The difficulty in finding suitable expatriates is likely to grow in the future. An increase in the numbers sent abroad to work is inevitable due to the rapid rise in Japanese direct investment overseas. The amount of foreign investment by all industries held stable at slightly under US $10 billion until 1985, after which it increased rapidly by almost five times. Since then the direct foreign investments of all sectors have risen sharply, reaching US $47 billion in 1988 for all sectors and US $13.8 billion for manufacturing.

A further source of friction is the high concentration of this investment in the USA. In 1988, for example, 46.2 per cent of Japanese foreign direct investment by all industries was made in the USA and a level of 66 per cent had been reached by manufacturing alone.

Japan's overseas direct investment is likely to rise in the future. Japan's GNP is 66 per cent of the USA's, but its stock of overseas investment is only 33 per cent of the US level. Or, taking the ratio of non-domestic to domestic production quoted above, the Japanese figure at 5 per cent is about one-fourth of the US level (18 per cent).

OFFSHORE VERSUS LOCAL OVERSEAS INVESTMENT

The term 'offshore' is commonly used outside of Japan to describe overseas business activities, financing and making goods abroad and returning goods and/or profit to the home country. In many cases, overseas facilities are regarded as being subsidiary to the activities in the home country. This view is much less evident in Japanese corporations.

Indeed, there is no Japanese equivalent to match the term 'offshore'. When describing overseas production, the Japanese use the term 'local' production and overseas operations are referred to as 'the site of the market'. An overseas site, rather than a base for production, is resolutely regarded as a market itself, while the manufacturing facilities are regarded as a place where production takes place within the prospective market.

The bulk of overseas production by Japanese corporations thus far has been to secure local markets. Little thought has been given to reverse imports. The highest region of non-local sales is Asia, but, even so, at least 70 per cent of local production by Japanese firms is sold there. Sales inside the actual country of production amount to 60 per cent, and only 8.7 per cent and 13.7 per cent are exported to the USA and Japan respectively. This pattern has changed little over many years. Sales destinations of local subsidiaries in North America (94 per cent) and Europe (96 per cent) are also overwhelmingly local. Globally, the ratio of local sales to local production is 82 per cent. The export ratio, therefore, approximates to the export ratio of domestic production by Japanese companies.

The electronics industry in Asia comes closest to the 'offshore' image. Its local sales ratio is the lowest of all the principal Japanese industries represented there. Nevertheless, even this industry's behaviour in Asia is a far cry from the offshore image of USA firms. Compared with the 60 per cent ratio of local sales to local production in 1988, and a ratio of 43 per cent for Japanese electronics manufacturers, the comparable USA manufacturers' ratio was 32 per cent. What is particularly interesting is that the Japanese electronics industry in Asia only exports 19 per cent of its production back to Japan. In contrast, USA subsidiaries in Asia repatriate 45 per cent of their production, a factor, of course, in the persistent trade deficits of the USA (Japan Export–Import Bank 1990). Thus, even the atypical electronics industry sells most of its Asian-made products in Asia.

This local market orientation of Japanese corporations is closely linked to the recent rapid increase in Japanese direct investment in the USA and Europe. The basic pattern (cause and effect) of Japanese internationalization is exporter ⇒ economic friction ⇒ local production. Japan created its markets in the USA and Europe via exports, but later switched to local production in response to protectionist threats. In all cases the market is outside Japan, therefore production is local, not 'offshore'.

Western style 'offshore' activities by Japanese corporations are unlikely. One reason is that Japanese firms will continue to respond to the needs of the local market rather than use local production facilities as a base for other markets. Another reason is that the Japanese market will continue to be hard to penetrate even for Japanese subsidiaries overseas. What happened to the USA will not happen to Japan.

THE IMPACT OF EXTERNAL SHOCKS

In the period from 1960 to 1988, Japanese exports grew at an average of just less than 13 per cent per year. But in 1974 and 1980 the growth of exports exceeded 30 per cent. These two spurts were due to the preceding oil price 'shocks'. Another shock occurred in 1985 when the yen rapidly appreciated. This led to a sharp decrease in yen-dominated exports, but a corresponding spurt in Japanese foreign direct investment in manufacturing, the financial sectors and real estate.

These three shocks all induced major changes in the international price mechanism to the detriment of Japan's competitiveness. The oil crises led to multiple increases in the price of petroleum, a natural resource almost non-existent in Japan. Yen appreciation brought about price changes in the opposite direction. The dollar price of land and human resources in Japan paralleled the 100 per cent appreciation of the yen's international purchasing power.

The oil crises contributed to the internationalization of Japanese companies which intensified efforts to penetrate foreign markets, particularly those of automobiles and electronics. The strong yen, on the other hand, promoted the internationalization of Japanese production and other investment activities, that is to say, the 'globalization' of Japanese corporations.

The oil crises contributed to the process of internationalization of Japan's companies in several ways. Exporting intensified to compensate for a slowdown in the growth of domestic demand. In the search for energy-saving techniques, firms began to streamline their operations and reduce costs. Overseas, oil price increases found expression in increased product prices more so than in Japan. In consequence of these influences, Japanese companies were more competitive internationally after each oil crisis than they were before. In addition, demand grew in foreign markets for energy-efficient Japanese products. A typical example would be the automobile market. Small, fuel-efficient Japanese cars rapidly gained favour in the USA after each oil crisis.

The link between the 'strong' yen and the globalization of Japanese firms is quite simple. Japan's trade surpluses, which were responsible for the appreciation of a floating yen, had already generated trade friction, in the face of which Japanese firms with significant foreign market dependence had already begun to move production overseas as a countermeasure. The strong yen made investment in Japan less attractive relatively and speeded up the flow of foreign direct investment.

Thus three characteristics are apparent in the globalization of Japanese industry: concentration, sudden spurts in activity and relatively low levels of foreign trade and investment, poised for future growth. All these suggest that Japan will remain a target for protectionists and that cross-border transactions will be more difficult for Japanese companies than for companies from other countries. Sudden spurts and concentrated activity have been most pronounced in the USA and, more recently, the European Community (EC), and it is in these regions that appeals for protection against Japanese firms will continue to be heard.

THE ROLE OF THE MACHINERY INDUSTRY IN TRADE FRICTION

Japanese firms have responded rationally to events as they have impacted on international prices and competitiveness, moving into foreign markets at greater or lesser speed via exporting or foreign direct investment, as dictated by price movements. The leading actor in these flexible responses has been the machinery (mechanical engineering) industry. This leadership is yet another characteristic of the internationalization and globalization of the Japanese firms.

Of all Japanese export industries, the first to achieve post-war global superiority was the shipbuilding industry. Eleven years after the close of the Second World War, Japan's shipbuilding tonnage was number one in the world. Shipbuilding was also Japan's major exporter, and this remained so until the late 1970s when shipbuilding was displaced by the automotive industry. Manufacturers of machinery continue to lead Japan's internationalization, as Table 3.1 makes clear.

Overall, the machinery sector accounted for 78 per cent of manufacturing exports in 1988 and for 65 per cent of overseas production and overseas hiring. These figures indicate an importance in trade and foreign direct investment far beyond the industry's domestic significance, which was only to 41 per cent of manufacturing output in 1987. Despite the high ratio of overseas production attributed to machinery, the export dependence of the industry exceeds those of all other industries. Foodstuffs and textiles offer examples of industries where overseas production is relatively more important than exporting.

The high export status of the machinery industry is not unique to Japan. The same is true in many advanced nations. But in Japan's case, the importance of the machinery exports (78 per cent of manufactured exports) is much greater than in the USA (69 per cent) or Germany (57 per cent).

A particular structural feature of the machinery industry is worthy of comment. Whether in capital goods or consumer goods, the final markets for machinery are situated towards the last link of the vertical value-added chain from raw materials to final goods. Due to its multi-stage nature, the industry is capable of generating high value added. When this final product is exported, all the value added remains in Japan. Overseas, products which capitulate to Japanese competition have their value added absorbed by Japanese firms. In other words, a large share of the earnings of the global machine industry accrues to Japanese firms and is retained in Japan. Not surprisingly, countries everywhere are inclined to argue that as much production as possible in this kind of industry is done within their own country, hence we have yet another source of friction between nations.

A second structural element also stems from the industry's multi-stage nature, namely the time and effort it takes to transfer many stages of production overseas. A simple example would be 'parts supply'. Machinery cannot be assembled efficiently unless parts are properly supplied. When one considers that the video cassette recorder contains some 3,000 parts and the automobile over 30,000, the seriousness of the problem becomes apparent. Final production and assembly locations require competent systems support, a further reason for the relatively slow growth of overseas production and the tendency for parts manufacturing to remain in Japan. But when parts manufacturing stays in Japan, much of the value added stays in Japan, giving rise to 'local content' restrictions in overseas markets. The fact that Japanese internationalization and globalization has been led by the machinery industry has made Japan more vulnerable to economic friction than would otherwise have been the case.

THE FUTURE OF JAPAN'S GLOBALIZATION

It is unlikely that the penetration of global markets by Japanese firms has reached saturation. Exports have further to grow due to Japan's competitiveness in price and quality. Those Asian nations that are replicating Japan's industrial policies are likely to join Japan in the further penetration of global markets rather than threaten the continued growth of Japan's exports. In addition, as Asian exports to non-Asian destinations increase, exports of intermediate and capital goods from Japan to Asia needed for such production will likewise increase. Since the strengthening of the yen from 1985 this division of labour in production is already under way in Asia, signifying a further consolidation of Japan's export base.

At the root of this export competitiveness lies Japan's accumulation of technology in electronic components and dies, the backbone of so much manufacturing output. A symbolic example is Japan's overwhelming share of global video cassette recorder production. Industry experts predict that by the millennium 40 per cent of dies will be made in Japan. NEC, Toshiba and Hitachi are the three leading manufacturers in the world of semiconductors, of which Japan is responsible for half of global output. Japan's machine tool industry, a specialist in computerized machine tools, is the world leader, and it is certain that Japan will continue to dominate the major markets in electronics and precision machinery.

The process of internationalization via foreign direct investment is spreading to small and medium-sized firms, and industries new to the process have begun to invest overseas, the timing being strongly influenced by the strong yen throughout the latter half of the 1980s. For example, in 1988 the largest overseas investment was made by 'other' industries, namely manufacturers of general merchandise and processed goods. The $4 billion invested by this sector compares with $3 billion for electronics and $1.4 billion for transport equipment. Investment in steel, other metals, chemicals and textiles is also increasing. The number of overseas ventures started up by small and medium-sized firms increased by 30 per cent in 1985, 42 per cent in 1986 and 50 per cent in 1987.

Where will this all end? At the very least, Japan's ratio of overseas to domestic production might be expected to rise from 5 per cent to match Germany's non-EC ratio of 10 per cent, perhaps even approach Germany's total overseas ratio of 20 per cent. Even a ratio for Japan of 15 per cent would be about 5 per cent lower than the ratio for the USA. A doubling of Japan's overseas production over the current level would not be an unusual international phenomenon. If this happens, overseas employees in Japanese subsidiaries would exceed 2 million and the number of Japanese employees working overseas would exceed 30,000. The current ratio of domestic to overseas employment is ten to one. A ratio of five to one is conceivable if the strong trend continues towards Japanese investment in labour-intensive manufacturing in Asia.

The internationalization of Japanese firms will bring forth internal and external problems and challenges with which they will be required to cope. The internal challenge will concern how to design and operate management systems necessary for managing across borders. The external challenge concerns the response of firms to trade friction.

A doubling of international employees will demand major reform in the international management of Japanese companies. Externally, increases in Japanese exports will lead to further trade friction. Direct investment overseas in response to this will often generate investment-related friction. One unintentional consequence of the internationalization of Japanese firms has been the retreat and often the demise of other companies, primarily those of the USA, where the view persists that Japan has successfully targeted US firms in a zero-sum game. Trends in the share of world GNP show that gains by Japan have been matched by decreases for the USA. At the corporate level, there were 217 US firms in the *Fortune* Top 500 in 1980 and 176 in 1988, compared with 66 and 102, respectively, in the case of Japanese firms.

Persistent trade surpluses in Japan and deficits in the USA are another serious issue. The US trade deficit accounted for by the deficit with Japan was 45 per cent in 1989; the percentage of the US trade deficit reflected in Japan's trade surplus was 58 per cent. Despite the illogicality of bilateral trade comparisons in a multilateral trading world, such comparisons, being made, feed the protectionist lobby. From a US perspective, balanced trade with Japan would eliminate half the US deficit. Similar comparisons are possible with EC countries. The likelihood of a continuing Japanese trade surplus and the further growth of Japanese exports and overseas production clearly indicate that the problems and challenges faced by Japanese companies will continue to grow.

NOTES

1 Most of the data, throughout the paper, is from MITI (1990), unless otherwise noted. The MITI survey covered 1,047 companies, including 375 out of Japan's 400 top exporters, representing 85 per cent of Japan's total exports.

REFERENCES

Japan Export–Import Bank (1990) *Rapid Rise in Direct Investment and the Globalization of Management*, Tokyo: Foreign Investment Research Institute, Tokyo.

MITI (Ministry of International Trade and Industry) (1990) *Survey on Trends of Business Operations Abroad by Japanese Companies*, No. 19, Tokyo: MITI.

MITI (Ministry of International Trade and Industry) (1991) *White Paper on International Trade: 1990*, Tokyo: MITI.

Chapter 4

The trade effects of Japanese manufacturing investment in the UK economy

Roger Strange

ABSTRACT

There is widespread debate about the nature and scale of the benefits which accrue from inward direct investment by Japanese manufacturing companies in the UK. Proponents emphasize the additional output, employment and exports which such investment brings to the UK economy. In contrast, critics (particularly of Japanese investment) belittle the local content of mere 'screwdriver' assembly plants and maintain that the UK value added is but a small proportion of the output of the foreign affiliates. This paper provides estimates of the impact of Japanese manufacturing investment on UK output, employment and the trade balance in 17 industrial sectors. The main conclusion is that Japanese direct investment has had a disproportionate impact across industrial sectors but that the overall effect has been beneficial.

INTRODUCTION

Many proponents of inward investment (from whatever provenance) emphasize the additional output, employment and exports which such investment brings to the host economy. Moreover, they also stress the concomitant transfer of advanced technology and production skills and the introduction of new products and superior management and organization methods. In short, the net effect is found to be unquestionably beneficial, with the inward investors also assumed to demonstrate high levels of productivity, efficiency and profitability. In contrast, critics (particularly of Japanese direct investment) belittle the local content of mere 'screwdriver' assembly plants and maintain that the UK value added is but a small proportion of the total value of the output of the foreign affiliates. They draw attention to the imports of raw materials, parts, components, sub-assemblies and knockdown kits which are purchased by the assembly plants, question the extent of technology transfer on the grounds that it is usually the production of more standardized products which is transferred abroad, and suggest that a large part of the overseas production is undertaken simply as a means to circumvent trade barriers. Furthermore, they compare the operations of the Japanese-owned plants with the activities of hypothetical UK firms which undertake 'full' UK manufacturing, which source their inputs exclusively in the UK, which retain all their profits in the UK, and whose interests are assumed to be identical to those of UK labour and the overall UK economy. Such firms are dubbed 'hypothetical' because they either never came into existence (due to the overbearing competition) or because they were forced out of existence by the 'unfair trading practices' of the foreign firms.

This introduction presents something of a caricature of the different attitudes towards Japanese direct investment in the UK: attitudes which are often reinforced by substantial doses of myth, misunderstanding and xenophobia. The reality is rather more complex and involves elements of both stylized views, and is moreover subject to continual evolution. Nevertheless, this discussion of the conceptual issues does focus attention on the importance of the counterfactual position – i.e. the question of 'what would have happened if the Japanese company had not set up production facilities in the UK?' – in the assessment of the impact of Japanese direct investment. If the hypothetical UK company referred to above could have captured or retained an equivalent share of the market, then it is feasible that the net effects of Japanese investment on UK national income, employment and the balance of payments might be negative. It is more probable, however, that such a vulnerable UK company would have suffered anyway from US and European competition even in the absence of the Japanese production facilities, or that the Japanese firm might have been able to retain at least some proportion of the market through direct exports or licensing. Given the UK's membership of the European Community (EC), there is also the possibility that the Japanese firm might have established a production facility in an alternative EC location and shipped its output from there to the UK market.

This latter possibility focuses attention on the choice of the appropriate geographical unit for assessment. From the viewpoint of the EC as a whole, it makes little difference whether a Japanese company locates its EC production facilities in the UK, in France, in Germany, or wherever. As regards the potential benefits for the UK economy, however, the choice is critical with a UK location likely to be far more favourable than a location on the Continent. Furthermore, it is likely that the positive effects for the UK economy will be offset, at least partially, by negative effects for other EC economies. And, at a more local level, it is feasible that an investment by a Japanese company in Scotland, for example, may have adverse repercussions for employment etc. in other parts of the UK.

These questions clearly cannot be tackled at the macroeconomic level, as the answers depend upon the industrial spread of the investment and upon the competitive situation in each industry. This paper presents an analysis of the trade effects of Japanese manufacturing investment which concentrates on the narrow interests of the UK economy, and which examines the effects on UK output, employment and the trade balance in 17 industrial sectors.

THE OVERALL STATISTICAL PICTURE

The available data on foreign direct investment (FDI) in the UK[1] are not very revealing about the UK activities of foreign affiliates. A more helpful and detailed perspective is provided by the statistics on net output and employment in foreign-owned enterprises in the UK generated by the annual Census of Production. These show (Table 4.1) that 21 per cent of the net output of UK manufacturing industry in 1989[2] was produced by foreign enterprises who, moreover, employed almost 15 per cent of the workforce. UK employment in foreign-owned enterprises fell steadily through the 1980s (largely as a result of a fall in employment in US-owned firms), but appeared to be increasing again in the later years of the decade. Net output also appeared to rise sharply after several years of sluggish growth. The major investor is the USA which accounts for 12–13 per cent of net output, with the EC accounting for a further 3–4 per cent. Both the USA and the EC make rather smaller contributions to UK employment, which indicates that their enterprises have rather higher per capita output levels than domestic firms. In contrast, Japanese firms only accounted for 0.05 per cent of both UK net output and employment in 1981, but these proportions had increased twelvefold by 1989. Per capita output in these firms is similar on average to that for UK manufacturing industry as a whole. Moreover, it is worth noting that, in 1989, Japanese-owned companies still only produced 0.6 per cent of the net output, and employed only 0.56 per cent of the employees in UK manufacturing industry. These proportions will have risen since, and the concentration of Japanese companies in certain industrial sectors is quite high. Nevertheless, the aggregate *direct* impact of Japanese-owned companies on both output and employment in UK manufacturing

Table 4.1 Net output and employment in UK manufacturing industry accounted for by US, EC and Japanese enterprises, 1981–9

Year	Nationality of enterprise			All foreign enterprise[a]	
	USA	EC [b]	Japan		% of total
(A) Net output as percentage of total net output					
1981	12.91	2.44	0.05	13,099.3[c]	18.6
1983	12.69	2.50	0.08	15,322.2[c]	19.0
1984	13.30	2.45	0.09	17,120.4[c]	20.3
1985	12.29	2.45	0.12	17,279.3[c]	18.8
1986	11.68	2.49	0.15	17,392.3[c]	17.7
1987	12.11	2.98	0.21	20,298.1[c]	19.1
1988	11.52	2.71	0.37	22,385.6[c]	18.5
1989	12.88	3.48	0.60	28,430.8[c]	21.5
(B) Employment as percentage of total net output					
1981	9.83	2.20	0.05	858.1[d]	14.9
1983	9.05	2.14	0.07	736.0[d]	14.5
1984	9.25	2.05	0.11	716.3[d]	14.8
1985	8.60	1.96	0.13	677.1[d]	14.0
1986	8.25	1.93	0.16	621.1[d]	13.0
1987	8.22	2.15	0.22	624.7[d]	13.4
1988	7.69	2.15	0.36	635.2[d]	13.1
1989	8.10	2.74	0.56	724.1[d]	14.9

Notes: [a] Foreign enterprises are defined as those controlled or owned by companies incorporated overseas. The percentage figures are proportions of total net output (employment) in all private sector enterprises in UK manufacturing industry – i.e. excluding public sector enterprises.
   [b] The figures for the European Community (EC) exclude Spain and Portugal before 1986.
   [c] £ millions.
   [d] Thousands.
Source: Business Monitor PA1002: Report on the Census of Production – Summary Volume

industry is relatively small, and is still far exceeded by that of USA- and EC-owned companies.

JAPANESE MANUFACTURING INVESTMENT IN THE UK ECONOMY

It should be stressed at the outset that any quantitative analysis[3] (such as that presented in this paper) is only as good as the assumptions on which it is based. Given the acknowledged lack of detailed official UK data on Japanese FDI, a number of heroic assumptions have had to be made to arrive at what must be considered very approximate estimates.

The starting point is to present a 'naive' analysis based upon

Table 4.2 A naive analysis of the effects of Japanese manufacturing investment on UK employment, output and the trade balance

Industry	Employment	Net output (£ million)	Total sales (£ million)	Exports (£ million)	Purchases (£ million)	Imports of parts etc. (£ million)	Trade balance (£ million)
Textiles and clothing	3,892	53.94	115.31	32.29	61.70	38.80	−6.51
Motor vehicles	5,013	200.23	608.30	364.30	417.68	228.35	+136.63
Bearings	4,774	110.38	220.66	176.53	112.37	45.33	+131.20
Consumer electronics	11,679	445.86	1,361.65	816.99	985.35	639.29	+177.70
Machine tools	304	7.06	14.94	11.94	8.10	3.40	+8.54
Construction equipment	458	16.25	48.95	39.16	33.59	13.20	+25.96
Electronic office equipment	3,814	93.50	228.79	137.27	141.56	96.61	+40.66
Electronic components	7,167	144.74	315.39	126.16	171.81	111.23	+14.93
Automotive components	6,394	131.60	302.15	105.75	171.47	91.61	+14.14
Computers	2,532	150.09	388.28	232.97	239.39	163.38	+69.59
Chemical and allied products[a]	3,685	113.62	248.15	62.04	136.34	65.38	−3.34
General machinery[b]	846	21.79	44.23	17.25	22.94	9.32	+7.93
Electrical machinery[b]	834	19.24	40.62	18.69	21.80	12.78	+5.91
Precision machinery	970	21.42	40.53	21.89	19.43	11.00	+10.89
Food and related products	146	4.31	13.38	1.61	9.12	5.15	−3.54
Rubber products	2,080	65.40	124.52	59.77	57.29	29.02	+30.75
Other manufacturing	2,126	39.78	79.88	23.96	40.46	22.42	+1.54
Total	56,714	1,639.21	4,195.71	2,249.25	2,650.40	1,586.27	+662.98

Notes: [a] Excluding firms classified to the 'bearing', 'machine tools' and 'construction equipment', industries.
[b] Excluding firms classified to the 'consumer electronics', 'electronics', 'electronic components' and 'automotive components' industries.
[c] See Appendix F of Strange (1993) for details of sources and calculations.

employment data largely derived from the survey published by the Japan External Trade Organization (JETRO) of UK-based manufacturing affiliates of Japanese companies at the end of January 1991.[4] The total figure of 56,714 employees[5] relates to the end of January 1991, and has been broken down into 17 industrial sectors (Table 4.2). The categorization of most affiliates was fairly straightforward. For example, Hitachi Consumer Products (UK) Ltd is clearly part of the 'consumer electronics' industry. Some affiliates are, however, more difficult to classify because of lack of information, and some involve production in more than one 'industry' – NEC Technologies (UK) Ltd, for instance, manufactures both electronic office equipment and consumer electronic products. The most populous sector is 'consumer electronics' as might be expected, but there is also substantial employment in the 'motor vehicles', 'electronic office equipment', 'electronic components' and 'automotive components' industries. Employment in the 'bearings', 'textiles and clothing' and 'computers' sectors has been boosted by the recent acquisitions of United Precision Industries, Daks-Simpson and ICL respectively. And the 'rubber products' sector is dominated by the presence of Sumitomo Rubber Industries.

It was noted above that Japanese enterprises in the UK accounted for 0.56 per cent of total employment, and 0.60 per cent of total net output in UK manufacturing industry in 1989. Per capita output in these affiliates was thus similar on average to that for UK manufacturing industry as a whole. This observation is surprising given the high levels of per capita output shown by US and EC firms, and the fact that, a priori, one would expect foreign firms to show higher productivity than their domestic counter- parts. Perhaps, however, the figures reflect the fact that much of the production by Japanese companies in the UK is still (at least in 1989) of a relatively unsophisticated, assembly nature. If it can also be assumed that the per capita net output of Japanese affiliates is similar to the UK average in *each* industry, then it is possible to derive estimates of net output (in 1989 prices) by Japanese companies in each of the 17 sectors.[6] If it is also reasonable to assume that the Japanese affiliates purchase the same proportion of inputs as the UK average in *each* industry, then it is further possible to derive estimates of total sales and purchases in each of the 17 sectors. Total aggregate sales (in 1989 prices) on the basis of the January 1991 employment data thus amount to £4,195 million, while aggregate net output (a better guide of the contribution to gross domestic product (GDP)) was £1,639 million. These figures compare with those reported for Japanese companies in the 1989 Census of Production (see Table 4.1): employment = 27,200; net output = £797.7 million.

As regards the balance of trade, two direct effects may be attributed to the location of Japanese manufacturing investment in the UK. On the one hand, there are the exports of finished goods from the UK production facilities. The export sales ratios for the Japanese affiliates have been estimated on the evidence of information provided by the companies themselves.[7] In most of the industries, these estimates have been higher than the average export sales ratios for the UK industries of which they are a part. The ratios range from 80 per cent for the 'bearings', 'machine tools' and 'construction equipment' industries to only 12 per cent for 'food and drink manufacturing'. Total exports (in 1989 prices) thus amount to £2,249 million, of which over 50 per cent is provided by the 'consumer electronics' and 'motor vehicles' sectors.

On the other hand, there are the induced imports of raw materials, parts, sub-assemblies etc. One of the major criticisms of Japanese manufacturing facilities in the EC is their alleged low level of local content. The JETRO survey (JETRO 1991: 46) provides disaggregated sectoral data on the proportion of parts and materials sourced within the EC. If these data are combined with estimates of the average proportion of purchases bought by UK companies within the UK, it is then possible to derive estimates of the imports of parts etc. by Japanese companies within each industrial sector. Thus, for example, Japanese affiliates within the 'consumer electronics' sector typically purchase 51.8 per cent of their parts and materials within the EC, and it is assumed that 67.8 per cent of these purchases are met within the UK. Almost 65 per cent of purchases of parts etc. (£639 million) are accordingly imported. In contrast, the 'bearings' industry only imports 40 per cent (£45 million) of its requirements. Total imports (in 1989 prices) thus amount to £1,586 million,[8] of which the 'consumer electronics' sector accounts for 40 per cent.

Finally, it is possible to derive simple estimates of the effect of Japanese manufacturing investment on the UK trade balance. All but three sectors show surpluses. 'Textiles and clothing', 'chemicals' and 'food and related products' all show deficits, but those deficits are small enough to be insignificant given the level of approximation in the calculations. In contrast, the 'motor vehicle', 'bearings' and 'consumer electronics' sectors all show substantial surpluses. The above analysis ignores imports of capital equipment by the Japanese companies associated with the establishment of their UK production facilities – these imports would typically be one-off expenses. Furthermore, no assessment is made of the extent to which profits are repatriated from the UK affiliates to the Japanese parent companies. However, what little evidence exists suggests that such financial flows are limited as most Japanese companies have been reinvesting their profits in their overseas affiliates, and have even been providing additional capital from Japan.

The figures quoted in Table 4.2 provide only a naive analysis of the effects of Japanese manufacturing investment on the UK economy. They take no account of the extent to which UK production by the Japanese firms has substituted for imports from overseas, or for production by indigenous UK firms. In the analysis that follows, an hypothetical counterfactual position is described (Table 4.3) in which no Japanese manufacturing investment has been undertaken in the UK. In general, the UK production by the Japanese firms will have led to some reduction in output/sales by other UK-based companies. Or to put it in a different way, if there had been no Japanese FDI, the hypothetical UK company (or companies) would have produced and sold some portion of the output, both domestically and overseas, currently provided by the Japanese affiliates. Thus it is possible to distinguish three indirect effects of Japanese manufacturing investment on the UK trade balance. First, there is the 'import substitution effect' whereby the UK production by the Japanese firms reduces the import of finished goods. Second, the gross exports of the Japanese companies (from Table 4.2) need to be reduced by the exports which the hypothetical UK company would have made in their absence – the 'export effect'. Third, the import bill of the Japanese companies (from Table 4.2) also needs to be reduced by the imports of parts etc. purchased by the hypothetical UK company – the 'import effect'.

It is first assumed that the UK sales of the Japanese companies constitute the 'available' market in the absence of the Japanese FDI. Some of this market will be taken by imports, and this part may be calculated with the aid of the import penetration ratios for each sector. Total imports (in 1989 prices) of finished goods thus amount to £1,186 million, much of which consists of 'consumer electronics', 'electronic components' and 'motor vehicles'. The remainder of the 'available' market may be assumed to be captured by the hypothetical UK company. Given its low level of import penetration, 'chemicals' emerges as the sector with the highest UK sales under this scenario. The hypothetical UK companies will also export a proportion of their output, though typically a rather smaller percentage than their Japanese counterparts. Here again 'consumer electronics', 'computers' and 'electronic components' are to the fore, but exports from the 'motor vehicles' sector are assumed to be low. Total exports (in 1989 prices) thus amount to £783 million, and total sales (UK and overseas) to £1,543 million. Purchases will, in general, be

Table 4.3 The hypothetical situation without Japanese manufacturing investment

Industry	Employ-ment	Net output (£ millions)	Total sales (£ millions)	Exports (£ millions)	Imports of finished goods (£ millions)	Imports of parts etc. (£ millions)	Trade balance (£ millions)
Textiles and clothing	2,156	29.88	63.88	18.22	37.36	16.03	−35.17
Motor vehicles	1,344	53.70	163.14	46.35	126.53	34.61	−114.79
Bearings	950	21.97	43.91	30.67	30.89	3.47	−3.69
Consumer electronics	2,762	105.46	322.09	191.37	413.94	75.05	−297.62
Machine tools	56	1.30	2.74	1.34	1.58	0.27	−0.51
Construction equipment	102	3.62	10.91	7.39	6.27	1.05	+0.07
Electronic office equipment	1,888	46.29	113.48	91.52	69.56	27.17	−5.21
Electronic components	2,774	56.03	122.08	97.48	164.63	24.41	−91.56
Automotive components	3,694	76.02	174.54	58.66	80.52	30.61	−52.47
Computers	1,008	59.73	154.43	117.16	118.04	36.85	−37.73
Chemical and allied products	2,764	85.22	186.11	46.53	46.53	35.48	−35.48
General machinery[a]	510	13.14	26.68	10.49	10.79	2.20	−2.50
Electrical machinery[b]	400	9.23	19.49	8.96	11.40	3.08	−5.52
Precision machinery	389	8.58	16.23	8.77	11.18	1.56	−3.97
Food and related products	120	3.53	10.96	1.31	2.12	1.26	−2.07
Rubber products	1,141	35.88	68.32	33.36	29.79	11.85	−8.28
Other manufacturing	1,168	43.88	13.12	13.12	25.16	8.04	−20.08
Total	23,226	1,542.87	782.70	782.70	1,183.29	312.99	−716.58

Notes: [a] Excluding firms classified to the 'bearing', 'machine tools' and 'construction equipment', industries.
[b] Excluding firms classified to the 'consumer electronics', 'electronics', 'electronic components' and 'automotive components' industries.
[c] See Appendix F of Strange (1993) for details of sources and calculations.

Table 4.4 A more sophisticated analysis of the effects of Japanese manufacturing investment on UK employment, output and the trade balance

Industry	Actual situation with Japanese investment[a]			Hypothetical situation without Japanese investment[b]			Effects of Japanese investment		
	Employment (£ m)	Net output (£ m)	Trade balance (£ m)	Employment (£ m)	Net output (£ m)	Trade balance (£ m)	Employment (£ m)	Net output (£ m)	Trade Balance (£ m)
Textiles and clothing	3,892	53.94	-6.51	2,156	29.88	-35.17	+1,736	+24.06	+28.66
Motor vehicles	5,013	200.23	+136.63	1,344	53.70	-114.79	+3,669	+146.53	+251.42
Bearings	4,774	110.38	+131.20	950	21.97	-3.69	+3,824	+88.41	+134.89
Consumer electronics	11,679	445.86	+177.70	2,762	105.46	-297.62	+8,917	+340.40	+475.32
Machine tools	304	7.06	+8.54	56	1.30	-0.51	+248	+5.76	+9.05
Construction equipment	458	16.25	+25.96	102	3.62	+0.07	+356	+12.63	+25.89
Electronic office equipment	3,814	93.50	+40.66	1,888	46.29	-5.21	+1,926	+47.21	+45.87
Electronic components	7,167	144.74	+14.93	2,774	56.03	-91.56	+4,393	+88.71	+106.49
Automotive components	6,394	131.60	+14.14	3,694	76.02	-52.47	+2,700	+55.58	+66.61
Computers	2,532	150.69	+69.59	1,008	59.73	-37.73	+1,524	+90.36	+107.32
Chemicals and allied products	3,685	113.62	-3.34	2,764	85.22	-35.48	+921	+28.40	+32.14
General machinery[c]	846	21.79	+7.93	510	13.14	-2.50	+336	+8.65	+10.43
Electrical machinery[d]	834	19.24	+5.91	400	9.23	-5.52	+434	+10.01	+11.43
Precision machinery	970	21.42	+10.89	389	8.58	-3.97	+581	+12.84	+14.86
Food and related products	146	4.31	-3.54	120	3.53	-2.07	+26	+0.78	-1.47
Rubber products	2,080	65.40	+30.75	1,141	35.88	-8.28	+939	+29.52	+39.03
Other manufacturing	2,126	39.78	+1.54	1,168	21.85	-20.08	+958	+17.93	+21.62
Total	56,714	1,639.21	+662.98	23,226	631.43	-716.58	+33,488	+1,007.78	+1,379.56

Notes: a See Table 4.2.
   b See Table 4.3.
   c Excluding firms classified to the 'bearings', 'machine tools' and 'construction equipment' industries.
   d Excluding firms classified to the 'consumer electronics', 'electronic components' and 'automotive components' industries.

Table 4.5 The effects of japanese manufacturing investment on the UK trade balance

	Import substitution effect (£ million)	Export effect (£ million)	Import effect (£ million)	Total effect on trade (£ million)
Textiles and clothing	+37.36	+14.07	−22.77	+28.66
Motor vehicles	+126.53	+318.63	−193.74	+251.42
Bearings	+30.89	+145.86	−41.86	+134.89
Consumer electronics	+413.94	+625.62	−564.32	+475.32
Machine tools	+1.58	+10.60	−3.13	+9.05
Construction equipment	+6.27	+31.77	−12.15	+25.89
Electronic office equipment	+69.56	+45.75	−69.44	+45.87
Electronic components	+164.63	+28.68	−86.82	+106.49
Automotive components	+80.52	+47.09	−61.00	+66.61
Computers	+118.04	+115.81	−126.53	+107.32
Chemicals and allied products	+46.53	+15.51	−29.90	+32.14
General machinery[a]	+10.79	+6.76	−7.12	+10.43
Electrical machinery[b]	+11.40	+9.73	−9.70	+11.43
Precision machinery	+11.18	+13.12	−9.44	+14.86
Food and related products	+2.12	+0.30	−3.89	−1.47
Rubber products	+29.79	+26.41	−17.17	+39.03
Other manufacturing	+25.16	+10.84	−14.38	+21.62
Total	+1,186.29	+1,466.55	−1,273.28	+1,379.56

Notes: [a] Excluding firms classified to the 'bearings', 'machine tools' and 'construction equipment' industries.
[b] Excluding firms classified to the 'consumer electronics', 'electronic components' and 'automotive components' industries.

sourced rather more from within the UK than was the case with the Japanese companies. For example, it was noted above that Japanese firms in the 'consumer electronics' industries imported about 65 per cent of their parts etc. In contrast, the hypothetical UK company in the industry only imports 32 per cent of its requirements. Thus total imports of parts etc. (in 1989 prices) are only £313 million. All but one of the 17 sectors in this hypothetical situation show trade deficits; the exception is the 'construction equipment' industry where an insignificant surplus is registered. Furthermore, UK employment and net output are both much reduced to 23,226 and £631 million respectively. The sectors with the largest employment are 'automotive components', 'electronic components', 'chemicals', 'consumer electronics' and 'textiles and clothing'.

It is in comparison with this counterfactual position that the 'naive' data from Table 4.2 should be judged. Table 4.4 provides this more sophisticated analysis of the effects of Japanese manufacturing investment. As regards employment, the total figure amounts to 33,488. The largest effect is clearly in the 'consumer electronics' sector, though there are sizeable contributions from the 'electronic components', 'bearings', 'motor vehicles', 'automotive components' and 'electronic office equipment' industries. The total addition to net output is estimated (in 1989 prices) to be £1,008 million, with the same six sectors again prominent. The greater relative importance of the 'motor vehicles' industry is occasioned by the fact that net output per employee is high in this sector. And the total effect on the trade balance is +£1,380 million (cf. the UK deficit on manufacturing trade of £13 billion in 1990). The breakdown of this improvement into its various components is shown in Table 4.5.

In aggregate terms, the 'export effect' and the 'import effect' are roughly in balance – i.e. the additional exports generated by Japanese affiliates in the UK are largely offset by the companies' higher propensity to import parts etc. from overseas. At the industry level, however, there is rather more variation. In five sectors ('textiles and clothing', 'electronic office equipment', 'electronic components', 'automotive components' and 'chemicals') the additional imports of parts etc. are much larger than the concomitant increase in exports. In all five, though, the 'import substitution effects' are much stronger and so all register substantial trade surpluses overall. In the 'motor vehicles', 'bearings', 'consumer electronics', 'machine tools' and 'construction equipment' sectors, the opposite situation pertains where the additional exports associated with Japanese FDI outweigh the increased purchases of parts from overseas. In these cases, the 'import substitution effects' are also rather weaker in relative terms. These results reflect the efforts made by Japanese affiliates in these sensitive sectors to localize their operations. The other seven industries show no obvious pattern, largely because of the assumptions used in the calculations.

A number of final points should be made about the above assessment. First and foremost, it must be stressed again that the conclusions of such a numerical analysis are only as good as the accuracy of the assumptions on which the analysis is based. It was acknowledged at the outset that many of the figures were ball-park estimates, and the final conclusions should thus be interpreted with great caution. One conclusion that does bear close scrutiny is that there is considerable variation in the effects of Japanese manufacturing investment across industrial sectors. This observation validates the disaggregated approach adopted in this paper – any failings in the final analysis merely highlight the need for further sectoral research.

Second, the analysis focuses on the trade effects of Japanese manufacturing investment, and assumes that the Japanese affiliates are identical to their indigenous UK counterparts in terms of total sales, net output and purchases per employee. Thus the reported effects on employment etc. rest upon the assumptions regarding the level of import penetration in the absence of Japanese investment, and upon the different propensities of UK and Japanese firms to export from their UK base and to source their inputs from within the UK economy. A more comprehensive analysis should also take account of differences in productivity, differences in pricing and any multiplier effects upon the rest of the UK economy.

Third, the calculation of the trade effects of Japanese manufacturing investment rests crucially upon the assumptions of the counterfactual position. This has been specified for all industries in terms of an hypothetical situation where the 'available' UK market may be satisfied in part by imports. Yet in many of the sectors considered, imports have not only been restricted but those restrictions have also played a pivotal role in the promotion of inward investment. This raises the question of whether the appropriate counterfactual position in these industries should instead envisage the 'available' UK market being fully satisfied by imports. This would correspond to the optimal 'free-trade' solution in which production is located in the most efficient location. If such a counterfactual position was adopted then any direct investment provoked by trade restrictions would necessarily accompany a net loss of economic welfare for the host country. The approach adopted in the above analysis, however, considers the effects of the trade restrictions (and the consequent loss of economic welfare) to be distinct from the effects of any subsequent direct investment. It should therefore be stressed that the analysis should not be interpreted as validating the use of trade restrictions to promote direct investment.

Finally, it is interesting to speculate on the possible scale of the Japanese contribution to the UK economy at the turn of the century, as Japanese FDI seems certain to rise considerably through the 1990s. It has been suggested (Dillow 1989) that output might well rise to £16 billion (at 1989 prices) in the year 2000, and that the UK trade balance might

Table 4.6 The effects of an increase in Japanese manufacturing investment on UK employment and net output

	Actual employment (January 1991)	Change in net output per additional employee (£)	Change in trade balance per additional employee (£)
Textiles and clothing	3,892	+6,182	+7,364
Motor vehicles	5,013	+29,230	+50,154
Bearings	4,774	+18,519	+28,255
Consumer electronics	11,679	+29,146	+40,699
Machine tools	304	+18,947	+29,770
Construction equipment	458	+27,576	+56,528
Electronic office equipment	3,814	+12,378	+12,027
Electronic components	7,167	+12,378	+14,858
Automotive components	6,394	+8,693	+10,418
Computers	2,532	+35,687	+42,385
Chemicals and allied products	3,685	+7,707	+12,329
General machinery[a]	846	+10,225	+13,705
Electrical machinery[b]	834	+12,002	+15,320
Precision machinery	970	+13,237	−10,068
Food and related products	146	+5,342	+18,764
Rubber products	2,080	+14,192	+10,169
Other manufacturing	2,126	+8,434	+10,169
Total/average	56,714	+17,770	+24,325

Notes: [a] Excluding firms classified to the 'bearings', 'machine tools' and 'construction equipment' industries.
  [b] Excluding firms classified to the 'consumer electronics', 'electronic

benefit by over £13 billion. These projections seem unduly optimistic. If it is assumed that Japanese FDI rises globally at an annual cumulative rate of 14 per cent (MITI 1988: 2) through the rest of the decade, then this will imply a doubling of the stock of investment every five years. If this growth rate also applies to Japanese FDI in the UK economy, and if employment rises proportionately, then Japanese affiliates may well employ over 200,000 people by the year 2000. The effects upon net output and the trade balance depend crucially upon the industries in which this additional employment is found (Table 4.6). Moreover, the potential crowding-out of UK firms becomes greater as the scale of Japanese involvement increases. The potential benefits are greatest in the high-technology sectors, and are much smaller in the components (both electronic and automotive) industries and many of the other low- and medium-technology sectors. Thus additional employment in the 'motor vehicles' sector will bring greater than average improvements in both the trade balance and in net output. It is in this light that the establishment of UK manufacturing facilities by Toyota and Honda should be viewed.

Any attempt to predict the industrial spread of Japanese FDI in the year 2000 would be fanciful in the extreme. Instead, the average increments of £17,770 per employee to net output, and £24,325 per employee to the trade balance will be assumed. These assumptions then imply that Japanese affiliates will contribute annually about £3.5–4 billion (in 1989 prices) to UK net output, and about £5 billion (in 1989 prices) to the UK trade balance at the end of the century. These estimates are rather more modest than those put forward by Dillow, and certainly do not suggest that Japanese manufacturing investment will alone eradicate the UK trade deficit.

CONCLUDING REMARKS

This paper has presented a statistical analysis of the contemporary economic impact of Japanese manufacturing investment in the UK economy. It has been shown that Japanese FDI has already had a major impact upon output and employment across a range of industries. However, the analysis probably underestimates the full impact of Japanese FDI because it ignores any productivity differentials between the Japanese affiliates and other UK firms, because it takes no account of future trends towards greater local sourcing by the Japanese affiliates and because it makes no quantitative assessment of the indirect benefits which accrue from the 'demonstration effect' associated with the Japanese presence – the so-called phenomenon of the Japanization of British industry (Oliver and Wilkinson 1988).

In the future, the scale of the Japanese presence is likely to grow, and its influence is likely to deepen and broaden. The potential benefits of such increased Japanese involvement are substantial, but there are also associated dangers. For example, Japanese companies have recently criticized the skill levels of UK job applicants, and have suggested that the UK might lose its dominant share of EC-destined inward investment as the Japanese companies start to produce more sophisticated goods overseas. If that were to be the case, then the fears of some commentators that the UK might become a mere offshore assembly plant would start to gain credence.[9]

Furthermore, while the Japanese presence in many industries is to be welcomed for the substantial additional employment etc. that it brings, and while there is every prospect of further productivity increases at these plants in the future, it would nevertheless be a very risky policy to assume that benefits will continue to flow uninterrupted and in the absence of concerted efforts to promote the UK as a viable manufacturing base. Promotion in this sense does not refer to the activities of the Invest in Britain Bureau or the various Regional Development Organizations, but rather it means the provision of an educated and well-trained workforce, an environment in which firms are encouraged to invest in research and new capital equipment and a government which is actively committed to the long-term regeneration of UK manufacturing industry. The potential impact of Japanese manufacturing investment will be fully realized only if the UK Government and UK manufacturing industry can respond to this challenge.

ACKNOWLEDGEMENTS

The paper is derived from work undertaken while the author was Visiting Professor at the Institute of Social and Economic Research, Osaka University, Japan. The visit was made possible by a Foreign Visiting Scholarship funded by the Japanese Government and by additional financial assistance from the UK Economic and Social Research Council (Award reference number F00232430).

NOTES

1 As reported in *Business Monitor MO4: Census of Overseas Assets and Business Monitor MA4: Overseas Transactions*.
2 The latest year for which the summary report of the Census of Production has been published.
3 An extended version of the analysis in this paper is presented in Chapter 10 of Strange (1993).
4 See JETRO (1991) and Table 5.4 of Strange (1993).
5 Companies where the equity participation by Japanese firms is less than 40 per cent (e.g. Rover Cars, Laura Ashley) have been excluded, as have those companies for which employment data are not available. Also excluded is Toyota Motor Manufacturing (UK) Ltd. as production is not due to start until 1993.
6 Using the disaggregated sectoral data available in *Business Monitor PA1002: Report on the Census of Production – Summary Volume 1989*.
7 Again see Chapter 10 of Strange (1993) and the case studies of 27 Japanese companies presented in the book.
8 Given the assumptions above, it is likely that this is a high estimate as the figures for the proportion of UK purchases relate to total imports not just imports from the EC.
9 *Financial Times*, 14 January 1992: 7.

REFERENCES

Dillow, Chris (1989) *A Return to a Trade Surplus? The Impact of Japanese Investment on the UK*, London: Nomura Research Institute.

JETRO (Japan External Trade Organization) (1991) *7th Survey of European Operations of Japanese Companies in the Manufacturing Sector*, London: JETRO.

MITI (Ministry of International Trade and Industry) (1988) 'The progress of Japan's structural adjustment and prospects for the industrial structure,' *News from MITI*, NR–354 (88–02).

Oliver, Nick and Wilkinson, Barry (1988) *The Japanization of British Industry*, Oxford: Basil Blackwell.

Strange, Roger (1993) *Japanese Manufacturing Investment in Europe: its Impact on the UK Economy*, London: Routledge.

Chapter 5

International alliances as a strategic tool of Japanese electronic companies

Fred Burton and Freddy Saelens

ABSTRACT

The paper explores the motives of Japanese electronics firms for entering into strategic alliances with Western partners, identifies the key characteristics of these alliances and considers some of the consequences for industry structure and the ability to compete of Western firms. The analysis suggests that Japanese companies accord a high priority to strategic alliances in support of policies of technology acquisition and global market penetration.

INTRODUCTION

There is a growing literature on the scope, purpose and consequences of international strategic alliances, particularly those involving Japanese and Western partners (e.g. Hamel *et al.* 1989), although there continues to be a dearth of empirical studies. Of these, Harrigan (1985, 1988) provides evidence that alliances between otherwise competing firms in related business activities have a better than average success record, and Dunning (1988) has claimed that the function of the decision-making 'nexus' of new-style multinational firms is to advance global competitive strategy by forming alliances with other firms. Porter and Fuller (1986) argue that alliances are likely to be technology inspired because the pace of technological change is such that access to the technologies of other firms is necessary to enable a major player to create and sustain a competitive advantage in the pursuit of market share, profitability or, as argued by Kogut (1986), the minimization of transaction costs.

For whatever reasons, alliances are entered into as a preferred option to independence or merger or to arm's-length relationships with suppliers and customers. As a 'hybrid' between markets and hierarchies (Turner 1987), alliances may embrace various forms of coalition, including joint ventures, licensing agreements, franchising, original equipment manufacturing (OEM) sales, technical agreements, standardization agreements, sub-contracting, joint pre-competitive research programmes, joint development, joint production, joint marketing and second sourcing. Hymer (1968) anticipated the hybrid nature of international alliances: 'A firm can agree with others to divide the market into spheres of influence . . . or it can establish tighter co-operative links and share with others the risks of certain operations' (p. 973).

What are these 'certain operations' (activities) likely to be? Dunning and Porter offer some clues. Dunning (1988) argues that the motive for international alliances is to assist firms to globalize their value chain. Porter's value chain framework (1985) and his concept of 'five competitive forces' (1980) helps to isolate alliances by type. In the value chain, namely the *support activities* (firm infrastructure, HRM, technology, development, procurement) and the *primary activities* (inbound logistics, operations, outbound logistics, marketing and sales, service), the great majority of alliances are confined to technology, operations (production agreements) and marketing activities, but Pucik (1988) has emphasized the necessity of a human resource strategy that supports the process of organizational learning to ensure that maximum benefit is gained from collaboration. Of the potential linkages in the five forces (rivalry, buyer power, supplier power, threat of new entrants, threat of substitutes) upstream and downstream alliances will have their primary impact on the 'positioning' of the partners in their industry, diversification into new areas of business will permit economies of scope and the benefit of horizontal alliances with competitors or potential competitors will be confined to economies of scale.

The traditional forms of alliance in the manufacturing sector, typically licensing agreements or joint ventures involving a more or less equal partnership between Western firms and partners in the third world, involve the transfer of Western technology and know-how in exchange for a smoother entry by Western firms into third world markets. A distinguishing feature of traditional coalitions is their tactical nature, such as seeking to satisfy government regulations, gaining access to otherwise closed markets or achieving economies of scale. Strategic alliances, which became apparent in the late 1970s, in contrast, feature coalitions between developed country multinationals competing globally in the same markets, even in the 'alliance' market, where the partners, for example, may collaborate to sell their own brands through each other's distribution outlets (Bradley 1991).

International alliances carry potential risks and costs, including the disruption of a core competence, a loss of control (Ohmae 1989), the erosion of a firm's competitive position and the creation of an adverse bargaining position (Porter and Fuller 1986). The possibility will always exist that a partner, having gathered up information and know-how, may renege on an alliance and reposition itself in the market as a more powerful competitor. Given these potential risks and costs, why should firms seek to enter into alliances in preference to independence, arm's-length transactions or merger and acquisition? Klein *et al.* (1978) and Williamson (1988), drawing on theories of market failure, argue that alliances occur because open-market contracts cannot accommodate a wide range of contingencies.

Clearly, both partners expect to gain from an alliance and to learn more about the possible benefits during its lifetime (Westney 1987; Lyles 1987). Always intended as a means to an end, the literature offers several specific motives for an alliance: economies of scale through a pooling of resources, risk reduction, shaping competition by choosing with whom to co-operate or compete against and gaining access to technology or production techniques (Porter and Fuller 1986). To these can be added the desire to surmount market barriers (Badaracco 1991), a reduction in political risk (Hennart 1986) and enlarged market access (Robock and Simmonds 1989). Some of these motives are clearly more tactical than strategic, and many so-called strategic alliances may be neither 'strategic', i.e. compensating for weakness and creating competitive strength and serving the long-term strategic plans of the partners (Devlin and Bleakley 1988), nor 'alliances', i.e. coalitions directed towards a common objective. The contribution of an alliance to the pursuit of a long-term objective does not preclude the possibility that the alliance may itself be short term, transitory, even an unstable coalition. Even so, the termination of an alliance may not indicate failure but rather a successful transfer of competencies. Some alliances may be entered into to achieve a specific purpose in a specific period of time. In other cases the time period may be undefined, with the arrangement terminating when changed circumstances render the relationships no longer desirable or necessary.

This investigation was undertaken to gain insight into the motives of Japanese electronics firms for entering into international strategic alliances with Western competitors and to gauge some of the consequences for the partners and for their respective industries. For our purposes, we define an international strategic alliance as a collaborative arrangement in which partner firms of different nationality are major players in the same industry and where at least one partner regards the alliance as a means to safeguard or improve its competitive position at the global level. A strategic shift is considered to occur when an alliance influences the structure of the industry or when one or both partners enjoy an improvement in 'relative position' (Porter 1991).

In what follows, we explore the notion that Japanese firms enter alliances to acquire and/or to leverage competitiveness.[1] An example would be a pre-emptive alliance in which a Japanese firm links up with a foreign partner in possession of a unique market position, technology or cost advantage.[2] We then consider the economic implications of Japanese alliance policy and draw some conclusions.

STRATEGIC GROUPS: ESTABLISHMENT FIRMS AND ENTREPRENEURS

For analytical purposes, we divide Japanese electronics firms into two broad strategic groups (Table 5.1). The first group consists of firms which historically were members of large conglomerates (the pre-war zaibatsu) and which continue to maintain ties with firms – mostly in other industries – formerly belonging to the same zaibatsu (or present keiretsu).[3]

Table 5.1 A classification of the Japanese electrical and electronics industry

	Establishment	Entrepreneurial
Typical firms	Hitachi, Toshiba, NEC, Fujitsu, Matsushita Electric	Matsushita, Sharp, Sony, Sanyo
Government involvement	Large	Small
Core competence	Technology	Technology and marketing
Initial product range	Capital equipment Communication equipment	Consumer durables
First product extension	Professional electronics Component-ICs, tubes, etc.	Consumer electronics
Second product extension	Consumer electronics	Component-ICs Professional electronics

Electronics firms in this category usually owe their existence to initiatives of former Japanese governments to establish a communications infrastructure in Japan.

With the arrival of mass-electronics many of these companies made the transition towards telecommunications and other industrial applications of electronics technology, such as computers, while simultaneously integrating vertically in high value-added components, such as television tubes and, later, integrated circuits. In addition to this diversification into industrial electronics and components, these firms also entered at an early stage into consumer products, such as refrigerators, and subsequently consumer electronics equipment. Even so, the emphasis of these firms remains on industrial electronics and components, which we presume to be a consequence of a company culture that emphasizes technology rather than mass-marketing. The relative inadequacy of marketing competence, however, is not restricted to consumer markets but also manifests itself in industrial markets, one reason being that many of these firms are heavily dependent on sales to the (Japanese) government sector.[4]

We argue that these 'establishment' firms engage in strategic alliances with Western partners primarily to compensate their weaknesses in international marketing and/or to leverage their technological strengths. Our analysis of this group centres on Hitachi, Toshiba, NEC and Fujitsu.

The second strategic group consists of firms which started off primarily as producers of electrical domestic appliances and/or consumer electronics equipment. In recent years these companies have begun to enlarge their scope by moving into industrial electronics, in response to mediocre growth of the consumer electronics market, and high-technology components such as television displays and integrated circuits. Vertical integration into these components is gaining in importance as technology has begun to become a more prominent source of competitive differentiation. The historical emphasis of these firms on consumer products implies that they are relatively weak in technologies for professional applications and components.

These observations lead us to argue that these firms enter into strategic alliances with Western partners to compensate their technological weaknesses and/or to leverage their skills in consumer marketing. The firms we analyse, Matsushita, Sony and Sharp, which still identify with their founders, we refer to as 'the entrepreneurs'.

Given the well-established global market penetration strategies of these two groups of firms, we shall suggest that their alliances with a Western partner are primarily likely to reflect their strategic diversification and the corresponding strengths and weaknesses related to these strategies. This implies that the type of alliance within each strategic group will reveal a considerable degree of uniformity while, conversely, significant differences between the two groups can be expected.

To explore this compensation-leverage focus, a database was constructed of the strategic alliances between the seven Japanese firms and Western partners during the period 1978–87.[5] Only alliances with large Western electronics firms in direct global competition with the Japanese firms were considered. The database contains only those alliances for which public information is available. The extent to which this constraint introduces bias is difficult to gauge.

The sectors of the electronics industry for which alliances are recorded are consumer electronics, industrial electronics (mainframe computers, office computers, computer peripherals, telecommunications and industrial automation) and active components (semiconductors, including integrated circuits). While these sectors do not fully encompass the industry (e.g. passive components such as resistors and capacitors are not included), all the 208 recorded alliances in the database – with two exceptions – are covered by these sectors.

One problem in constituting the database centred on which alliances to include. As a general rule, only agreements which were regarded as important (by a panel of European electronics executives) and which went beyond a simple sales transaction were included.[6] Some business agreements could be dissected into separately discernible components, namely marketing, production or technology. In such cases, each of the components was treated as a separate alliance.

To understand the motives behind them, the strategic alliances were divided into three categories: transfer of technology, production and marketing alliances. In the transfer of technology category there were three kinds of transactions mode: joint development, licensing and second sourcing. In cases of joint development the partners decide to jointly develop a new product or process. For the two other modes the key element is the transfer of technology, occasionally in exchange for another technology, but usually against the payment of royalties. Second sourcing arrangements differ from licensing in that they are not entirely voluntary in nature. Companies developing a unique product or process may succumb to pressure from potential customers to transfer their technology to competitors in order to reduce the dependence of customers on a single source.[7]

The production category did not contain discernibly different transaction modes. Among the marketing alliances there were some joint marketing agreements, but the dominant modes were OEM and standardization agreements. With OEM, a producer supplies goods to its alliance partner for resale under the partner's name. In essence, the second partner acts as a marketing agent for the first. With standardization agreements a number of competitors decide on the common specifications for a new product which each of them intends to produce and market separately. In effect, each supplier trades in a potential monopoly status in exchange for enhanced market acceptability of the product.[8]

These transaction modes and types of strategic alliances cover all the cases in the database. Other types of collaborative agreements, such as pre-competitive research, technical assistance agreements and franchising, did not occur.

MOTIVES AND CONSEQUENCES

Categorizing the strategic alliances leads to the distribution shown in Table 5.2. A surprising feature, perhaps, is the low incidence of production alliances, all of which, with one exception, relate to joint production in Western countries. Most of these alliances were a response to trade controls or other market access barriers. More than 80 per cent of all transfers of technology occurred within the semiconductor/integrated circuit sector, the majority being concerned with the flow of microprocessor technology from the USA to Japan. The 'marketing' category is dominated by OEM contracts which allow Western firms to sell Japanese products under their own label.

The physical location of marketing and production alliances and the direction of technology flows show that the dominant motives of the Japanese firms for entering alliances are:

- in marketing and production alliances, to safeguard and enhance Japanese exports to the West.
- in technology alliances, to transfer Western semiconductor/integrated circuit technology to Japan.

Table 5.2 Strategic alliances by category

Category	Number	Percentage
Marketing	95	45.7
Transfer of technology	79	38.0
Production	34	16.3
Total	208	100.0

The major exception to these conclusions is the telecommunications sector, where many of the marketing and production alliances are associated with the strategy of Western firms, particularly from the USA, to enter the Japanese market. A minor exception relates to the transfer of integrated circuit technology from Japan to the West.[9]

The dominant interpretation of the executive panel was that the Japanese firms in question used alliances primarily to maintain or strengthen their export positions or global market shares but revealed a reluctance to export technology. In contrast, through alliances, Western firms have become increasingly dependent on Japanese products.

The capitulation of the US colour television industry offers a pointer to the further decline of Western industries which, we concede, is the likely consequence of strategic alliances between Japanese and Western partners. Figure 5.1 traces out the strategic error made by the industry. In the early 1970s the US colour television industry, under pressure from Japanese exports, initiated a rapid replacement of own production by OEM imports from Japan, rather than free the necessary resources to enable it to compete.[10] Consequently, the US industry lost its production skills, quickly followed by the loss of its innovation capabilities. When Japanese firms subsequently set up their own distribution channels and in many instances terminated existing collaboration agreements, the US partners lost their strategic freedom and the ability to compete, leading inevitably to the collapse of the US industry (Burton and Saelens 1987). A similar pattern can be observed in mainframe computers, where important US and European firms are becoming ever more dependent on vital components and products from their Japanese competitors.

STRATEGIC ALLIANCES AND CORPORATE POLICY

From the quantitative information in the database, we can infer that Japanese electronics firms assign high priority to collaborative arrangements with competitors. However, the emphasis differs as between the 'establishment' and the 'entrepreneurial' groups.

Characteristics of the 'establishment' group are:

- frequent use of strategic alliances
- intensive use of OEM arrangements to compensate for weakness in international marketing
- acquisition of Western semiconductor/integrated circuit telecommunication technologies

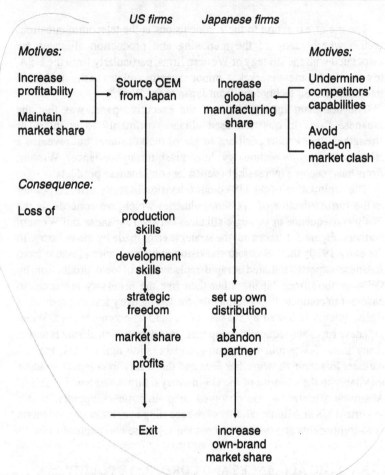

Figure 5.1 The decline of the US colour TV industry

As we supposed, the establishment group of Japanese firms make intensive use of alliances to penetrate international markets. Less expected was the frequent use of alliances to compensate weaknesses in technology portfolios.

The most important characteristics of the 'entrepreneurial' group are:

- relatively little use of strategic alliances
- no alliances formed to increase their power in domestic consumer markets through acquisition of Western products

- use of Western OEM channels to leverage existing production capabilities[11]
- acquisition of Western technology to accelerate the process of diversification into industrial electronics and components

This group can be observed to seek technology compensation but not to leverage in consumer marketing.

In addition to differences *between* the groups, there are significant differences *within* them. Among the establishment firms, Fujitsu makes a much larger use of (large-scale) strategic alliances than NEC, although they have comparable business portfolios and growth in turnover. Among the entrepreneurial firms a similar difference exists between Matsushita (a renowned low-cost producer) and Sony (which focuses on technological and market differentiation). Sony, for example, makes less use of foreign OEM channels. These examples show that there are considerable differences between Japanese firms as concerns the priority accorded to strategic alliances. In any case, the expectation that the patterns of strategic alliances of individual firms within a group would show a high degree of uniformity cannot be maintained.

CONCLUSIONS

First, Japanese companies generally accord a higher priority to strategic alliances than Western partners. A possible explanation is the greater Japanese affinity for collaboration between groups in general and between corporations in particular. Second, the firms analysed concentrate their alliance policy on exporting products and importing technology – a conclusion hardly surprising in view of Japan's industrial history. Third, the alliance policy of individual firms is the complex result (which could not be disentangled in view of the small samples) of various factors as identified earlier in the literature, such as diversification strategies, competitive strategy (e.g. low cost versus differentiation), functional capabilities (especially marketing and technologies) and a vision of alliances as a strategic tool to enhance global competitiveness.

It may be plausible to argue that the firms formulate strategies which find expression in alliances to export products and import technologies, the fundamental objective being to execute corporate policy, not to export and import, as described, *per se*. This represents a reversal of previous trends where this import/export pattern was clearly a national industrial policy objective with Japanese firms as the executors. That is to say, the current pattern is an 'unintended' consequence of *private* corporate strategies, whereas before it was a primary objective of *national* policy, enforced by the Ministry of International Trade and Industry (MITI) and others on the private sector. Alliances may involve lower transactions costs than other instruments of strategy, such as acquisitions, due to past learning experiences enforced upon Japanese firms by former industrial policies.

It is our view that Japanese firms will (a) try to reduce their dependence on Western partners, for example, by absorbing the partner's skills or concluding alliances with several partners; (b) see a collaboration agreement usually as a temporary expedient to acquire certain competencies or to leverage existing capabilities; and (c) use alliances to make partners dependent on both products and technology.

NOTES

1 According to Porter (1991: 97) the notion of competencies originates with Selznick (1957). The concept is treated at length by Itami (1987).
2 The Mitsubishi Motor Corporation, for instance, entered a strategic alliance for the production of low end cars with Hyundai of South Korea to prevent collaboration between Hyundai and one of Mitsubishi's main competitors (Devlin and Bleakley 1988).
3 A company in this category is the Mitsubishi Electric Company, which continues to bear the same name and logo as her former sister companies, e.g. Mitsubishi Heavy Industries, the Mitsubishi Corporation (general trading), the Mitsubishi Bank etc.
4 A view that is derived from interviews with company executives.
5 A strategic alliance was included if it was initiated within the period 1978–88, regardless of whether the alliance was terminated within that time.
6 An agreement was considered to be 'important' if, in the opinion of Western company executives, it could lead to a change in competitive positions in the sector concerned and/or required a re-evaluation of strategy by incumbent firms.
7 The competitors to which the technology is licensed are then known as second source suppliers.
8 For instance, three different types of video recorders were introduced more or less simultaneously, whereas the compact disc was introduced on a common format.
9 For example, the transfer of integrated circuit memory technology from Toshiba to Siemens.
10 The only US firm of any consequence to produce televisions, Zenith, announced some time ago that it would sell this loss-making activity.
11 For example, Matsushita.

REFERENCES

Badaracco, J.L. (1991) *The Knowledge Link: How Firms Compete Through Strategic Alliances*, Boston, MA: Harvard Business School Press.

Bradley, F. (1991) 'Competitive alliances to enter international markets', Chapter 13 in *International Marketing Strategy*, London: Prentice Hall International.

Burton, F.N. and Saelens, F.H. (1987) 'Trade barriers and Japanese direct investment in the colour television industry', *Managerial Economics*, 8: 285–93.

Devlin, G. and Bleakley, M. (1988) 'Strategic alliances – guidelines for success', *Long Range Planning*, 21 (5): 20.

Dunning, J.H. (1988) 'The new style multinational – circa the late 1980s and early 1990s', in J.H. Dunning (ed.) *Explaining International Production*, London: Unwin Hyman, ch. 13.

Hamel, G., Doz, I.L. and Prahalad, C.K. (1989) 'Collaborate with your competitors – and win', *Harvard Business Review*, 67 (1): 133–9.

Harrigan, K.R. (1985) *Strategies for Joint Ventures*, Lexington, MA: Lexington Books.

Harrigan, K.R. (1988) 'Strategic alliances and partner asymmetrics', *Management International Review*, 28, special issue: 53–72.

Hennart, J.F. (1986) 'A transactions cost theory of equity joint ventures', Proceedings of the Research Colloquium on Corporate Strategies in International Business, The Wharton School, University of Pennsylvania.

Hymer, S. (1968) 'La Grande corporation multinationale: analyse de certaines raisons qui poussent a l'Integration Internationale des Affaires', *Revue Economique*, 14 (6): 949–73.

Itami, H. (1987) *Mobilizing Invisible Assets*, Cambridge, MA: Harvard University Press.

Klein, B., Crawford, R. and Alchian, A. (1978) 'Vertical integration, appropriable rents and the competitiveness contracting process', *Journal of Law and Economics*, 21: 297–326.

Kogut, B. (1986) 'Joint ventures: a review and preliminary investigation', Proceedings of the Research Colloquium on Corporate Strategies in International Business, The Wharton School, University of Pennsylvania.

Lyles, M.A. (1987) 'Learning among joint venture sophisticated firms', in F.J. Contractor and P. Lorange (eds) *Cooperative Strategies in International Business*, Lexington, MA: Lexington Books.

Ohmae, K. (1989) 'The global logic of strategic alliances', *Harvard Business Review*, 67 (2): 143–54.

Porter, M.E. (1980) *Competitive Strategy: Techniques for Analysing Industries and Competitors*, New York: Free Press.

Porter, M.E. (1985) *Competitive Advantage: Creating and Sustaining Superior Performance*, New York: Free Press.

Porter, M.E. (1991) 'Towards a dynamic theory of strategy', *Strategic Management Journal*, 12: 95–117.

Porter, M.E. and Fuller, M.B. (1986) 'Coalitions and global strategy', in M.E. Porter (ed.) *Competition in Global Industries*, Boston, MA: Harvard Business School Press, ch. 10.

Pucik, V. (1988) 'Strategic alliances, organizational learning and competitive advantage: the HRM agenda', *HRM*, 27 (1): 77–93.

Robock, S. and Simmonds, K. (1989) *International Business and Multinational Enterprise*, Homewood, IL: Richard D. Irwin.

Selznick, P. (1957) *Leadership in Administration: A Sociological Interpretation*, New York: Harper and Row.

Turner, L. (1987) *Industrial Collaboration with Japan*, London: Routledge.

Westney, D.E. (1987) 'Domestic and foreign learning curves in managing international co-operative strategies', in F.J. Contractor and P. Lorange (eds) *Co-operative Strategies in International Business*, Lexington, MA: Lexington Books.

Williamson, O.E. (1988) 'The vertical integration of production: market failure considerations', Chapter 6 in O.E. Williamson (ed.) *Economic Organization: Firms, Markets and Policy Control*, Brighton: Wheatsheaf.

Chapter 6

Global strategy in the Japanese semiconductor industry
Knowledge creation through strategic alliances

Yoshiya Teramoto, Frank-Juergen Richter, Naoto Iwasaki, Tohru Takai and Yukihiro Wakuta

ABSTRACT

Japanese firms dominate many parts of the semiconductor industry and they have formed many strategic alliances. The study shows how Japanese firms create knowledge through strategic alliances. A framework for understanding and analysing knowledge creation by alliance partners is proposed. There are three sequential processes – internalization, distribution and evolution. The framework is then illustrated with examples of knowledge creation by Japanese companies such as Toshiba, Hitachi, NEC and Fujitsu and contrasted with the lack of attention that Western companies pay to knowledge creation in strategic alliances. Because the alliances between Japanese and Western firms are frequently unbalanced, the view is developed that more balanced relationships would be desirable in the future.

INTRODUCTION

Within the information technology industries, the semiconductor industry has shown stormy growth during the 1980s. Semiconductors can be considered to be a focal point of the high-tech industry, because the computer and electronics industries use the products provided by the semiconductor industry as basic input materials. Hence, semiconductors can be seen as the 'crude oil' for today's industries (Okimoto *et al.* 1984).

The convergence of information technologies has provoked the emergence of a global network of firms linked through a wide variety of strategic alliances (Hamel 1991; Teramoto *et al.* 1993). This network binds US, European and Japanese firms into a structure of overlapping equity arrangements that increasingly blurs the traditional locus of competition.

The semiconductor industry is characterized by rapid innovation and the life cycle of semiconductors is very short. To meet the need for rapid innovation firms are building technological linkages and entering joint research and development (R&D) projects. Investment in production facilities is so huge that single companies on their own often cannot provide the necessary financial resources. They are sharing the financial burden and are entering alliances with competitors.

Historically, Japanese companies linked up with their American and European competitors to acquire technical knowledge. Today, almost all Japanese semiconductor manufacturers are bound in alliances, so that huge networks of firms have appeared. Alliances are the institutional arrangement that best allows Japanese firms to implement strategies for effectively acquiring knowledge (Jones and Shill 1991; Hamel 1991).

Previous research on strategic alliances focused, above all, on the transaction cost aspect of strategic alliances (Harrigan 1985; Casson 1990). Such a perspective, however, considers trade-offs between organizations in a static way.[1] A better source of competitive advantage comes from knowledge creation.

The first section of the paper proposes a framework for understanding and analysing knowledge creation in strategic alliances. Then, after an introduction to alliances in the semiconductor industry, the way Japanese companies carry out knowledge creation is explained and illustrated. The paper ends with a discussion of the problems which arise and future developments.

STRATEGIC ALLIANCES AND KNOWLEDGE CREATION

In order to create new markets, develop new products and respond to customers, the creation of new knowledge is essential in the semiconductor industry. New knowledge emerges in all areas of human life and changes the basic conditions of human behaviour. The rapid increase of knowledge leads to a competition for knowledge because practically everybody becomes able to obtain knowledge due to the spread of information in society (Boulding 1981).

The importance of knowledge

Companies which create new knowledge quickest can develop long-lasting competitive advantages. Beside the creation of knowledge within the narrow boundaries of industrial organizations, the possibility of grafting knowledge from the business environment also exists.

Table 6.1 Different kinds of knowledge

Operational knowledge	Quantifiable data, codified procedures
Strategic knowledge	Core competencies, policy direction
Meta-knowledge	Basic assumptions, inherent values

Strategic alliances, in particular, are an effective way to graft knowledge from other firms in the same industry. Companies are abandoning their competitive stances and are entering strategic alliances with former competitors in order to share knowledge and to create new forms of knowledge (Badaracco 1991).

Knowledge to be shared by co-operating firms can occur in three forms: operational knowledge, strategic knowledge and meta-knowledge (Table 6.1). Operational knowledge is knowledge about products and markets, e.g. all the knowledge which is linked to production and marketing. Most of this knowledge is formal and quantifiable. Alliance partners expect to receive readily usable operational knowledge. Strategic knowledge, on the other hand, is less tangible. It is about core competencies and policy directions. Alliance partners can improve their strategies through exchanging this knowledge. Meta-knowledge, finally, contains the basic assumptions which guide corporate behaviour. Reconsideration of these basic assumptions can lead to a total change of a company's values.[2]

The learning system

The creation of knowledge demands the willingness of firms to learn (Argyris and Schon 1987). When knowledge is internalized by an organization, corporate growth is not guaranteed. Knowledge has to be interpreted and memorized in order to transform it into manageable forms (Huber 1991). Sometimes, however, old knowledge first has to be unlearned in order to make room for new knowledge (Hedberg 1981). Hence, well-worn routines, which could hinder learning, have to be abandoned in order to release learning potentials.

Existing literature often compares strategic alliances with learning systems (Lyles 1988; Hamel 1991; Parkhe 1991) because through such alliances firms aim to acquire their partners' knowledge. Knowledge is an information-based asset and its market value is uncertain. It is not enough if companies transfer knowledge as a kind of interfirm trade. They have to utilize knowledge from their partners by integrating it within their own organizational boundaries. As seen in Figure 6.1, the sub-routines leading to new knowledge are as follows. The figure shows

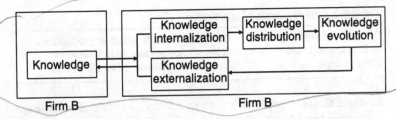

Figure 6.1 The creation of knowledge through strategic alliances

the processes which take place when Firm B receives knowledge from Firm A and creates new knowledge. Generally, the first step of knowledge creation occurs when Firm B internalizes the knowledge of Firm A.[3] The internalization is a result of intentional, systematic efforts to acquire knowledge that is new to the organization. Organizations can acquire operational, strategic or meta-knowledge according to their capabilities and preferences.

In the next step, the acquired knowledge becomes linked with already existing knowledge when it is distributed throughout the organization. The distribution mechanism is important because knowledge remains useless if it is not recallable in the right place at the right time.[4] Organizational sub-units can further develop new knowledge by piecing together items of knowledge that they obtain from other organizational units. Thus, knowledge distribution leads to a broader range of knowledge.

The internalization and the distribution of knowledge leads to the evolution of the organizational knowledge. In this perspective, evolution means an increase of adaptability and a more highly developed organizational form which is better than the firm's initial state.[5] Organizations graft knowledge from the outside but evolve it within their organizational boundaries.

In a last step, the knowledge is externalized towards the partner who initially provided the knowledge. The partner, in his turn, proceeds in enriching the knowledge and returns it. Knowledge is passed back and forth and becomes mutually fruitful. The firms elicit behaviour from their counterparts, which allows both to do well. The firms co-create knowledge.

STRATEGIC ALLIANCES IN THE JAPANESE SEMICONDUCTOR INDUSTRY

Strategic alliances have been an important reason behind the increased competitiveness of the Japanese semiconductor industry. Although Japanese companies entered many alliances with foreign companies, there are only a few domestic alliances and the intensity of competition among Japan's semiconductor firms is high. One of the few co-operation projects among the major Japanese semiconductor makers was the Ministry of International Trade and Industry (MITI)-initiated VLSI project from 1976 to 1980 which involved optical technology research.

Toshiba's most important strategic alliances are its partnerships with Motorola and Siemens. The agreement with Siemens started as a licensing agreement for Toshiba's direct random access memory (DRAM) technology and was later enlarged to include joint second sourcing agreements. In the alliance with Motorola, on the other hand, Toshiba obtained Motorola's microprocessor unit (MPU) technology and became the first manufacturer, besides Motorola and Intel, to sell 32-bit MPUs.

In 1965 Hitachi started to develop integrated circuits under a technological tie-up with RCA and continually expanded its semiconductor business. During the late 1980s, Hitachi's semiconductor earnings faltered and it promoted a strategy to enhance R&D capabilities. Hitachi invested heavily in international alliances to realize this strategy. In 1988, for example, Hitachi formed an alliance with Texas Instruments to jointly develop 16M DRAM.

Since about 1987 the alliance strategy of NEC has been briskly carried out. Co-operative and wide-ranging alliances, including joint design or development, have increased since 1989. In 1989 NEC entered a licensing agreement for reduced instruction set computer (RISC) processors with MIPS Computer Systems in order to catch up in this field. In 1990 NEC made an agreement with AT&T concerning wide-ranging products related to the semiconductor business. The contract included technology exchanges and tie-ups in manufacturing and sales.

By the mid-1980s Fujitsu entered into a very strong relationship with Sun Microsystems, a company successful in the workstation business. Semiconductors used for workstations have been supplied by Fujitsu through an OEM agreement since 1989. To expand its product lines Fujitsu has relied heavily on technological transfer through strategic alliances.

Recent shifts in alliance patterns

Because the Japanese companies have broad product ranges they are important consumers of semiconductors themselves. The existence of a strong domestic market is indispensable for maintaining economies of scale. However, given the capital involved, there has been a spontaneous division of labour in semiconductor manufacturing. For example, Hitachi attained a large market share in 256-byte chips, Toshiba in 1-megabyte chips and Fujitsu in application specific integrated circuits (ASICs). In order to catch up, where the market is dominated by competitors, Japanese firms are increasingly entering alliances with Western companies.

As a consequence, the scope of alliances has broadened. Narrow relationships focusing on the development of just one product, such as gate arrays, for one market are being enlarged to complex co-operative arrangements, which often include joint development, joint production and joint marketing.

The alliance between Toshiba and Motorola in Japan was first conceived to produce semiconductors for the Japanese market. Today, the alliance focuses on joint developments for global markets. In 1990 both companies even decided to build a joint venture in Scotland in order to enter the European market. Closely related to the broadening of the scope of alliances are recent technological trends within the semiconductor business. Alliances were first formed to develop the hardware for producing semiconductors. The new alliances include the joint development of the necessary software. Software tools have to be provided especially for ASICs, which enable customers to develop chips with unique functions. NEC is promoting tie-ups with the American company Keidaence to stimulate the necessary integration of hardware and software components.

KNOWLEDGE CREATION OF JAPANESE FIRMS

Japanese companies are said to be talented in knowledge creation and to tackle knowledge in holistic ways. The Japanese approach is based on the recognition that creating knowledge is not a matter of handling objective information, but of mobilizing the tacit and subjective insights related to information. Japanese firms convert tacit to explicit knowledge (Nonaka 1991).

Although Japanese firms are actively creating knowledge through strategic alliances, their internal capabilities to create knowledge are advanced, too. By the beginning of the 1980s, they had already reached a high level of technological expertise. If this was not the case, they would not have been able to internalize, distribute and evolve knowledge. The following sections will show the ways Japanese semiconductor firms create knowledge through strategic alliances.

Knowledge internalization

Fujitsu supplies MPU units to the American Sun Microsystems and receives Sun's workstation technology. Such a product exchange is related to quantifiable data rather than to more abstract forms of knowledge, such as corporate strategies and values. As in the case with Sun Microsystems, Fujitsu generally prefers to utilize OEM agreements or to build up product links. Hence, Fujitsu's intention when entering strategic alliances is to strengthen its product lines. The same conditions can be seen in the case of Hitachi in an alliance with Texas Instruments. Hitachi supplies SRAMs to Texas Instruments and receives the American firm's semiconductor technologies. In its alliance with Goldstar, on the other hand, Hitachi uses the Korean firm as second source supplier for assuring production capacity. Both Fujitsu and Hitachi have managed very successfully to internalize operational knowledge. Additionally, all Japanese semiconductor companies make efforts to acquire operational knowledge through reverse engineering and the systematic collection and analysis of product and market data.

Hitachi entered a further alliance with Texas Instruments to broaden its background in the development of 64M and 256M DRAMs. Both companies are combining their R&D expertise to develop new products. Hitachi engaged in other alliances, as with the American company RCA and with Motorola, to reduce R&D costs and lower risk. Hitachi hopes to acquire strategic knowledge through such alliances. In the development of flash memories, a whole new set of alliances have been recently concluded: Toshiba tied up with IBM, Fujitsu with AMD and Sharp with Intel. These alliances all focus on joint R&D. The companies are striving to obtain strategic knowledge in order to strengthen their core competencies and to reconsider their policy directions.

Compared with other firms, NEC is strong in acquiring knowledge related to its basic assumptions and values. Although NEC has been reluctant to enter alliances for a long time, it recently linked with AT&T. Through this alliance, NEC not only got knowledge from products or patents, but also through human resources. NEC sent expatriates to foreign laboratories like AT&T's Bell laboratories and scouted out key persons from other companies. By doing so, NEC learned how to create knowledge at these sites. Through its link with the Bell laboratories, NEC gained insight into new ways of advancing its business operations. The American approach of basic research has been transferred to the Japanese company. Hence, NEC acquired meta-knowledge.

Knowledge distribution

According to their strategies, Japanese semiconductor companies internalize different types of knowledge from their overseas partners.

They then start actively to distribute the acquired knowledge within their organizational boundaries. Knowledge distribution is essential to enable Japanese manufacturers to benefit from their alliances. The following examples show how units that possess knowledge and units that need this knowledge can find each other quickly.

At both Toshiba and Hitachi relationships with other companies are basically managed at the divisional level. In high-tech industries, technology and market conditions are subject to rapid change, so that the speed with which an agreement can be worked out is of the utmost importance. However, managing alliances at the divisional level is not so efficient in terms of knowledge distribution, because knowledge gained from alliances is not shared by the whole company.

To overcome this problem, both Toshiba and Hitachi restructured their organizations in order to enable each division to share information better. Both companies recognized that divisions have only a partial view of the knowledge gained from alliances. Toshiba's international legal department, for example, has become involved in partner selection and in monitoring the further development of alliances. At Hitachi interdivisional project teams and working groups support the development and maintenance of alliances.

At NEC and Fujitsu, strategic alliances are managed by corporate headquarters. Alliances in the semiconductor field are connected with computers, the core business of the companies. Both firms have special divisions whose main tasks are the co-ordination and observation of the alliances. The divisions formulate long-term visions and align them with the corporate headquarters' growth strategies. Hence, the planning of alliance making becomes flexible.

The four Japanese semiconductor makers differ in the kind of knowledge acquired from their alliance partners and in their approach to guiding the distribution of knowledge within their organizations. There are distinctive linkages among the divisions which manage strategic alliances and different divisions take the initiative in forming the alliances. However, all four Japanese companies have built mechanisms to spread knowledge on alliances throughout the organizations.

For example, internal reports concerning the different alliances are actively distributed among the employees. The strategic intent linked to each alliance is communicated throughout the organization. Whenever the renewal of an alliance is being considered, such news is consciously spread within the organization. Through this mechanism, the firms get an active evaluation system which guides decision making.

Japanese firms usually define specific responsibilities of knowledge creation for managers transferred to strategic alliances.[6] The managers are required to transmit their personally acquired knowledge to predetermined contact persons within the main organization as well as in other alliances. The managers and their contact persons function as gatekeepers of knowledge. They bundle it and stimulate its further transmission.

Managers who have served in strategic alliances for a couple of years are often moved to other departments which are indirectly related with the alliances in order to communicate their experiences. Hence, the transfer of knowledge spans the career of the gatekeepers. Their business experiences remain preserved and they continue to transmit knowledge throughout the company.

These features show that new knowledge in Japanese firms always begins with individuals. The creation of knowledge, however, must be tackled by the whole organization. Organizational learning is more than the sum of the learning activities of single individuals and is realized by the continual interaction of the firms' employees.

Knowledge evolution

The benefit of the knowledge acquired by a Japanese company seems often to be doubtful at the start of the alliance. The tie-up of NEC with AT&T was not based on a foreseeable competitive position, but formed rather to create opportunities for the future. At the start of a partnership, knowledge is obtained from alliance partners in order to be transferred by distribution mechanisms throughout the entire organization and to be linked with already available knowledge. The evolutionary development of knowledge is then enhanced. The R&D efforts of most Japanese semiconductor firms have relied on basic technologies developed in the West, but Japanese technology is not a mere copy. Most Japanese firms have put considerable effort into the conscious evolution of knowledge. Knowledge evolution is the main reason why Japanese semiconductor firms can refine and use the knowledge grafted from their alliance partners. The refined knowledge is often superior to the originally acquired knowledge. Fujitsu, for example, started to produce transistors through a licensing agreement with Siemens in 1958. The transistors were produced for in-house use and for supply to customers. In 1966, Fujitsu started producing semiconductors and used the experience gained from its early alliance with Siemens.

As mentioned above, most Japanese information technology companies have comprehensive business lines. They manufacture semiconductors for in-house use, so that their semiconductor departments closely interact with various other departments (Teramoto and Kanda 1991). By doing so they gain knowledge from these departments. This linkage leads to the sophistication and evolution of knowledge.

The evolution of knowledge is supported by corporate visions, such as NEC's 'C&C' and Toshiba's 'W' strategies. Both visions lead to world leadership in semiconductors and related technologies. Visions stimulate the transformation and upgrading of grafted knowledge in order to give rise to competitive advantage. Japanese firms' visions guide the corporate growth and ensure that the Japanese way of knowledge creation is evolutionary in nature (Kagono *et al.* 1985).

The grafted knowledge is distributed within the organization and consciously evolved towards totally different knowledge. The systematic evolution of knowledge, gained through strategic alliances, is similar to the practice of 'kaizen', the continuous improvement of production processes. Both are special cases of the general attitude to knowledge evolution.

PROBLEMS FOR STRATEGIC ALLIANCES

It has often been argued that the balance of power within strategic alliances lies clearly with the Japanese partners and that the responses of the Western firms are rather defensive (Pucik 1988; Hamel 1991). The Japanese partners are more adept at learning and asymmetries in learning occur quite often. What are the reasons for such differences in learning outcomes?

Unbalanced knowledge creation

The evolution of knowledge has enabled Japanese companies to catch up with their Western partners and even surpass them. Although Japanese contributions to basic research and to the development of new semiconductor technologies have been rather small, Japanese firms have become strong players. Hence, the flow of technology has been from the USA to Japan up to now (Okimoto *et al.* 1984).

Fujitsu, for example, was initially a joint venture initiated by Siemens and Fuji Electric and at first was supplied with Western technology. Today, Fujitsu has surpassed its former teacher. In its second alliance with a Japanese semiconductor firm, Siemens has fallen back as well: in its alliance with Toshiba, Siemens received the Japanese firm's 1-megabyte DRAM technology. However, Siemens was not able to catch up, because Toshiba was already about to develop the future generation of semiconductors. The technology gap was not shortened, but was, in reality, expanded during the time of co-operation.

Through access to the operational knowledge of Sun Microsystems, Fujitsu's ASIC technology was crucially enhanced. In addition, Fujitsu enhanced its competitiveness by introducing Sun's workstation technology. Supplied by Fujitsu's MPU, however, Sun Microsystems could not yet realize a big breakthrough in the field of processor units.

In its alliance with AT&T, NEC gained access to meta-knowledge. Equipped with AT&T's approach of radical innovation, NEC will probably become an even stronger player in the future. As to its alliance with MIPS Computer Systems, NEC has already improved the internalized RISC technology, and NEC is about to overhaul its technology supplier. Japanese semiconductor firms seem to be more experienced in reaping the benefits from alliances because they are more accustomed to growing on the basis of internalized knowledge and to exploiting co-operative relationships with foreign firms.[7] Other examples, such as the alliance between Hitachi and Texas Instruments, provide similar results. Toshiba's alliance with Motorola, however, seems to be more balanced.

When the number of alliances with Western partners increased dramatically in the late 1980s, the business positions of Japanese companies improved considerably. This proves that Japanese semiconductor firms used their Western alliance partners. In terms of sales NEC, Toshiba, Fujitsu and Hitachi occupy top positions. American companies, such as Texas Instruments and Motorola, which held top positions as late as the beginning of the 1980s, fell to lower positions. Similarly, among European companies, Philips is clinging to tenth place (Hobday 1989). Japanese firms, the former students of their partners, are stronger than their teachers. During the past ten years, the competitive landscape of the semiconductor industry has changed dramatically.

Japanese firms could advance so far because they have been able to obtain knowledge from their alliance partners, distribute it throughout their organizations and further evolve it. Western companies, on the other hand, have not been able to enhance organizational learning to the same degree as the Japanese. The capability to distribute knowledge, in particular, is less developed in Western firms.[8] Western firms normally manage their alliances on the divisional level and attach little importance to internal reports about strategic alliances, gatekeepers of knowledge and career planning for alliance cadres.

The missing link: knowledge externalization

Co-operation between Western and Japanese semiconductor companies seems to be a zero-sum game. The Japanese firms are winning and the Western ones are losing. All too often Japanese firms perceive themselves as learning systems entitled to receive knowledge from their alliance partners but not required to externalize knowledge. A more equal relationship between Japanese and Western companies would require a tighter linkage between the knowledge-creating systems of the firms with mechanisms to externalize knowledge.

Then, there would no longer be an exploited and an exploiting firm, but rather a situation in which both firms jointly create knowledge. In such a positive-sum game, both partners can advance their knowledge. The firms' knowledge evolves at the same speed and intensity. In the long run such 'weak altruism' (Simon 1983) will help to ensure a healthy business environment.

FUTURE DEVELOPMENTS

As Akio Morita, the chairman of Sony, argues, Japanese firms have to respect their American and European partners more and should initiate learning activities based on mutuality (Morita 1992). Strategic alliances have to be two-way streets by definition. One company can no longer exploit the assets of its partners. Industrial society has to be based on symbiosis[9] and global co-operation among market participants. Japanese companies should not only learn from their partners but should teach them, too.

Keidanren (Japanese Federation of Economic Organizations) has recently begun to stress symbiosis and promotes this concept within society. Some companies have already incorporated the idea of symbiosis. Canon adopted this new concept for its corporate vision for the 1990s: 'Symbiosis with global partners.'

Other companies, such as Toshiba, have shown tentatively how symbiosis in general and the externalization of knowledge in particular can be realized. Toshiba entered into a global alliance with IBM and Siemens in the summer of 1992 to develop new generation chips. Although Toshiba profits from the alliance, too, the alliance should strengthen the technological background of its partners. Toshiba has begun to teach its partners and to contribute to the easing of trade conflicts.

Japanese firms of the semiconductor industry have been able to evolve their knowledge by entering strategic alliances with Western companies. Because the actors in the semiconductor industry are quite inter-dependent, the firms have established many linkages (Okimoto *et al.* 1984; Warshofsky 1989). Although Japanese semiconductor firms have developed an expertise concerning knowledge creation through strategic alliances, their ability to share this expertise with their Western alliance partners remains limited. Increased knowledge externalization should become a goal of Japanese semiconductor firms in order to promote symbiosis.

NOTES

1 There are, however, some dynamic models of strategic alliances. Lorange and Roose (1992) and Kogut (1988) proposed life-cycle models of strategic alliances, but do not describe the learning activities and the creation of knowledge within strategic alliances.
2 The classification of different levels of knowedge follows the practice of distinguishing between different levels of learning. Learning within organizations is the acquiring of knowledge and occurs within a frame of reference or the learning of a new frame of reference, see Argyris and Schon (1978).
3 The perspective of knowledge internalization adopted here has nothing to do with traditional internalization theory, which concerns transaction costs, see also Casson (1990).
4 See also Nonaka (1991).
5 See Nelson and Winter (1982). For a discussion of the usefulness of evolutionary models in management see Richter and Teramoto (1993).
6 For a further discussion see also Pucik (1988).
7 Reich and Mankin even argued that alliances with Japanese firms harm Western ones, see Reich and Mankin (1986).
8 Other studies, as Pucik's analysis of the human resource agenda within strategic alliances, came to similar results. See Pucik (1988).
9 Symbiosis (in Japanese: kyosei) is a current buzzword and has triggered discussion among Japanese businessmen, see Fukunaga (1993).

REFERENCE

Argyris, C. and Schon, D.A. (1987) *Organizational Learning: A Theory of Action Perspective*, Reading, MA: Addison Wesley.

Badaracco, Jr, J.L. (1991) *The Knowledge Link*, Cambridge, MA: Harvard University Press.

Boulding, K. (1981) *Ecodynamics – A New Theory of Societal Evolution*, Beverly Hills: Sage.

Casson, M. (1990) *Enterprise and Competitiveness – A Systems View of International Business*, Oxford: Oxford University Press.

Fukunaga, H. (1993) 'Kyosei: Japanese firms must pick up the social tab as well'. *Tokyo Business Today*, January/February: 33–4.

Hamel, G. (1991) 'Competition for competence and inter-partner learning within international strategic alliances', *Strategic Management Journal*, 12: 83–103.

Harrigan, K.R. (1985) *Strategies for Joint Ventures*, Lexington, MA: D.C. Heath.

Hedberg, B. (1981) 'How organizations learn and unlearn', in P. Nystrom and W.H. Starbuck (eds) *Handbook of Organizational Design*, vol. 1, York: Oxford University Press, pp. 28–64.

Hobday, M. (1989) 'Corporate strategies in the international semiconductor industry', *Research Policy*, 18: 225–38.

Huber, G.P. (1991) 'Organizational learning: the contributing processes and the literatures', *Organization Science*, 2 (1), February: 88–115.

Jones, K.K. and Shill, W.E. (1991) 'Allying for advantage', *The McKinsey Quarterly*, 3: 73–99.

Kagono, T., Nonaka, I., Sakakibira, K. and Okumura, A. (1985) *Strategic Versus Evolutionary Management: A U.S.–Japan Comparison*, Amsterdam: North-Holland.

Kogut, B. (1988) 'A study of the life cycle of joint ventures', *Management International Review*, special issue: 39–51.

Lorange, P. and Roos, J. (1992) *Strategic Alliances: Formation, Implementation and Evolution*, Cambridge, MA: Blackwell.

Lyles, M.A. (1988) 'Learning among joint venture sophsticated firms', *Management International Review*, special issue: 85–98.

Morita, A. (1992) 'Partnering for competitiveness: the role of Japanese business', *Harvard Business Review*, 70 (3), May/June: 76–83.

Nelson, R.R. and Winter, S.G. (1982) *An Evolutionary Theory of Economic Change*, Cambridge, MA: Harvard University Press.

Nonaka, I. (1991) 'The knowledge-creating company', *Harvard Business Review*, 69 (6), November/December: 96–104.

Okimoto, D.I, Sugano, T. and Weinstein, Franklin (1984) *Competitive Edge: The Semiconductor Industry in the U.S. and Japan*, Stanford, CA: Stanford University Press.

Parkhe, A. (1991) 'Interfirm diversity, organizational learning, and longevity in global strategic alliances', *Journal of International Business Studies*, 22 (4), Fourth quarter: 579–601.

Pucik, V. (1988) 'Strategic alliances, organizational learning, and competitive advantage: the HRM agenda', *HRM*, 17 (1): 77–93.

Reich, R.B. and Mankin, E.D. (1986) 'Joint ventures with Japan give away our future', *Harvard Business Review*, 64 (2), March/April: 79–86.

Richter, F.J. and Teramoto, Y. (1993) 'Population ecology versus network dynamics: from evolution to co-evolution', *Research Report of Graduate School of Systems Management*, 93–15, August.

Simon, H.A. (1983) *Reason in Human Affairs*, Stanford, CA: Stanford University Press.

Teramoto, Y., Richter, F.J. and Iwasaki, N. (1993) 'Learning to succeed: what European firms can learn from Japanese approaches to strategic alliances', *Creativity and Innovation Management*, 2 (2): 114–21.

Teramoto, Y. and Kanda, M. (1991) 'Nichiou jouhougijitsu sangyou no senryakuteki linkeiji – missingu link ka, soretomo shi no butou ka', *Business Review*, 38 (4): 43–61.

Warshofsky, F. (1989) *The Chip War*, London: Macmillan.

Chapter 7

Japanese joint ventures in Italy
A second-best strategy?

Corrado Molteni

ABSTRACT

So far Italy has not attracted a large flow of Japanese direct investment. However, recently a small but growing number of companies have chosen Italy as the location for their manufacturing operations. These investments present distinctive characteristics. In particular, there is a clear preference for joint ventures with Italian interests, while in other European countries wholly owned subsidiaries are preferred. Through the analysis of relevant cases, the paper points out how these investments are the result of a positive, assertive strategy reflecting sector and firm specific conditions, rather than a second-best solution adopted in order to overcome obstacles preventing the establishment of wholly owned subsidiaries.

INTRODUCTION

In the literature on Japanese direct investment in Europe, joint ventures are usually presented as a second-best strategy versus wholly owned greenfield investments.

Joint ventures are not viewed as an optimal choice but as a second-best solution to be accepted because of the existence of external constraints or entry barriers. In this perspective, the preponderance of joint ventures with minority participation in some countries like Italy is related more to host country regulations than to any desire to benefit from the expertise and the resources of the local firms.[1] Is this really the case? By looking at the Japanese manufacturing base in Italy, we can observe how joint ventures can provide competitive advantage to both Italian and Japanese firms through the exploitation of complementarities, the reduction of risks and investment costs and the attainment of economies of scale.

First, we shall examine the sectoral composition and type of ownership of Japanese direct investments in Italy, and then we will focus on the objectives of major joint ventures between Italian and Japanese interests.

JAPANESE MANUFACTURING INVESTMENTS IN ITALY: AN OVERVIEW

So far Italy has been relatively neglected by Japanese companies investing abroad. As shown in Table 7.1, only 1.8 per cent of the cumulated total of Japanese direct investment in Europe in the post-war period (1951–91) has been channelled to Italy. The situation has hardly changed in recent years, with Italy still attracting only about 2 per cent of the annual flow of Japanese investment in Europe.

The reluctance to choose Italy as an investment location is also evident if we consider the number of manufacturing units established there by Japanese firms. According to JETRO (1992), at the end of January 1992, out of 721 European establishments with Japanese capital affiliation (more than 10 per cent of the capital invested) only 47 were located in Italy. This is less than 7 per cent of the total, and far less than the 195 located in the UK, 128 in France, 111 in Germany and 67 in Spain. Even if the actual number of manufacturing units in which Japanese companies have invested is definitely higher (several small and medium-sized companies in metalworking machinery are not listed in the JETRO survey), the fact remains that the Japanese presence in Italy is far smaller than in other major European countries. This is confirmed by other

Table 7.1 Japanese direct investment in Europe (US$ million)

	FY 1989		FY 1990		FY 1991		1951–1991 (cumulated total)	
	Value	*%*	*Value*	*%*	*Value*	*%*	*Value*	*%*
UK	5,239	(35.4)	6,806	(47.6)	3,588	(38.3)	26,168	(38.2)
Netherlands	4,547	(30.7)	2,744	(19.2)	1,960	(20.9)	14,776	(21.5)
Germany	1,083	(7.3)	1,242	(8.7)	1,115	(11.9)	5.805	(8.5)
France	1,136	(7.7)	1,257	(8.8)	817	(8.7)	4,973	(7.2)
Spain	501	(3.4)	320	(2.2)	378	(4.0)	2,245	(3.3)
Belgium	326	(2.2)	367	(2.6)	222	(2.4)	1,941	(2.8)
Italy	314	(2.1)	217	(1.5)	322	(3.4)	1,222	(1.8)
Total	14,808	(100.00)	14,294	(100.00)	9,371	(100.00)	68,636	(100.00)

Source: Ministry of Finance

indicators such as the average amount of capital invested and the number of employees (JETRO 1992).

On the other hand, the JETRO figures show that the 15 Japanese plants located in Italy at the end of December 1987 had more than trebled to 47 by 1992. Thus, a small but growing number of Japanese companies are choosing Italy as a site for their manufacturing operations in Europe. What is the main reason for this choice? What are the major objectives of these investments? To answer these questions it is necessary to examine the sectorial composition and type of ownership, which, as we will see, present distinctive characteristics when compared with Japanese direct investment in other European countries. No such distinctive characteristics emerge with regard to the period of entry. In fact, except for a few pioneering companies such as YKK, Honda and Toray, which invested in the late 1960s and early 1970s, most of the investment in manufacturing activities took place in the second half of the 1980s.

Turning to the sectorial composition, several interesting points can be detected. First, there have been no significant investments in the car and consumer electronic sectors. Among Japanese car-makers only Daihatsu has a participation in a joint venture (with Piaggio of the Fiat Group) for the manufacturing and sale of small commercial vehicles. In the field of consumer electronics, there are only two Japanese factories for the production of components and accessory products; Sony making audio cassette tapes and Seiko Instruments making liquid crystal displays, both in regions close to the border with France and Austria. The limited number of investments in this sector is particularly striking, as the electronics industry – an industry in which Japanese firms enjoy a clear

Table 7.2 Japanese manufacturing basis in Italy, August 1992

Industry	Japanese investor's capital share				Total
	10–49%	50–99%	100%	n.a.	
Chemicals – pharmaceuticals	5	2	4	–	11
Machinery	4	2	2	–	8
Clothing – textiles	2	3	2	1	8
Electric and electronic equipment	4	3	–	–	7
Electric and electronic components	2	1	1	–	4
Transport equipments' components	3	–	1	–	4
Transport equipments	2	–	1	–	3
Others	–	1	5	1	7
Totals	22	12	16	2	52

Source: JETRO and author's own findings

Table 7.3 Major Japanese investments in Italy, January 1992

Company name	Japanese investor (capital share)	Italian investor (capital share)	Number of employees	Year of establishment or acquisition	Capital (million lira)	Main product
Fiat Hitachi Excavators	Hitachi Kenki (44%) Sumitomo Shoji (5%)	Fiat Geotech (51%)	1,151	1986	73,800	Excavators
P&D	Daihatsu Motor (49%)	Piaggio VE (51%)	n.a.	1991	30,000	Small commercial vehicles
Bridgestone Firestone Italia	Bridgestone (100%)	–	1,116	1988	27,000	Tyres
Sanyo Argo Clima	Sanyo Denki (39%) Sumitomo (10%)	Elfi (51%)	n.a.	1991	23,000	Air conditioners
Tecdis	Seiko Instruments (74.75%)	Finaosta (12%) Teknecomp (10%) Alenia (3%)	230	1985	18,000	Liquid crystal displays
Borletti Climatizzazione	Nippon Denso (25%)	Magneti Marelli (75%)	1,008	1990	18,000	Car air conditioners
Honda Italia Industriale	Honda Motor (100%)	–	332	1971	16,000	Motorcycles
Belgarda	Yamaha Motors (40%)	Intfaco (60%)	202	1989	13,000	Motorcycles
Miteni	Mitsubishi Shoji (49%)	Enichem Synthesis (51%)	165	1988	13,000	Pharmaceuticals and chemicals
Minarelli	Yamaha Motors (30%)	Minarelli (70%)	160	1991	12,500	Motorcycle engines
Alcantara	Toray Industries (49%)	Enichem Fibre (51%)	430	1974	12,000	Synthetic leathers

Table 7.3 continued

	Japanese partner(s)	Italian partner				
Emblem Europe	Unitika (30%) Marubeni (10%)	Snia Tecnopolimeri (60%)	71	12,000	1988	Nylon films for food packaging
Marghera Butadiene	Mitsui Bussan (33.33%) Nihon Zeon (33.33%)	Enichem Anic (33.33%)	21	12,000	1985	Butadiene
Sony Italia	Sony (100%)	–	207	12,000	1981	Audio cassette tapes
Sapim–Amada	Amada (60%)	–	n.a.	12,000	1990	Metal panels
Galileo Vacuum Tec	Ebara Corp (20%)	Officine Galileo (80%)	190	11,900	1988	Vacuum equipments
Sun Chemical Inchiostri	Dainippon Ink & Chemicals (100%)	–	n.a.	10,720	n.a.	Printing ink
Olivetti Sanyo Industriale	Sanyo Denki (39%)	Olivetti (51%)	54	10,000	1989	Telefax
Olivetti–Canon Industriale	Mitsui Bussan (5%) Canon (50% – 1)	Olivetti (50% + 1)	500	9,800	1987	Copying machines and printers
Prima Industrie	Amada (40%)	Prima Industrie (51%)	140	8,382	1980	Laser robots

Source: JETRO and author's own findings

competitive advantage – has been the leading investor in Europe. In Italy, however, manufacturing investments have been concentrated in those sectors (machinery, chemicals, textiles, clothing and components for transport equipment) in which the Japanese presence in Europe is much less pronounced and where Italian firms maintain or are striving to maintain a competitive edge versus their Japanese competitors (Table 7.2).

This sectoral composition is closely related to the second distinctive characteristic of Japanese direct investment in Italy: the preference for minority shareholdings. While in Europe about 60 per cent of the Japanese manufacturing subsidiaries are wholly owned subsidiaries, in Italy wholly owned subsidiaries are less than one-third of the total (see Table 7.2). Furthermore, of the 20 major investments with a capital of more than 8 billion lira (approximately $6.5 million), only five (Bridgestone Italia, Honda Italia, Sony Italia, Sapim-Amada and Sun Chemical Ltd) are wholly owned subsidiaries. Two (Marghera Butadiene Ltd – a company set up by Montedison, Mitsui Bussan and Nihon Zeon – and Tecdis Ltd, established by Seiko Instruments and an Olivetti subsidiary) are majority controlled by Japanese interests, while the remaining 13 are joint ventures with a Japanese shareholding of 49 per cent or less (Table 7.3).

A third characteristic of Japanese manufacturing investment in Italy is the presence, as promoters, organizers and investors, of Japanese trading companies in many of the major joint ventures. In some cases the Italian subsidiaries of Marubeni, Mitsubishi Shoji, Mitsui Bussan and Sumitomo Shoji have been the actual promoters of the joint ventures, taking advantage of their knowledge of the Italian market and industry. As has already been pointed out, since investment has occurred in sectors where Japanese penetration of the European market is less advanced and where Italian firms have a competitive position in the market, the Japanese trading firms can play an intermediary role, finding new opportunities and suitable partners which can exploit them. Incidentally, it is also interesting to note that in their activity as intermediaries, the traders have gone beyond the boundaries of their *keiretsu*. Sumitomo Shoji, for example, organized a joint venture for the production of excavators between Fiat Allis and Hitachi Kenki, a company which does not belong to the Sumitomo group. Sanyo Denki (Sanyo Electric) has set up a joint venture with Olivetti for the production of telefax equipment with the support of Mitsui Trading, and another joint venture for the production of air conditioners with the co-operation of Sumitomo Shoji.

This strong presence of trading companies might be regarded as another indicator that joint ventures and minority participation are the only solution available to enter a country like Italy, where various external constraints and entry barriers (cultural differences, country regulations, complexity of industrial relations and labour management etc.) prevent the investing company from exploiting fully the available competitive advantage through a wholly owned greenfield investment, like in northern European countries. However, in many instances the decision to set up a joint venture with local interests is the result of a positive, assertive strategy of internationalization, reflecting sector and firm specific conditions. In other words, joint ventures are not aimed only at overcoming existing barriers through a passive adaptation to market, political and cultural conditions. Rather, through joint ventures firms try to acquire new competitive advantages via the exploitation of complementarities, the reduction of risks and the pursuit of economies of scale. This is particularly the case for many Italian–Japanese joint ventures which enable both partners to obtain complementary assets: access to advanced technology and managerial know-how for the Italian firms; market access and the use of already existing production facilities for the Japanese companies. The following cases clearly confirm this interpretation.

THE ADVANTAGES OF JOINT VENTURES

The case of Fiat–Hitachi Excavators S.p.A.

Fiat–Hitachi Excavator S.p.A. offers an example of how two companies can develop a competitive advantage through the exploitation of complementarities in a joint venture.[2]

The company was established in 1986 by Fiat Geotech (formerly Fiat Allis), the producer of earth-moving machines in the Fiat Group, Hitachi Kenki, a specialized producer of hydraulic excavators belonging to the Hitachi Group, and Sumitomo Shoji, the trading company of the Sumitomo Group, which acted as the initiator and the promoter of the initiative. From the beginning, Fiat Geotech has maintained a 51 per cent majority of the capital, with the rest divided between Hitachi Kenki (44 per cent) and Sumitomo Shoji (5 per cent). The company has more than 1,000 employees, producing hydraulic excavators from a plant located near Turin and selling them in Europe, the Middle East and Africa.

The joint venture was set up with the objective of strengthening both companies' competitive position in a global, mature market characterized by a high level of oligopolistic concentration: the share of Komatsu and

Caterpillar, the two major manufacturers, is more than 50 per cent. The rationale behind the joint venture was to combine the assets of Fiat and its strong base in the European market with the assets of Hitachi Kenki, a company with a leading technological edge, especially in the production of excavators, the most rapidly growing sector of the market, but with a limited presence in Europe.[3]

From the point of view of Fiat, the joint venture objectives were to gain access to Japanese technology and managerial know-how and to control the market entry of a potential competitor.

For Hitachi Kenki, the major goals were to enter the European market, avoid the risk of anti-dumping duties and local content requirements and at the same time gain the opportunity to offer a more diversified range of products through the alliance with a 'full-liner'. The avoidance of anti-dumping duties was particularly urgent as the EC Commission had started an anti-dumping investigation in 1984 against Japanese producers of hydraulic excavators, which resulted in the introduction of a countervailing duty in June 1985. Thus, the need to circumvent trade restrictions clearly represented a major reason behind the decision to undertake some kind of direct investment. On the other hand, the choice of a joint venture was related to the fact that this entry mode could provide additional advantages in comparison with a greenfield, wholly owned investment. For both partners the joint venture reduced the risk and cost of new investment, allowed economies of scale and improved their image with dealers and customers.

According to the managers of the company, despite the recession which has seriously hurt this sector, the above-mentioned objectives have been reached. Yearly production of hydraulic excavators based on Hitachi design and technology had climbed to 2,450 units in 1990, and the company is now one of the leading manufacturers in Europe. Further, the joint venture has witnessed a consistent transfer of technological and managerial know-how from the Japanese partner. One consequence has been a profound change in the internal organization of labour and the structure of the suppliers' network, whose number has been drastically reduced. This process has been made possible by the presence of Japanese managers in Italy and training at the Tsuchiura plant in Japan of Italian workers and technicians.

However, the process of technology and know-how transfer has not been just in one direction. As frequently mentioned by Japanese managers at Hitachi Kenki headquarters in Tokyo, the Japanese side too has been able to learn from the 'flexible' Italian approach to management problems. The joint venture has also benefited from Fiat's experience in the European market, which has made possible the adaption of products to the needs and requirements of local markets. Finally, both partners agree that the joint venture's success can be attributed to a considerable extent to the quality of management. Both sides have assigned to the joint venture excellent human resources, and avoided the frequent rotation of personnel which can become a source of serious friction between partners. In this way, stable and co-operative management has contributed to the positive performance of the enterprise. Satisfaction with this joint venture is confirmed by the decision, taken in July 1992, by Fiat and Hitachi to expand their co-operation and establish a new company (F. H. Construction Equipment S.p.A.) in Lecce, a town in the southern part of Italy.[4] In this new enterprise, Hitachi is expected to provide technical assistance in the areas of production technology, quality control and project planning, while Fiat's main contribution will be to provide production and distribution facilities.

Some other relevant cases

What we said for the Fiat–Hitachi case is also applicable to many other joint ventures between Japanese and Italian interests. For example, the Olivetti group has set up joint ventures with Japanese firms in order to gain access to advanced technology in the field of photocopiers and printers (with Canon), of facsimile (with Sanyo Denki) and of liquid crystal displays (with Seiko Instruments and a minority participation by Teknecomp). For the same purpose, the acquisition of production technology, Piaggio – the producer of scooters and motorcycles – has entered into a joint venture with Daihatsu for the production and sale of small commercial vehicles. Borletti Climatizzazione, a maker of car components, has entered a joint venture with Nippondenso to obtain Nippondenso technology for the production of air conditioners.

In all these cases, technology access considerations have been particularly important for the Italian firms, while, on the other hand, Japanese companies have been focusing their attention on the possibility of rapid and effective market access through the use of already existing production and distribution facilities. In some cases, as for Canon and Hitachi Kenki, the existence or the potential threat of market access restrictions through anti-dumping duties or local content requirements has been another relevant, if not a dominant, determinant. However, in most of the cases, genuine economic considerations have played a major role. In the case of Nippondenso, for example, the alliance with an Italian manufacturer, a traditional supplier to Italian and French car-makers, provides an important outlet for the attainment of the necessary economies of scale which probably cannot be reached by relying only on demand from Japanese 'transplants'.

Another interesting case is Alcantara, the joint venture between Toray Industries and the state-owned Enichem Fibre for the production of synthetic leather. Here too, the Japanese partner provided the technology, while the Italian side contributed to the success of the enterprise through its marketing expertise.

The reverse case: acquisition of Italian technology by Japanese investors

As we have just seen, technology access is the main Italian objective for entering a joint venture with Japanese partners, but there are also cases of Japanese firms investing in Italy for exactly the same purpose. This type of direct invest- ment is to be found in traditional sectors (clothing and textiles, in particular) and in machinery sectors in which Italian firms, including many small and medium-sized enterprises, are endowed with excellent technological and managerial resources. In the case of the textile and apparel industry, the major assets owned by Italian companies are mostly represented by the reputation of the firm and its brand name, as well as the expertise, the creativity and the knowledge accumulated and shared by its employees. In this sector Japanese direct investment through acquisition or joint ventures is specifically aimed at gaining access to these intangible resources. The ultimate objective is to secure a better competitive position in Japan's domestic market rather than in the European one.

From the point of view of the Italian firm, a joint venture represents a rapid and low-cost solution for penetrating the Japanese and, eventually, the Asian market. This strategy implies that, in most of the cases, the effective control of distribution and marketing policies in Japan has to be left in the hands of the Japanese partner. Among the Japanese companies which have undertaken this type of direct investment, it is possible to cite as significant examples those of Onward Kashiyama in the clothing sector and Amada in the metalworking machinery industry.

Onward Kashiyama, the largest maker of men's ready-made suits in Japan, has followed from the second half of the 1980s a policy of acquisition and capital participation in Italian apparel makers. Starting in 1986 with a minority participation (49 per cent) in Luciano Soprani S.p.A. – a company set up by the international fashion designer – Onward Kashiyama has rapidly expanded its investments in Italy, where it presently, partly or entirely, controls six companies operating in the design and production of high-quality men's and women's clothes.[5] The products of these companies, partly produced in Japan under a licence agreement and partly produced in the Italian factories, are then commercialized in the Japanese market. In the future, Onward Kashiyama is planning to use the manufacturing facilities in Italy to produce and sell in Europe clothes signed by Japanese fashion designers. Thus the direct investment could also become a vehicle for penetrating the European market.

In the case of Amada, a leading manufacturer of metalworking machinery, based in Tokyo, joint ventures have also been made mainly with the purpose of securing access to the technology and expertise of the Italian partners. It is interesting to note that Amada is a research-oriented company 'constantly striving to develop the latest technology' in its research and development (R&D) in Japan, the USA and Europe.[6] The Amada Group has also been the first Japanese metalworking machinery company to build an overseas production network, presently comprising several manufacturing subsidiaries in the USA, Taiwan, France, Austria and Italy. By end of 1991 Amada had invested in five manufacturing companies in Italy, of which four are also engaged in R&D activities. A sixth subsidiary, Altec S.r.l., is a rather small research unit established by Amada in order to conduct basic research in Italy on laser technology.

As can be seen from Table 7.4, except for one case, all the companies are joint ventures, since the primary aim of the investment is not to establish a production base in Europe – this objective has been assigned to two other companies owned by Amada in France and Austria – but to gain access to the original ideas and technical solutions proposed and developed by Italian engineers, especially in the crucial area of labour-saving technology. This aspect has been clearly admitted by Amada's managers during a visit to the company's headquarters and, in fact, in more than one case the advanced machinery produced and marketed by Amada incorporates important elements (robots and other labour-saving devices) originally developed by Prima Industries and other Italian partners of Amada. It is possible to say that in several cases Amada's leadership in the field of metalworking technology has been consolidated by Italian contributions in the area of factory automation: an important source of Amada's competitive power in the Japanese market which is affected by a chronic problem of labour shortage.

Capital participation, rather than the mere acquisition of the right to utilize the technology, is also a clear sign of Amada's long-term commitment to support the Italian partners. For both partners the joint

Table 7.4 Direct investment by Amada Co. Ltd in Italy, December 1991

Company name	Year of establishment	Activity	Amada's share (%)	Italian investor's share (%)
Prima Electronics S.p.A.	1978	R & D, manufacturing and sale of electronic industrial machinery	50	50
Prima Industrie S.p.A.	1980	R & D, manufacturing and sale of industrial machinery and robots	49	51
Sapri S.r.l.	1983	R & D, manufacturing and sale of welding robots	75	25
Altec S.r.l.	1989	R & D on laser technology	90	10
Gennelli-Allori S.r.l.	1990	Manufacturing and sale of metal moulds	50	50
Sapim-Amada S.p.A.	1990	R & D, manufacturing, sale of industrial machinery	100	–

Source: Amada Co. Ltd

venture can also guarantee a better exchange of information and a good opportunity for the training of employees. With regard to the latter point, it seems, however, that the Japanese side has been much more eager to use this opportunity, sending its employees to participate in R&D activities taking place in the laboratories of the Italian partners. Conversely, there has been less investment in the training of Italians in Japan: a regrettable fact considering that Amada has been introducing unique innovations not only in the manufacturing process, but also in sales and service systems.

CONCLUDING REMARKS

It is evident that the majority of the joint ventures between Italian and Japanese interests have been set up with two partners with the intent to gain new, additional competitive advantages. Beside the advantages of cost/risk-sharing and the economies of scale that can be attained, the joint venture is in fact the vehicle for the acquisition and the development of complementary resources, tangible and intangible. In this sense, the joint ventures cannot be considered as a second-best solution to be adopted whenever external constraints or entry barriers prevent the establishment of a wholly owned subsidiary. On the contrary, it seems to be the optimal choice for a company willing to exploit its available resources and the synergies that can be derived from a strategic alliance with a foreign partner. However, the success of a joint venture requires that both partners control one or more critical resources and are ready to transfer them to the new enterprise. Without these prerequisites the alliance will not be effective and successful, notwithstanding the quality and efforts of the management. This is the main reason behind those attempts at industrial and technological co-operation between Italian and Japanese firms which have failed.[7]

NOTES

1 See, for example, Thomsen and Nicolaides (1991: 16).
2 This case is based on materials and information provided by Paolo Sighicelli, former Chief Executive Officer of Fiat–Hitachi Excavators S.p.A., and the results of an interview in July 1992 with Hitachi Kenki's managers at the company headquarters in Tokyo.
3 Beside the joint venture with Fiat, Hitachi Kenki has a subsidiary (Hitachi Construction Machinery B.V.) in the Netherlands responsible for storage and distribution in the Dutch market and the manufacture of small-scale excavators.
4 Hitachi Kenki, News Release, 15 July 1992. In the new company, Fiat group's NH Geotech N.V. and Fiat–Hitachi Excavators S.p.A. have shares respectively of 80 per cent and 20 per cent.
5 Information and data provided by Onward Kashiyama Italia S.p.A.
6 Amada Co. Ltd, Annual Report, 1991, and an interview in July 1992 with Amada's managers at the company headquarters in Ishida.
7 A well-known case is the unsuccessful joint venture between Nissan and Alfa Romeo for the production of passenger cars in a factory located near Naples.

REFERENCES

JETRO (1992) *8th Survey of European Operations of Japanese Companies in the Manufacturing Sector*, London: Japan Trade Centre.
Thomsen, S. and Nicolaides, P. (1991) *The Evolution of Japanese Direct Investment in Europe: Death of a Transistor Salesman*, London: Harvester Wheatsheaf.

Chapter 8

The strategic role of Japanese R&D centres in the UK

David Cairncross

ABSTRACT

The UK, by European standards, has attracted a high proportion of Japanese manufacturing investment, and an even larger share of research and development (R&D) centres. 'Internationalization' of corporate R&D, which can include acquisitions, joint ventures and research contracts with higher education institutions, is a recent phenomenon, especially so for Japanese firms.

This paper describes Japanese overseas R&D in the context of the general trends applying to all international companies. It also presents the results of a preliminary survey of ten major centres in the UK. The centres were established for a variety of reasons including contact with the local science base and the benefits of a research environment favourable to creativity. Political factors are also relevant.

Further research is called for to clarify the role of such centres and their significance for the internationalization of R&D generally.

INTRODUCTION

In recent years, a considerable amount of interest has developed in 'global kaisha' and in the evolutionary trajectory which many Japanese firms are following in the course of becoming multinational enterprises. Much of this interest has concentrated on overseas activities by Japanese *manufacturers* (rather than, for example, banks or securities companies) and on the management, employment practices and so on that govern the manufacturing process itself. Recently, however, interest has also been expressed in design, development and research activities by these manufacturers. One aspect of these activities, still on a fairly small scale in the UK, is the move by Japanese firms to set up establishments specifically dedicated to R&D rather than manufacturing. This is a novel and interesting development in the case of Japanese firms.

It is only slightly less novel, and perhaps just as interesting, in the case of multinational firms in general. Compared with marketing and manufacture, R&D has tended to be concentrated in the home countries of multinational enterprises of all nationalities, and the 'internationalization' of R&D is recent and easily overstated. It is not surprising that it should be even more recent in the case of Japanese firms with very short histories of multinational operations.

For a variety of reasons, such activities by Japanese firms have attracted more attention than their scale alone would warrant. One of the reasons for this, and also one of the consequences of this extra attention, is that there is interest in the possibility that there may be something peculiarly Japanese, or particularly associated with Japanese circumstances, about the reasons for setting up R&D establishments in the UK, or about the way such places are managed, or both. This is partly a reflection of the view that Japanese overseas factories are managed by 'Japanese methods', which are different from and may be superior to traditional indigenous ones; and partly of the debate which is very lively in Japan on the obstacles to creative breakthroughs and basic research in company laboratories and indeed in universities and national research laboratories.

In order to begin to address these issues it is first necessary to develop a clear idea in general terms of the level and nature of the activities of Japanese R&D centres, and of how they compare with the parent firms' overall R&D activities and with overseas R&D by multinationals generally. This paper sets out to furnish some of the material necessary for this, as well as analysing the rationale for the establishment of overseas, especially British, R&D centres by Japanese firms.

It reports results of a preliminary survey of 10 of the 12 main known designated 'stand-alone' R&D facilities which Japanese firms have set up in the UK. The 12 are Aisin Seiki UK Research Laboratory (at the University of Sussex); Canon Research Centre Europe and Kobe Steel Europe Research Laboratory in Guildford; Eisai London Research Laboratories at University College, London; Fujitsu Europe Telecom R&D Centre near Uxbridge; Hitachi Cambridge Laboratory; Toshiba Cambridge Research Centre; Nissan European Technology Centre at Cranfield; NSK-RHP European Research Centre near Nottingham; Sharp Laboratories of Europe and the Yamanouchi Research Institute (both in Oxford) and Sony Broadcasting and Communications Advanced Development in Basingstoke. Centres were identified through a variety of sources; subject establishments were defined as those specifically constituted for research or development purposes, standing apart from any manufacturing facility. The existing establishments of firms which, through ownership changes, have come to be mainly or wholly owned by Japanese parents were not considered.

By choosing to focus on R&D centres which are specified as such, one may hope to exclude activities (such as minor modifications to the design of a product or of a manufacturing process) which are so closely tied to the production process as to be essentially an extension of it. Even so, the activities of designated R&D centres can embrace a wide spread of activity ranging from quite long-term and relatively basic research to very market-oriented development work, including various kinds of reverse engineering.

The directors or deputy directors, and in some cases additional members of staff, of each centre were interviewed on the understanding that no information given would be attributed to any named company, unless that information is already cited in publicly available sources. The centres are very diverse in terms of the kinds of work performed, in industries ranging from cars to pharmaceuticals, and at levels of application which vary from new product development to basic physical or biological science; this renders a standardized questionnaire survey relatively unhelpful in identifying the salient characteristics, particularly those that are shared, in the underlying strategic intentions and actual roles and styles of management of the different establishments. A number of issues have emerged from the initial study which are the focus of continuing research on this subject; some of these issues are identified later in this paper.

The second section of the paper describes the background to overseas R&D by Japanese firms in the light of global trends in R&D location generally and some of the factors which differentially affect Japanese firms. The third section sets out the current level and nature of R&D by Japanese firms in Europe generally and the fourth section reports in more detail on the situation in the UK. The fifth section offers an analysis of some aspects of the strategic rationale for overseas R&D which are of peculiar interest in the case of Japanese firms. The concluding section notes some of the unresolved questions, including impact on the host country.

OVERSEAS R&D BY JAPANESE FIRMS

The large and still growing importance of R&D for corporate strategy is a recent phenomenon. Between 1967 and 1988 the proportion of gross domestic product (GDP) accounted for by industry-financed spending on R&D increased by 37 per cent in the USA (from 1.01 per cent of GDP to 1.38 per cent), by 48 per cent in Western Europe (from 0.79 per cent to 1.17 per cent) and by 235 per cent (0.83 per cent to 1.95 per cent) in Japan (Keizai 1991: 26). Japan's consistently faster growth in GDP means that the absolute rate of growth of industrial R&D spending in Japan – starting from a low baseline – has been much faster than even these figures might suggest.

The growing importance of R&D is also particularly acute in Japan, where corporate R&D spending has reached remarkable heights (e.g. as mentioned above, nearly half again as much of the country's GDP as in the USA) and in many firms continues to grow even in the present stringent climate. Until recently Japanese corporate spending on R&D, though a higher proportion of GDP, remained lower in absolute terms than the total amount of corporate R&D spending in the USA.

Now, however, although Japan's GDP remains less than 60 per cent of that of the USA, private-sector R&D spending seems to exceed the US amount. In 1988 the Japanese private sector spent a total of $62.2 billion on R&D in Japan; the US figure was $60.5 billion (Keizai 1991: 26). Vigorous R&D is for many Japanese firms a critical aspect of the struggle for survival in an extremely competitive environment.

Moreover, because of their success in catching up with the countries and companies from which they used to import much of their technology, (and possibly because of increasing difficulty in accessing some foreign technology, which is now less likely than formerly to be available on favourable terms), Japanese firms are now increasingly reliant on their own resources for new technology, which obliges them to conduct in-house R&D to achieve the results which might once have been accessible by energetic technological scanning and licensing.

So the kind of importance which is now attached to corporate R&D is relatively recent; the internationalization of R&D is even more recent. This is graphically illustrated by a study of the patents granted in the USA to over 600 of the world's largest firms, in which by identifying the countries from which applications were made it was to some extent possible to determine the location of these large firms' R&D activities (Pavitt 1992). Between 1981 and 1988 about 92 per cent of the patenting by US firms was from the USA (5.7 per cent was from Europe); 66 per cent of the UK firms' patenting was from the UK; and more than 99 per

Table 8.1 Overseas R&D spending by Japanese firms

	N. America $million	%	Europe $million	%	Other $million	%	Total ($million)
1983	38	62	22*	38*	22*	38*	60
1986	169	49	99	29	64	22	342
1989	308	66	100	21	60	13	468

Source: MITI 1992; Nakasone 1991
    * Combined figure for Europe and other.

Table 8.2 R&D expenditure by foreign companies in Japan

	Manufacturing ($million)	Other ($million)	Total ($million)
1987	400	69	469
1988	507	120	627
1989	657	70	727
1990	791	51	842

Source: MITI 1992; Nakasone 1991

cent of the Japanese firms' patenting was from Japan. This implies that, if the country from which a patent is applied for is the same country as the one where the R&D leading to the patent was done, Japanese firms did less than 1 per cent of their R&D outside Japan during the 1980s.[1] Although analysis of this kind rests on a number of questionable assumptions, the conclusion seems likely to be true.

The fact that Japanese overseas R&D has grown so recently from a starting point of near zero is one reason why R&D activities by Japanese firms in the UK seem to be very visible. It is therefore easy to be surprised by the fact that Japanese firms spend less on R&D in all foreign countries than the total R&D expenditure of foreign companies in Japan. In 1983 the total R&D expenditure of overseas branches of Japanese companies was $60 million, in 1986 $342 million and in 1989 $468 million. As shown in Table 8.1[2] North America accounted for 62 per cent, 49 per cent and 66 per cent respectively, while Europe received 29 per cent of the total in 1986 and 21 per cent in 1989. In fact there are reasons for thinking this may overstate the European proportion, as the 1990 STA survey suggests (STA 1990).

These figures should be compared with the R&D expenditures of foreign companies in Japan, see Table 8.2,[3] which rose from $469 million in 1987 to $727 million in 1989 ($400 million and $657 million respectively if non-manufacturers are excluded). Thus foreign R&D spending in Japan exceeds the flow of funds in the opposite direction by a ratio of over 1.5:1. The extent of this investment, though widely reported in Japan, is not generally recognized elsewhere, particularly in Europe. A large proportion of the firms concerned are American, including Dow Chemicals, Du Pont, Eastman Kodak, IBM, Intel, Monsanto, Procter and Gamble, Texas Instuments, Upjohn, and many other major companies.[4] Only two British firms, Glaxo and ICI, have established R&D centres in Japan, but in both cases the scale of the investment is quite large, and smaller technical support or product development units are being set up by some other companies.

In terms of numbers of researchers there may be a similar imbalance: according to one survey foreign companies in Japan employed 6,581 researchers in 1991 (MITI 1992), whereas a 1989 survey of 833 Japanese companies with a capitalization of over 1 billion yen found that the 79 of them which described themselves as having overseas R&D centres (a total of 188 centres, since some firms had more than one) employed a total of 4,378 staff in them (STA 1990). Certainly some of the foreign laboratories in Japan are large, many of them having well over 100 technical staff, whereas the Japanese laboratories in the USA, UK and elsewhere are mostly on a much smaller scale, employing typically between 10 and 40 staff.[5]

JAPANESE R&D IN EUROPE

The annual JETRO surveys of Japanese-owned manufacturers in Europe show that in 1990 73 (out of 270 respondents) claimed to have design centres or R&D facilities, a figure which nearly doubled in 1991 to 140 (out of 323) and reached 203 in 1992 (out of 371 respondents). Just over one-quarter of these centres were described as 'independent', the remainder being associated with manufacturing facilities (see JETRO 1990, 1991, 1992).

Inevitably these centres are a heterogeneous assortment. The raw data are not available, but a careful examination of the statistics suggests some necessary qualifications. The large number and dramatic rate of growth may be misleading. 'R&D' centres may be little more than one or two staff monitoring market conditions, the broader political and economic environment or almost anything, including published reports of scientific and technological developments. 'Design centres' may do very minor modification of products or production processes to suit local market or supplier circumstances. The figures may include existing facilities which belong to concerns, such as Rover or ICL, in which a 10 per cent or larger interest has been purchased.

Of the 1991 total, 11 were said to have been established in 1970 or before, 14 between 1970 and 1980, eight between 1981 and 1985 and 49 between 1986 and 1990, leaving 58 unaccounted for. According to the 1991 survey, 22 out of 105 respondents among these centres claimed to be engaged in basic research (in 1992 the proportion was 18 per cent of those responding), 70 described themselves as doing product development (64 per cent in 1992), 67 (61 per cent in 1992) were involved in changes of product design specifications, 32 (31 per cent in 1992) in development of production processes and technologies and a small proportion in 'other activities'. (Multiple responses bring the total of the percentages to well over 100 per cent.)

Of the 73 'R&D facilities' in Europe in 1990, 23 were 'independent' or 'independently established' (the Japanese text uses *tandoku*, meaning separate) facilities; by 1991 this figure had risen to 42 'independent facilities' out of a total of 138 facilities; and by 1992 there were 54 out of 203. These R&D facilities are particularly numerous in the UK.

Of course, it is well known that by comparison with other European countries the UK has attracted a disproportionate share of Japanese investment in manufacturing generally. To take one measure of this, the UK accounted for 25 per cent of firms covered by the JETRO survey in 1990, and 27 per cent in 1992.

Meanwhile, however, the number of Japanese-owned R&D facilities in the UK has risen from 24 in 1990 (33 per cent of the European total) to 48 in 1991 (32 per cent) and to 73 in 1992 (36 per cent). If independent R&D facilities alone are looked at, the figures are 9 in 1990 (39 per cent of the European total), 15 in 1991 (36 per cent) and 19 in 1992 (35 per cent). Thus the UK has over a third of all Japanese R&D facilities.

The size and rate of growth of these figures should not obscure the fact that things are further advanced in this direction, and moving faster, in the USA. This applies at least as much to R&D centres as to factories. In 1986 Japanese firms spent 1.7 times as much on R&D in North America as in Europe, and in 1989 the figure was more than three times as much. The disparity may in fact be even greater than these figures suggest. The Science and Technology Agency's survey in 1989 found that, of the 80 largest overseas Japanese R&D centres, 66 were reportedly in the USA and nine in Europe (STA 1990: 23–4; see also Uenohara 1990).

What is the nature of the activities of the facilities covered by the JETRO surveys? The reasons given for localizing R&D strongly suggest that the centres of the majority of respondents are doing design or development work which is quite close to the market, rather than more long-term research. In percentage terms, the responses in 1992 (from 176 respondents – in other words from firms which in most cases had no 'independent facilities') were similar to those in previous years, although the total number of respondents in each category continued to grow. The main reasons specified (firms were asked to choose more than one from a menu of suggested reasons) were:

- locally produced products should be designed to satisfy local consumers' needs (77 per cent of respondents),
- information about what is going on in European markets has to be obtained as quickly as possible to meet intensifying competition for technological supremacy (58 per cent),
- our horizon of R&D activities in terms of ideas and ways of thinking must be broadened by employing foreign researchers (42 per cent),
- to shorten the lead time from R&D to the commercialization of products (34 per cent),

and (much lower in stated importance)

- as part of efforts to become an insider in the local market (14 per cent),
- implementing joint R&D with local companies and research institutes will become important in the future (14 per cent),
- to compensate for the shortage of R&D personnel in Japan (12 per cent in 1991).

MAIN R&D CENTRES IN THE UK: LOCATION AND INDUSTRIAL SECTOR

Of the 12 main Japanese firms which have set up designated, stand-alone R&D centres in the UK, five (Canon, Fujitsu, Hitachi, Sharp and Toshiba) belong broadly to the electronics and information and communication technology industries; two (Eisai and Yamanouchi) are pharmaceuticals companies; one (Nissan) is an automobile manufacturer; one (Aisin Seiki) is primarily an automotive parts manufacturer; and one (Kobe Steel) is a steelmaker which, like most of its Japanese rivals, is energetically seeking to diversify into a range of new products and activities, particularly in the field of new materials. Sony (in this case broadcast and communications equipment) and NSK-RHP (bearings manufacture) are both slightly anomalous, the former since it is in much closer proximity to other parts of the firm, and so only just qualifies as 'stand-alone'; the latter since it arises out of the acquisition of a British firm which possessed its own R&D centre, now merged in the new joint one, for which it furnished most of the staff.

These firms include some of Japan's largest, and some of the biggest spenders on R&D: according to one recent survey of R&D budgets, Hitachi (which accounts for 6 per cent of the total of Japanese corporate R&D spending) is in the top position, Fujitsu in fourth, Toshiba in sixth, Nissan in seventh, Canon in tenth, and Sharp in eleventh. Eisai is twenty-fourth, a strikingly high position for a company of modest size which, however, was planning to spend over 21 per cent of sales on R&D (*Nihon Keizai Shimbun* 1990).

Despite the size of the firms themselves, and of their R&D efforts, the centres opened in the UK are not particularly big, by comparison with, for example, foreign R&D centres in Japan. To take three instances, Glaxo, Goodyear and Texas Instruments announced plans to set up centres in Japan with research staffs of 70, 100 and 50 respectively.[6] This compares with numbers between 10 and 50 in all the Japanese establishments in the UK except Nissan, which has over 100 staff.

Three of the firms, namely Aisin Seiki, Kobe Steel and Eisai, do little or no manufacturing in the UK or elsewhere in Europe; and with the exception of Nissan and NSK-RHP most of the research activities of the other centres are comparatively remote in character from their major local manufacturing interests. The majority of them are concerned mainly with basic research and are on sites closely associated with a university or similar institution.

Thus, for example, the Sharp R&D centre in Oxford is concerned with optoelectronics, artificial intelligence and imaging technology. The Hitachi and Toshiba centres in Cambridge are concerned with aspects of semiconductor physics relevant to future high-speed devices. On the other hand, the Fujitsu Europe Telecom R&D Centre is not situated near a university (it is on a commercial science park, near Heathrow Airport) nor is it concerned with basic research.

Despite the low ranking of collaboration with local research institutes in responses to the JETRO survey, research so far confirms that many of the centres in the UK are quite active in developing their relationship with universities (and indeed that universities seek to woo them assiduously). In fact Japanese firms in general tend to take a keen interest in relations with overseas universities and other public research institutions. This may include research collaboration or contracts, or the seconding of a firm's researchers to work or study in a university laboratory, a common practice both within Japan and in Japanese firms' involvements with overseas universities.

Three of the more developmentally oriented centres (Fujitsu, NSK-RHP and Sony) have no formal or geographic ties with any one university. Of the other nine major centres in the UK all but one (Yamanouchi) are either located in a university science park or are in close association with a nearby university or other higher education and research institution. This does not of course prove or guarantee a research relationship, and indeed some of the centres tend to be fairly promiscuous, having nothing to gain by cultivating an exclusive relationship with one institution. Liaison with universities and semi-public research agencies, as well as the arrangement of participation in national or European collaborative projects, are functions for which locally situated R&D centres are well suited, since these activities may be more effectively and fruitfully performed by researchers who are local nationals based in the UK, whereas they are either more difficult or impossible for Japanese researchers based in Japan. Such considerations lead to a broader examination of the rationale underlying the choice of location of the centres in the UK.

STRATEGIC RATIONALE FOR OVERSEAS R&D

The rationale for conducting development activities in foreign markets is intuitively easy to conceive; that for research is less obvious. This paper explores three strategic reasons why Japanese companies conduct basic research overseas:

- proximity to the local science base
- concern about the creativity of Japanese researchers
- political response to host country pressure

Proximity to the local science base

This rationale applies particularly to the pharmaceutical industry, since new drugs and their development are particularly dependent on quite basic research, implying a closer link with the science base than in industries where production engineering is more crucial. Many USA companies came to the UK in the post-war years attracted by the quality and ease of access to British research (Sharp 1991). Despite their relatively small size compared with USA companies, a number of Japanese pharmaceutical firms have also established R&D centres overseas and Yamanouchi and Eisai have done so in the UK.

The drugs industry, and industries in related areas such as chemicals and possibly cosmetics, are highly research-intensive, 'science-based' and breakthrough-oriented. They seek the benefits of collaboration with local academic researchers and the opportunity to recruit local staff with appropriate competence. Although this rationale applies particularly to these industries, proximity to the science base is also important for firms in electronics and other sectors. The research centres which both Hitachi and Toshiba have set up in Cambridge are striking examples of this.

Japanese domestic research environment

The Japanese propensity (or alleged lack of one) for creative originality is a popular topic for discussion in Japan and elsewhere (Kinmonth 1987: 193–4).

To take a representative example, the president of Kobe Steel has explained his firm's establishment of a laboratory at Surrey University's research park by saying, 'The first reason we like to do R&D in the UK is because we are seeking basic research and creativity. Japanese research is better at improving technology, in applied research and commercialization.' This has been elaborated by the general manager of the laboratory, who is quoted as saying 'We are expecting original and innovative work here,' noting that, 'Most polymers were invented in Europe or the USA. Unfortunately, Japanese companies have never invented brand new polymers. The Japanese improved processes, for example we improved on catalysts, but no new polymers' (Kenward 1990).

It is widely argued, both in Japan and abroad, that the traditional style of R&D management in Japan is inclined to caution, conservatism, and an emphasis on incremental change; and that this style is far more suitable for a technological follower than for a leader.[7] It is certainly true that 'Japanese-style R&D' seems to have enjoyed remarkable success in industry during the period of Japan's 'followership': if that period is now at an end a new style may be more appropriate.

There is also a widespread perception, which has so far largely survived challenges to its underlying basis and justification (Dore 1986), that for reasons more deeply embedded in culture, or at any rate in the education system, basic research is something which Japanese corporate researchers do not do as well as some other people. This is sometimes couched in terms of the relationship between radical innovation and individualism: it is plausibly argued that Japanese society gives less encouragement to expressions of individual wishes and that this is a major barrier to creative scientific breakthroughs. This thesis depends so much on perceptions, definitions and prejudices that it is hard to discuss constructively. Nevertheless, the belief that foreign researchers, operating in a foreign environment, may be better able than many of their Japanese counterparts to come up with the breakthroughs which will be tomorrow's integrated circuits, carbon fibres, penicillin or magnetic resonance imagery has been stated or implied by several of those (both Japanese and British) concerned with setting up and running the Japanese R&D centres which have been surveyed.

Political response to host country pressure

The British government has been very welcoming to Japanese manufacturing investment, and particularly so towards the establishment of Japanese R&D centres. In some other parts of Europe this has been less true, but there is a widespread belief that R&D investment is politically more wholesome than investment in a manufacturing assembly plant (Seitz 1992: 338).

On the whole this has meant that for Japanese companies localization of R&D activities has appeared likely to win political approval in host countries. At the same time, some of them are aware of occasional media and academic criticism that foreign R&D centres do no more than capture scarce scientific talent to feed manufacturing elsewhere.[8] In the course of interviews conducted in the course of the present study, concern about the possible backlash effects of the negative arguments was sometimes recognized as an issue.[9]

In deciding whether to locate R&D overseas, linked or not linked to a manufacturing unit, Japanese companies have to judge the balance between these conflicting host country pressures and set this against the arguments in favour of keeping R&D at home. Clearly domestic R&D has the advantage of short and easy lines of communication between the key people involved.

CONCLUSIONS

R&D is growing in importance, volume and visibility throughout the industrial world. It is growing particularly rapidly in Japan. International firms conduct the great majority of their R&D in their home country. This means that compared with overseas manufacturing investment, overseas R&D is recent and small scale. In 1989 Japanese overseas R&D amounted to $468 million and the R&D expenditures of foreign firms in Japan came to $727 million.

Three-quarters of the Japanese R&D centres in Europe which figure in the latest JETRO survey are associated with manufacturing facilities, so that in 1992 there were only 54 'independent' centres and many of them were quite small. Several of the main R&D centres in the UK are located close to universities and many seek to benefit from this proximity. Concern about the creativity of Japanese researchers is a common theme, and some firms hope that British researchers will help them make breakthrough discoveries. At present it is too early to say whether the Japanese will gain a similar reputation for the effective management of British scientists as they have gained for the management of British factory workers. Some predictions are negative (Bloom 1990: 125), but evidence collected so far tends rather to support a positive forecast.

The growing body of literature on the internationalization of R&D has naturally focused on the activities of Swedish, American or other firms in which the trend has developed longer.[10] Theoretical accounts of the rationale underlying decisions to conduct R&D overseas are difficult to develop. The term R&D itself is not easy to define and the rationale for independent centres is different from that for centres associated with manufacturing. In addition the rationale differs by company and sector and may be influenced by pressure from the host country. The subject is one of increasing importance and raises a number of issues which current and future research must seek to clarify.

NOTES

1 Statistics like these should be treated with caution. For example, it is possible that patents have been applied for from Japan in respect of inventions made elsewhere. Indeed it seems that, for most multinationals, patenting is an even more centralized activity than R&D (Etemad and Dulude 1987). It may well be that this is more true of Japanese firms than others. In any case, the number of patents has only a limited amount to do with the quantity of R&D work that led to them, (and still less to do with its quality). Moreover, patents granted in the 1980s may have been in respect of work which was largely performed years earlier. Much – probably most, perhaps almost all – R&D may never lead to patentable results; or it may lead to results which provide a foundation for work done elsewhere (e.g. Japan) that eventually does lead to the grant of a US patent but which are not themselves patentable.

2 A full series of figures is to be found in earlier editions of MITI (1992), which is published annually.

3 For a complete set of figures, see successive editions of MITI (1991).

4 See, for example, DiCicco (1989); Bloom (1990: 124); and Moffatt (1991).

5 For the USA see, for example, Bloom (1990). The largest centre in the USA reportedly has a staff of 38 (Kumagai 1991).

6 See *Marketletter* (1991), Lammers (1991) and *Japan Economic Journal* (1991).

7 See, for example, Taylor (1989), and Sakakibara and Westney (1992).

8 Dreyfuss (1987) and Herbert (1989).
9 It is doubtful that US or Swiss investors have felt quite the same degree of concern about these issues, though their situation in many cases might be thought congruent.
10 See, for example, Ronstadt (1977); Behrman and Fischer (1980); Hirschey and Caves (1981); Pearce (1989); Casson (1991).

REFERENCES

Behrman, J.N. and Fischer, W.A. (1980) *Overseas R&D Activities of Transnational Companies*, Cambridge, MA: Oelgeschlager, Gunn and Hain.

Bloom, J.L. (1990) *Japan as a Scientific and Technological Superpower*, Potomac, MD: Technology International.

Casson, M. (ed.) (1991) *Global Research Strategy and International Competitiveness*, Oxford: Basil Blackwell.

DiCicco, R. (1989) 'Absorbing Japanese technology', *High Technology Business*, 9 (9), November–December: 9.

Dore, R.P. (1986) 'Where will the Japanese Nobel prizes come from?' *Science and Public Policy*, 13 (6): 347–61.

Dreyfuss, J. (1987) 'How Japan picks America's brains', *Fortune*, 21 December: 49–53.

Etemad, H. and Dulude, L.S. (1987) 'Patenting patterns in 25 large multinational enterprises', *Technovation*, 7 (1), December: 1–15.

Herbert, E. (1989) 'Japanese R&D in the USA', *Research Technology Management*, 32 (6), November–December: 11–20.

Hirschey, R.C. and Caves, R.E. (1981) 'Internationalization of research and development by multinational enterprises,' *Oxford Bulletin of Economics and Statistics*, 42 (2): 115–30.

Japan Economic Journal (1991) 9 March: 10.

JETRO (1990) *6th Survey of European Operations of Japanese Companies in the Manufacturing Sector*, Japan Trade Centre: London.

JETRO (1991) *7th Survey of European Operations of Japanese Companies in the Manufacturing Sector*, Japan Trade Centre: London.

JETRO (1992) *8th Survey of European Operations of Japanese Companies in the Manufacturing Sector*, Japan Trade Centre: London.

Keizai (1991) *Japan 1991: an International Comparison*, Tokyo: Keizai Koho Centre (Japan Institute for Social and Economic Affairs).

Kenward, M. (1990) 'A dip in the R&D pool', *Financial Times*, 11 December: 11.

Kinmonth, E. (1987) 'Japanese patents: olympic gold or public relations brass', *Pacific Affairs*, 60 (2): 173–99.

Kumagai, J. (1991) 'Several Japanese corporations establish new labs in USA', *Physics Today*, 44 (2), February: 81–3.

Lammers. D. (1991) *Electronic Engineering Times*, 7 October: 20.

Marketletter (1991) 30 September: 5.

MITI (Ministry of International Trade and Industry) (1991) Sangyō seisaku kyoku, Kokusai kigyō ka, *Kaigai jigyō katsudō kihon chōsa*, Tokyo: Ōkurashō insatsu kyoku.

MITI (1992) Sangyō seisaku kyoku, Kokusai kigyō ka, *Gaishikei kigyō no dōkō (Dai 25–kai)*, Tokyo: Ōkurashō insatsu kyoku.

Moffatt, S. (1991) 'Picking Japan's research brains', *Fortune*, 25 March: 54–9.

Nihon Keizai Shimbun (1990) European edition, 2 July: 17.

Nakasone, H. (1991) 'Japan's trade and industrial policy vision for the 1990s and the promotion of techno-globalism', Papers presented by the Parliamentary Vice-Minister of International Trade and Industry at the Royal Institute of International Affairs Conference: *The Internationalization of Research & Development: A British-Japanese Dialogue*, May 1991.

Pavitt, K. (1992) 'Internationalization of technological innovation', *Science and Public Policy*, 19 (2), April: 119–23

Pearce, R.D. (1989) *The Internationalization of Research and Development by Multinational Enterprises*, London: Macmillan.

Ronstadt, R. (1977) *Research and Development Abroad by USA Multinationals*, New York: Praeger.

Sakakibara, K. and Westney, D.E. (1992) 'Japan's management of global innovation: technology management crossing borders', in N. Rosenberg, R. Landau and D.C. Mowery (eds) *Technology and the Wealth of Nations*, Stanford: Stanford University Press.

Seitz, K. (1991) *Die japanisch-amerikanische Herausforderung*, Munich: Bonn Aktuell.

Sharp, M.L. (1991) 'Pharmaceuticals and biotechnology: perspectives for the European industry', in C. Freeman, M. Sharp, M. and W. Walker (eds) *Technology and the Future of Europe: Global Competition and the Environment in the 1990s*, London: Pinter, pp. 213–30.

STA (1990) *Minkan kigyū no kenkyō katsudō ni kan suru chōsa hōkoku: Heisei gannendo*, Tokyo: Science and Technology Agency, Kagaku gijutsu seisaku kyoku.

Taylor, M.S. (1989) 'A transaction costs analysis of Japanese employment relationships', Ph.D. Thesis, University of Washington.

Uenohara, M. (1990) 'The R&D invasion?', *Look Japan*, 413: 30–1.

Chapter 9

Organizational perestroika
Intra-company markets in Japanese multinational corporations

Tadao Kagono and Nigel Campbell

ABSTRACT

Japanese multinationals in the electronics sector keep production and sales divisions separate both at home and overseas. This creates an intra-company market regulated by the obligational nature of relationships between sister units and by the policies and interventions of top management. This organizational form facilitates innovation as the multiple sources of information and technologies, held by different production divisions, are retained as long as they are still viable.

INTRODUCTION

Japan's multinationals are increasingly important in world markets. Our research, involving interviews with more than 50 executives in 15 Japanese multinationals (mainly in the electronics sector) conducted over the last three years, suggests that they are developing a unique form of organization. They are achieving the original aims of perestroika, i.e. a loosening of the ties of the centre but without the breakup of the whole system. This involves an important role for intra-company markets; the most common of which occur where production and sales divisions[1] are separate profit centres. In consequence production divisions compete for the attention of the sales divisions and vice versa. The resulting inter-dependence requires complex co-ordinating mechanisms which Japanese multinational corporations (MNCs) are now in the process of developing. This organizational form has significant benefits for technical and managerial innovation.

Historically, as organizations have grown in size they have moved from a functional to a divisional structure (Chandler 1977). In today's textbooks the term divisional structure refers to self-contained units with their own manufacturing, accounting and marketing (Daft 1989: 230).

Normally the divisions are organized according to individual products or product groups, but, in some multinationals, structure reflects geography and self-contained units are created for different countries and regions.

In reality, few multinationals have divisional structures in purely a product or geographic form. More frequently they have a hybrid structure, or a matrix. In a hybrid, part of the organization is along product lines and part along geographic lines, whereas in a matrix, rather than divide the organization into separate parts, the product and country managers have equal authority. Most recently, Bartlett and Ghoshal (1989) have suggested that a decentralized federation may be a suitable structure for MNCs in the future. They have also stressed the danger of relying too heavily on organization structure to stimulate the necessary co-ordination, preferring to emphasize the need to create a 'matrix in the minds of the managers'.

Although there is no ideal solution, managers still have to choose some structure and many Western companies have global product divisions. The typical global product division has control of its own research, production and marketing at home and overseas. In the home country one profit centre handles all these functions. In overseas territories, which have manufacturing plants, the structure of one profit centre, handling all functions, is replicated. In territories without manufacturing plants the global product division controls its own salesforce, usually through its own sales subsidiary. However, sometimes sales are effected through a group sales company handling the products of more than one division. This is generally considered to be a second best solution, because it reduces the autonomy of the global product division.

This paper begins by describing, with examples, the nature of the divisional form we found in Japanese MNCs. This is followed by a description of the key co-ordinating mechanisms. These comprise a combination of hierarchical, market and relational processes. The advantages and implications of the structure and co-ordinating mechanisms for technological innovation are then discussed. The last section reflects on the reasons why this management system has developed in Japan and what may happen in the future.

INCOMPLETE DIVISIONS AND INTRA-COMPANY MARKETS

Although all the companies interviewed have formal profit centre structures, few of the divisions are fully self-contained and a strong functional emphasis prevails.[2] Most organizations comprise at least two kinds of incomplete divisions.[3] First there are the production divisions, which are usually divisionalized on the basis of technologies or products. Frequently, the number of production divisions is large, despite the relative narrowness of the product range. In 1989, Sony had 16 product groups, up from 12 a few years before, comprising a total of over 40 product divisions.

The production divisions control product development facilities and manufacturing plants. In most cases they have their own plants at home and overseas. Where they do not have a dedicated plant and instead have to share facilities, the production divisions will be intimately involved in the manufacture of their products. Frequently engineers from the production divisions are seconded to the plant, even if it is overseas. For example, several engineers from production divisions are based at Sharp's British factory, which manufactures for five different product divisions.

Second, there are sales divisions, handling a range of products suitable for particular customer groups and perhaps sold through a particular distribution channel. Thus Sharp has sales divisions for consumer products, industrial products and components. In Japan these sales divisions work through regional sales branches. Overseas there is usually a sales company in each country, which is divided into consumer, industrial and component divisions.

Relationships between production and sales are handled by negotiation. Production divisions negotiate with the domestic sales divisions and the overseas sales companies. The separate existence of production and sales divisions inevitably leads to competition between production divisions for the attention of the sales divisions. A few examples may help to clarify how this competition works.

Matsushita Electric

Matsushita Electric Industrial (MEI) has sales of 5 trillion yen and employs 45,000 people.[4] MEI and its major subsidiaries have divisional structures which are characterized by small production divisions that specialize in a narrow range of products, sometimes a single product. The divisions have a manufacturing function, a research and development function, and a minimal sales and marketing function. Except for original equipment manufacturing (OEM) customers, the sales and marketing teams are only indirectly linked with the end-users. Production divisions have first to sell their products to the domestic and overseas sales companies, which, in turn, sell them to distributors and retailers.

In overseas countries the production subsidiaries are separated from sales subsidiaries. The production plants report to their respective parent production divisions and sales companies report to sales headquarters.[5]

MEI's 36 production divisions and the additional 70 production divisions in subsidiary and affiliate companies are expected to manage themselves autonomously. Each has a clear profit responsibility evaluated by return on sales. Naturally the production divisions compete with each other indirectly to attract the marketing efforts of the sales divisions, which represent a scarce resource. The same is true of the sales divisions. They compete with each other to obtain the scarce product development resources of the production divisions.

Matsushita goes one step further, it allows direct competition between production divisions. For example, electric white boards are supplied by four divisions, personal computers by two divisions etc.

Canon Inc.

Canon Corporation, with a turnover of about 1 trillion yen and 16,000 employees, is basically a diversified manufacturing company with a small sales and marketing department. Canon's domestic sales are handled by the Canon Sales Company, a legally independent entity with sales of 510 billion yen and 6,800 employees. It is listed on the Tokyo Stock Exchange, but the majority of the shares (50.5 per cent) are owned by Canon. This sales company is divided into many profit centres around product lines and different regions of the country. Similar sales companies operate in major overseas markets. The production divisions sell their products to different sales companies which, in turn, sell the products through certain channels. Canon Sales Company sells the products of other companies, for instance Apple's computers. This is an exceptional case but exemplifies the autonomy of sales divisions.

Mitsubishi Electric

Mitsubishi Electric is a diversified manufacturer of electric equipment, electronics products and home appliances with sales of 2.7 trillion yen and 50,000 employees. Mitsubishi Electric's traditional multi-divisional structure was reorganized into a functional form in 1980. Originally the divisions were self-contained, with each having its own sales and marketing departments as well as departments for manufacturing and product development. After the reorganization the self-contained divisions were separated into two types of incomplete divisions –

marketing divisions and manufacturing divisions. The marketing divisions were organized around distribution channels, or customers, and the production divisions around products and technologies. The marketing divisions distributed the products of more than one manufacturing division.

The major reason for the reorganization was to change the power structure and to reduce duplication of effort in marketing. Mitsubishi Electric had a production-oriented culture which top management wanted to change. They hoped that separating production and sales would increase the relative power of the sales divisions. Instead of having to take what was offered by the production divisions, they could refuse to buy from the production divisions if their offer was not competitive enough.

The reorganization also helped to integrate the marketing efforts for a range of products of interest to one customer group or marketing channel. Previously these marketing efforts were carried out independently. For instance, the railroad sales division now sells, in addition to trains, elevators, audio and other equipment to railroad companies.

The specific historical contexts differ among the three companies. The structures of these companies, however, share a common characteristic of the functional division form; the production and sales operations are separately divisionalized. Other companies have developed similar organizational forms. In Hitachi the factories have profit responsibility and their products are distributed through divisions and sales companies. Sharp and Sanyo have manufacturing divisions and sales companies. Of course there are differences, resulting from differences in historical development, but the organizational forms are similar as are the co-ordination processes described in the next section.

CO-ORDINATION PROCESSES

Japanese multinationals use a variety of processes to co-ordinate production and sales divisions. We will categorize them as relational, hierarchical and market-based co-ordination.

Relational co-ordination

Co-ordination between production and sales divisions takes place in an atmosphere of trust and commitment. Relationships are similar to those which Sako (1991) has characterized as obligational contractual relationships, in contrast to arm's-length contractual relationships. Obligational relationships are fostered by the common striving to achieve the overall targets set for the parent company, and by the relationships built up during discussions about product development. The sales division can hardly refuse to sell a product which has resulted from a joint development effort.

Co-ordination is frequent because operating plans are revised every six months. Twice a year detailed discussions are held between production and sales divisions and the central staff. At these so-called 'line-up' meetings transfer prices are renegotiated, new forecasts of sales are made and plans for the launch of new products updated.

The chairman of one European sales subsidiary attended the latest line-up meeting for overseas subsidiaries with a team of six people. After formal meetings with the president and senior managers the team attended a series of bilateral meetings with the production divisions. Each meeting lasted half a day and two meetings were scheduled for each negotiation. The whole exercise lasted two weeks. This may seem excessive, but the exchange and sharing of information is as important as the actual outcome. Such extensive exchange of information helps each side to cope with problems which arise during the intervening six months.

Negotiations can take place overseas as well as in Japan. For example, one sales company in Britain negotiates prices and terms with manufacturing plants in Europe, including the plant in Britain.

Hierarchical co-ordination

Bilateral relationships in Japanese multinationals are not free from the interventions of senior management. First, top management determines the domain of each division and uses regular reorganizations to ensure that the structure stays in tune with the needs of the market place. Sometimes two production divisions are merged to realize technology synergy. For instance, Matsushita merged the tape recorder division and the radio division into the general audio division. At other times a production division is split up to give greater autonomy to competing technologies.

Second, top management can use resource allocation to promote the desired strategic direction.

Third, top management influences co-ordination by maintaining pressure on the divisions. Demanding goals for overseas production, new product development, quality improvement and cost reductions are set and used to prod and provoke middle managers into achieving what seems impossible. The rationale is that the healthy Japanese organization needs to maintain a certain 'stress' amongst its members. Mr Yamashita, the former president of Matsushita, was well known for insisting on both short-term performance and long-term development.

Fourth, the head office may intervene directly, as Matsushita did when it ordered one of two divisions making radio cassettes to cease production. In this case the head office only came to a decision after competition in the market place had made clear which product was the winner.

Market-based co-ordination

Markets are uniquely efficient mechanisms for co-ordinating a diverse set of demands. The separation of production and sales divisions creates multiple centres whose co-ordination would be difficult to achieve effectively without the existence of intra-company markets. Top management allows the intra-company market to sort out the prices and features required to be successful. Linkages are created, through the initiative of the divisions, and maintained because of their contribution to the strategic goals of each party. Hence the intra-company market becomes a market-place for strategic ideas and initiatives.

ADVANTAGES FOR INNOVATION

The separation of sales and production and the associated co-ordination processes create a market place for new ideas. Conflict between the needs of the market and the trajectories of the technologies are not suppressed, but are rather brought into the open to stimulate innovation. As the sources of information are multiple, there is a high probability of gaining better ideas concerning new products. As the relationships are bilateral and obligational each side listens attentively to the other's concerns. In the development and manufacture of most products there is a choice of technologies. When alternative technologies are kept in one division, which is subject to short-term profit pressure, the division tends to choose the 'best' technology, invest in it and allow the others to atrophy and eventually disappear from the division and later from the firm. When technologies are held by different production divisions, competing technologies are retained as long as they are still viable.

For instance, Matsushita allowed four different divisions to make air purifiers. Competition between the divisions enhanced technical development. As the president of one of the divisions explained:

[The other divisions] are tough competitors and tougher than the other competitors. The domain of each division is differentiated by agreement between the three, but the borders are not clear. We fight each other around the borders. Naturally we watch each other closely and if the technology of one division proves more successful we have to make every effort to improve our own technology.

The communication channels which result from this choice of structure and process also assist technological innovation. Competitive information is accessed more quickly and shared more widely. Diagonal as well as vertical and horizontal communication takes place. Managerial innovation and entrepreneurship also become easier when it is no longer necessary to integrate sales and production to achieve co-ordination. Small units can co-exist. The extreme case is Kyocera, in which each working unit in the factory is profit responsible.

DISCUSSION AND CONCLUSION

The relationship and co-ordinating mechanisms which we have described between production and sales divisions are similar to subcontract relationships (Asanuma 1989; Sako 1991) and to relationships between in-house divisions and wholly or partly owned subsidiaries. We believe that the ability of Japanese MNCs to spin off some activities as wholly or partly owned subsidiaries, but to retain them in 'the family', is accomplished through the co-ordination mechanisms we have described. In other words the Japanese MNC seems to be evolving a form of organization which blurs the distinction between intra- and inter-company relationships. Both are obligational in nature, but with market-based incentives and some hierarchical intervention.

Further research is needed to understand the circumstances in which this organizational form is an advantage. Its emergence in the electronics sector suggests that it is best suited to situations of continuous change in technical and competitive conditions. In other circumstances the high cost of co-ordination could become a burden and could lead to duplication and lack of a dedicated, focused effort.

Multinational companies are increasingly having to manage more complex portfolios of products and more varied customer requirements. Simple organizational solutions are not adequate. Bartlett and Ghoshal (1989) have proposed a move towards a federated structure with clearly defined roles for each subsidiary. Developments in Japanese MNCs suggest that another model may be evolving in which top management orchestrates a series of intra- and inter-company markets, seeking to maintain a balance between the conflicting requirements of customers and production engineers.

NOTES

1 The term 'production division' is used throughout this paper to refer to the divisions of Japanese MNCs which are engaged in manufacturing, product development sales to in-company sales divisions and, in some cases, sales to original equipment manufacturing customers. Production divisions are therefore 'incomplete' as they have only limited direct contact with end-users. The term 'product division' refers to the divisions of Western MNCs which control sales and marketing as well as manufacturing and product development.

2 Recently the Japan Development Bank (1989) surveyed the organization structure of 874 manufacturing companies listed on the Tokyo Stock Exchange. Most of the companies have a functional structure. For example, according to the survey, out of 74 companies in the electric machinery industry which had a divisional structure, two-thirds had 'incomplete' divisions.

 The functional division form is adopted by large Japanese firms in various industries, including steel, automobile and pharmaceuticals. This form is most widely adopted by the large diversified, multinational firms in electronics, home appliances, office equipment and related industries, such as Matsushita Electric, Canon, Sharp, Hitachi, Mitsubishi Electric, Kyocera and so on.

3 In some organizations independent R&D and technical service divisions also exist.

4 MEI is a diversified manufacturer of home appliances, audio and visual products, office equipment, telecommunications equipment and audio-visual software. MEI has three basic roles in the Matsushita Group. First, MEI undertakes the headquarters function for the group as a whole. Second, MEI manufactures a wide range of products. Third, MEI controls an extensive distribution network, through which it distributes its own products and those of Matsushita's wholly or majority owned subsidiaries and affiliates. Some of these affiliated companies are public corporations, like JVC or Matsushita Seiko, listed on the Tokyo Stock Exchange.

5 Regional headquarters are being established in Europe, America and South-east Asia, to manage relationships among the subsidiaries and between them and their Japanese parents.

REFERENCES

Asanuma, B. (1989) 'Manufacturer–supplier relationships in Japan and the concept of relation-specific skill', *Journal of the Japanese and International Economies*, 3 (1): 1–30.

Bartlett, C. and Ghoshal, S. (1989) *Managing Across Borders*, Cambridge, MA: Harvard Business School Press.

Chandler, A.D. Jr. (1977) *Visible Hand*, Cambridge, MA: Harvard University Press.
Daft, R.L. (1989) *Organisation Theory and Design*, St Paul, MN: West Publishing.
Sako, M. (1991) 'The role of trust in Japanese buyer–supplier relationships', *Ricerche Economiche*, 45 (2–3): 449–74.

Strategies for human resource management and supply relationships

Part II

Strategies for human resource management and supply relationships

Chapter 10

The best of both worlds? Human resource management practices in US-based Japanese affiliates

Schon Beechler and Allan Bird

ABSTRACT

Japanese management practices have received considerable attention and notoriety over the past 15 years as Westerners have searched for an understanding of Japan's meteoric economic success. As Japan's foreign direct investment has accelerated in the last few years, attention has shifted from what the Japanese are doing at home to what they are doing overseas. In spite of this, however, relatively little empirical research has actually been conducted on the management of foreign affiliates of Japanese firms.

This chapter reports the results of an exploratory study examining the characteristics of human resource management (HRM) practices and policies in 49 Japanese manufacturing and service affiliates located in the USA. It describes the policies and practices of personnel selection, compensation, appraisal and development in terms of three archetypal strategies for managing human resources. Also examined is the extent to which policies and practices conform to predications for the three HRM strategy types, as well as the degree of consistency found between stated organizational policies and actual practice.

INTRODUCTION

Japanese management practices have received considerable attention and notoriety over the past 15 years as Westerners have searched for an understanding of Japan's economic success (e.g. Ouchi 1981; Pascale and Athos 1981). More recently, attention has shifted from what the Japanese are doing at home to how they are managing their overseas operations (e.g. Boyacigiller 1990; DeNero 1990). This attention is due, in part, to the increased level of overseas investment by a large number of Japanese firms, who have moved aggressively into a global business arena once dominated by European and American multinational companies (MNCs).

Today, Japanese MNCs represent a formidable international presence around the world. Total direct foreign investment by Japanese firms increased from $47 billion in 1988 to $67.54 billion in 1989, more than a fivefold increase over the 1985 investment level (JETRO 1991). Investment in the USA, the largest recipient of Japanese foreign direct investment (FDI), accounted for over 48 per cent of Japan's total FDI worldwide in 1989 (JETRO 1991).

Although the rapid and very visible increase in Japanese FDI has, in and of itself, spawned a closer look at Japanese overseas operations, this increased attention is also due to the successes a number of Japanese firms have had in the management of their foreign operations. One such example is NUMMI, the Toyota–GM joint venture which has effectively implemented Japanese management techniques with an 'unmanageable' United Automobile Workers workforce.

Most American managers, the business press and the general public believe that Japanese MNCs are superbly managed and that they share common management characteristics. The implicit assumption has been that Japanese companies have a single common approach to management and that this approach is more successful than the prototypical 'Western' management style. However, there is little empirical evidence to support these conclusions and, indeed, there is some evidence to the contrary. For example, DeNero (1990) argues that most Japanese MNCs do not perform nearly as well in the USA or Europe as they do in Japan. He states that

> despite their massive investments in USA sales and marketing, manufacturing and even R&D facilities – few of these companies possess the full range of institutional skills needed for globalization. The necessary approaches to planning, measuring, rewarding, communicating, and day-to-day decision making all fly in the face of the centralized, functionally-driven style of most Japanese MNCs.
>
> (DeNero 1990: 157)

Much of what we know about Japanese operations in the USA comes from the popular press and is primarily anecdotal. The empirical studies which do exist are generally descriptive in nature and very little progress has been made toward developing and applying discipline-based theoretical paradigms to Japanese MNCs.

One consequence of this empirical deficiency has been an assumption by some writers that Japanese management is culturally deterministic, i.e. that Japanese companies have instituted specific types of policies and practices both at home and abroad simply because they are Japanese.

Such an assumption overlooks the potential influence of company-specific distinctive competencies, industry effects or other variables which have been shown to be significant in determining organizational structures and processes in research on American and European firms.

In order to help close this gap in our knowledge, research was undertaken to examine Japanese management practices and policies in American affiliates. Using a theoretical model which incorporates recent thinking in strategy and international HRM, this exploratory study of 64 US-based Japanese affiliates examines the similarities and differences between them and explicitly attempts to explain the relationships between business-level strategies and HRM strategies, policies and practices. We report on a subset of the research results, focusing our attention on the HRM strategies in use in the affiliates in our sample and on the nature of the HRM policies and practices in place in these firms.

HRM STRATEGIES

We begin with the premise that Japanese firms are *not* all alike, and that they have different philosophies, policies and practices, and strategies. Because we begin with this premise and reject the assumption of cultural determinism, we can apply existing theory in this area, although decidedly domestic in its orientation, to Japanese organizations. It then becomes an empirical question whether these frameworks actually apply to Japanese firms or not. Although a number of schemes have been suggested for categorizing HRM strategies (Dyer 1984; Schuler and Jackson 1987; Schuler 1988; Carroll 1991; Cascio 1991; Wright forthcoming), one typology in particular (Schuler and Jackson 1987) is consistent with previous theoretical and empirical writings on Japanese firms (e.g. Hatvany and Pucik 1981; Kagono *et al.* 1985). This typology defines three general types of HRM strategies.

A *Utilizer* strategy is predicated on minimal employee commitment and high skill utilization. It seeks to deploy the human resources of the firm as efficiently as possible through the acquisition and dismissal of personnel in accordance with the short-term needs of the firm and the matching of employee skills to specific task requirements. Hiring decisions are based primarily on the technical fit of candidates and there is little organizational support for employee development. Schuler (1988) concluded that a Utilizer HRM strategy is common in many American firms and Kagono *et al.* (1985) suggest that this strategy is more likely to be found in firms based in the USA than in Japan.

An *Accumulator* strategy is based on maximum employee

involvement and skilled execution of tasks. It attempts to build up the human resources of the firm through the acquisition of personnel with large, latent potential and through the development of that latent potential over time in a manner consistent with the needs of the organization. This HRM strategy exhibits strong parallels with accepted conceptions of Japanese HRM practices (e.g. Abegglen 1958; Rohlen 1974; Kagono *et al.* 1985; Lincoln and Kalleberg 1990).

Finally, a *Facilitator* strategy is focused on new knowledge and new knowledge creation. It seeks to develop the human resources of the firm as effectively as possible through the acquisition of self-motivated personnel and the encouragement and support of personnel to develop, on their own, the skills and knowledge which they, the employees, believe are important. Schuler (1988) suggests that this strategy may reflect an emergent movement in American firms' HRM practices.

HRM DIMENSIONS

The implementation of any HRM strategy requires the formulation of specific policies and practices addressing each of the functional areas of human resources management: planning, staffing, compensation, appraisal and training and development. These policies and practices may vary according to a number of dimensions. Although a number of writers have identified dimensions within particular HRM functions (e.g. Schuler and Jackson 1987), none have systematically applied those dimensions across all of the HRM functions, nor have they provided any theoretical framework with which to link the dimensions and the observed HRM policies or practices. The work in this area has thus been fragmented, descriptive and atheoretical in nature. Only recently are we beginning to see the emergence of paradigm development in this field.

To both address the gap in theory and to explore the linkages between theory and practice, we first identified eight dimensions on which HRM policies and practices in each of the HRM functional areas could vary: participation, time horizon, formality, explicitness, scope, individualism, frame of reference and equity. These eight dimensions were derived by cataloguing and classifying statements of HRM practices and policies found in the practitioner and academic literatures. Each dimension was identified on the basis of its ability to be broadly applied and yet be clearly distinguishable from the other dimensions. In other words, a policy's position on one dimension would not necessarily restrict its position on any of the other dimensions. These eight dimensions are briefly described below.

Participation is defined as the extent to which employees and non-related personnel and departments participate in HRM decisions. For instance, in some organizations employees are involved in setting their own performance objectives, whereas in others performance measures are established and applied across employees by the personnel department.

Time horizon refers to the relative time horizon of HRM activities, i.e. the extent to which such activities are focused on immediate concerns as opposed to future concerns. For example, in some organizations the incentive component of compensation packages is based on achievement of short-term goals (i.e. 3–6 months) as opposed to long-term goals (i.e. 18–24 months).

Formality is defined as the extent to which HRM activities are codified and/or follow set procedures or sequences. For instance, when conducting performance appraisals, some organizations use standardized forms and conduct interviews in a formal fashion at regular intervals while in others there is little standardization and interviews are conducted in a less systematic fashion.

Explicitness refers to the extent to which HRM policies, decision-making criteria and activities are clearly stated and communicated throughout the organization. In some organizations, HRM plans are stated clearly and in great detail. In other organizations, although the plans may still be well understood, they are neither articulated in detail nor explicitly defined.

Scope pertains to the relative focus of HRM activities, i.e. the extent to which such activities are concentrated on or directed at a limited set of goals or purposes versus concentrating on a wide range of goals, or are confined to a specific group of individuals as opposed to encompassing a large group of individuals. For example, training employees for specific skills constitutes a narrow scope whereas training which provides employees with general skills or abilities exemplifies a broad scope.

Individualism is defined as the extent to which HRM activities are directed toward, or oriented around, the individual as opposed to the group (i.e. work group, project team, section etc.). For example, employees can be compensated based primarily on their own performance or based on the performance of their unit, section or department in which they work.

Frame of reference refers to the extent to which the basis for comparison or evaluation of HRM activities is *within* the organization rather than *between* organizations. In the area of appraisal, for example, an employee's performance could be compared with his/her peers' performance within the firm or with some industry or professional standard.

Finally, *justice* is the extent to which HRM activities are concerned with fairness as opposed to equality, i.e. how they take into account individual differences as opposed to applying a single standard or criteria across all employees. For instance, training can be provided to employees on the basis of individual need or to all those who qualify, regardless of need.

MATCHING HRM STRATEGY AND POLICIES AND PRACTICES ON THE EIGHT DIMENSIONS

Implementation of any HRM strategy requires the formulation of specific policies and practices addressing each of the functional areas of HRM. Using a contingency perspective (e.g. Van de Ven and Drazin 1985), we predict that a firm's HRM policies and practices should match with its HRM strategy. That is, under norms of rationality, managers will adopt policies and practices which will facilitate the implementation of the firm's HRM strategy. Thus, different HRM strategies should lead to systematic variations in human resources policies and practices. In the following section we outline a profile of HRM policies and practices for each of the three HRM strategic types (Accumulators, Utilizers and Facilitators), using the eight dimensions of HRM described above. The relationship between each of the three HRM strategies, their policy implications and each strategy's relative position on the eight dimensions are presented in Table 10.1.

Accumulator profile

An Accumulator strategy focuses on providing employee skill development in an evolutionary fashion in accordance with the firm's slowly evolving human resource needs. Once employees with large latent potential are selected into the firm, attention shifts to developing employees' abilities, skills and knowledge in ways that will serve company purposes.

The internal development of human resources over time requires the firm to exercize care in the selection of new employees. The firm searches for employees with both future potential and personal fit with the firm since the relationship between employer and employee is expected to be long term. The result is a selective hiring process, an emphasis on job security and the application of compensation and promotion policies containing a strong seniority component. These, in turn, call for extensive

Table 10.1 HRM strategies, their HRM policy implications, and predicted scores on the eight HRM dimensions

Human resources strategy	Human resources policy implications	Position on strategic dimensions
Accumulator strategy *Strategy based on building maximum involvement and skilled execution* Acquisition of employees with large latent potential Development over time of employee abilities, skills, and knowledge	Internal development of human resources Careful selection of procedures on basis of personal fit Creation of functional specialists Heavy emphasis on on-the-job and job rotation Slow, steady promotion Long-term employment and job security Policy of egalitarianism among workers High levels of training Salary based on job level and seniority	Participation: Moderate Time horizon: Long Formality: High Explicitness: Low Scope: Broad Individualism: Low Frame: Internal Justice: Equality
Facilitator strategy *Strategy based on new knowledge and new knowledge creation* Acquisition of self-motivated personnel Encourage and support self-development of abilities, skills and knowledge Co-ordinate between accurate placement and flexible team structures	Mixture of outside hires and internal development of employees Selection of employees based on technical and personal fit Hire self-motivators Organizational attractiveness used to retain employee Emphasis on groups, informal interaction Careful placement and development Design of flexible teams Heavy emphasis on employee development focused on individual and facilitated by the firm	Participation: High Time horizon: Intermediate Formality: Low Explicitness: Moderate Scope: Broad Individualism: Moderate Frame: Mixed Justice: Mixed
Utilizer strategy *Strategy based on minimal commitment and high skill utilization* Employ ready-to-use talent Move employee to match abilities, skills, and knowledge to specific tasks	Closely match employee skills to task requirements in hiring Selection of employees based on technical skills Employment at will Low emphasis on employee training Appraisal and rewards based on results Compensation based on external market referents External recruitment at all levels	Participation: Low Time horizon: Short Formality: Moderate Explicitness: High Scope: Narrow Individualism: High Frame: External Justice: Equity

training which, because it is directed at internal company-employee fit, is biased toward on-the-job training and the development of a skill set which is firm specific.

Because Accumulators emphasize maximum employee involvement and skilled execution of tasks, we predict that policies and practices in these firms will be characterized by moderate levels of participation, long time horizons, high formality, high explicitness, a broad scope, low individualism, an internal frame of reference and be based on principles of equality. As an example, if we apply this profile to the function of training and development, we would expect Accumulators to have a set of policies and practices which would (a) encourage moderate participation by employees in determining the type and amount of training they receive; (b) emphasize training to develop skills for jobs which employees do not currently occupy or which do not exist; (c) provide training within a well-defined framework or programme; (d) clearly define the nature of the training and its content; (e) carry out training that enhances general skills, abilities and knowledge of the employee; (f) address training to the development of individual, as opposed to group competencies; (g) conduct training in-house with content that is firm specific; and (h) provide training to all employees equally.

Facilitator profile

A Facilitator strategy seeks to create flexible team structures and is concerned with managing human resources in a way that facilitates the creation and management of new knowledge. Facilitators must balance their need to keep up with technological change with long-term effectiveness considerations. Because Facilitators seek to develop the human resources of the firm as effectively as possible through the acquisition of self-motivated personnel and the encouragement and support of personnel to develop their skills on their own, we predict that policies and practices in these firms will be characterized by high levels of participation, moderate time horizons, low formality, moderate explicitness, a moderate scope, moderate individualism, a frame of reference which balances an internal and external orientation and a balance between equity and equality considerations.

Utilizer profile

A Utilizer strategy places minimal emphasis on employee commitment while trying to ensure immediate and high skill utilization. As a consequence, selection policies focus on closely matching employee skills to immediate task requirements. The need for rapid deployment of manpower also reduces the company's emphasis on training. The Utilizer's view of employees as just another resource of the firm and their emphasis on resource utilization and deployment encourage the development of appraisal and reward systems based on results (Kagono *et al.* 1985). Additionally, compensation is likely to be referenced to the external market since the firm relies on an external, rather than an internal, labour market. Because Utilizers deploy human resources as efficiently as possible in accordance with the short-term needs of the firm, we predict that policies and practices at these firms will be characterized by low levels of participation, a short time horizon, moderate formality, high explicitness, a narrow scope, high individualism, an external frame of reference and principles of equity.

Figure 10.1 presents ideal profiles of the three HRM strategies in terms of the eight strategic dimensions. It should be noted here that the three HRM strategies occasionally overlap with respect to the positions along some dimensions. For example, both Accumulators and Utilizers have a nearly equal emphasis on formality. Although overlap may occur on a single dimension, overall, the three profiles are markedly different from each other.

The three HRM strategy profiles described above can, we believe, be applied to domestic and international situations and to Western and non-Western firms alike. Given that the Accumulator profile closely matches what many authors have described as typical Japanese practice, we expect that the majority of Japanese affiliates in our sample will be following an Accumulator strategy. We also expect that very few firms, if any, will be following a purely traditional American approach, a Utilizer strategy, although some firms may have adopted the 'hybrid' approach of the Facilitator.

THE RESEARCH STUDY

A written questionnaire survey of senior-most American personnel managers and their immediate Japanese supervisors in US affiliates of Japanese firms was carried out between November 1990 and February 1991. One of the initial objectives of this study was to examine differences in perceptions of Japanese and American managers towards management issues. For this purpose, questionnaires were mailed in both Japanese and English and we asked respondents to return both. However, a low response rate from Japanese managers removed the possibility of carrying out a comparative analysis by respondent nationality.

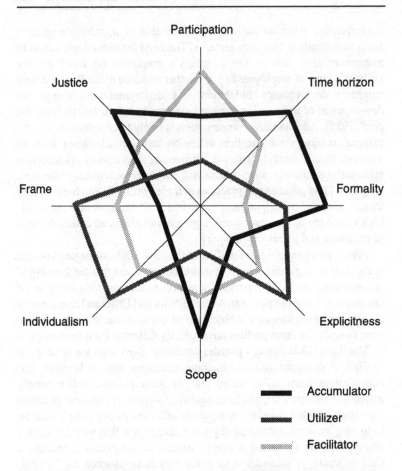

Figure 10.1 Ideal profiles for Accumulators, Facilitators and Utilizers on the eight HRM dimensions

Because the research was exploratory, firms included in the survey were selected from a subset of all Japanese subsidiaries in the USA where top-level executives had previously indicated an interest in participating in a study of HRM issues. Out of this sub-sample, we randomly selected equal numbers of manufacturing and service affiliates and questionnaires were mailed to a total of 219 firms. A total of 69 responses were received after two mailings, yielding a response rate of 32 per cent. Of these 69, five were deleted due to missing data. The remaining 64 firms include 33 manufacturing affiliates and 31 non-manufacturing affiliates. An analysis of the basic characteristics of the respondent and non-respondent firms, including average size, length of tenure in the USA and location, revealed no significant differences between the two groups.

RESULTS FOR THE TOTAL SAMPLE

Individual demographic profile

Survey respondents were 45 years old on average and a majority (80 per cent) held bachelor degrees while an additional 12 per cent had masters degrees. Almost all of the respondents, 66 out of 69, were male. On average, respondents had 13 years experience with their firm and six years with their current business unit.

Nearly 60 per cent of the respondents held the position of chief executive officer (CEO) in their affiliate and the remaining 40 per cent reported to the affiliate's general manager. In terms of functional specialization, almost half of the respondents were in general management, 17 per cent were in HRM and 20 per cent were in finance. In 72 per cent of the cases the respondents had an American superior while 28 per cent had a Japanese superior.

The predominance of American superiors in this sample of firms is surprising considering the widely held belief that a 'bamboo ceiling' in overseas affiliates prevents American managers from reaching top management positions in Japanese companies (e.g. Boyacigiller 1990). However, we did find a sizeable difference in staffing patterns according to whether the affiliate was a manufacturing unit or not. In non-manufacturing affiliates 92 per cent of the respondents had an American superior, whereas in the manufacturing affiliates only 54 per cent had an American boss. These results may reflect differences in the affiliates' tasks or the difficulty Japanese managers have reportedly had in managing American white-collar employees in service operations (e.g. Pucik *et al.* 1989; Taylor 1989; Beechler and Yang 1992).

Parent firm profile

The average sales volume of the parent organizations of affiliates in the sample totalled $5,648 million in 1991. These Japanese parent companies employed an average of 16,500 employees worldwide and an average of 700 employees in the USA. Fifty per cent of the sample companies had established operations in the USA prior to 1981 and the remainder had established operations between 1981 and 1990.

Affiliate profile

Forty-two per cent of the affiliates were established prior to 1981 and the remaining affiliates were established between 1981 and 1990. In the majority of cases (75.4 per cent) the affiliate was established as a greenfield site. Only ten companies reported that 80 per cent or less of the total capital of the branch/subsidiary was held by the Japanese parent company when the affiliate was first established. The vast majority of firms, 54 of the 64 affiliates, were 100 per cent owned at the time of establishment and, by 1991, 57 of the 64 affiliates were 100 per cent owned.

The affiliates in the sample had an average sales volume of $130 million and employed 256 employees. In terms of staffing, on average, two to three Japanese dispatchees and three American personnel occupied the top three management levels in the sample affiliates. There were an average of 50 managers below the top tier, 44 of whom were American managers, four of whom were Japanese dispatchees and two of whom were third-country nationals.

HRM STRATEGY

Using the paragraph method, respondents were asked to indicate which HRM strategy was in use at their affiliate: Accumulator, Utilizer or Facilitator. As described in detail above, an Accumulator strategy is based on maximum involvement and skilled execution of tasks. It focuses on attracting and retaining good employees. There is also an emphasis on continual employee development. This strategy has been traditionally associated with Japanese management and 42.6 per cent of the American affiliates in our sample identified their firm's HRM strategy as that of an Accumulator.

A Utilizer strategy is based on minimal employee commitment and high skill utilization. It focuses on the efficient deployment of human resources by placing people in positions where they will be able to make an immediate contribution to the firm. Hiring decisions are often based primarily on the technical fit of candidates and there is little support for employee development since employees are hired and fired according to the short-term needs of firms. Historically, this strategy has been associated more with an American management style. Only about 13 per cent of the responding affiliates identified their firm's HRM strategy as Utilizer.

Finally, a Facilitator strategy is focused on new knowledge and new knowledge creation. It concentrates on helping people work together. Skill and knowledge development are valued under this philosophy, but are not directly provided by the organization. Employees receive guidance and support from the organization in their individual development activities, so this strategy may be thought of as a hybrid approach. Forty-four per cent of the respondents identified their firm's HRM strategy as one of a Facilitator.

In summary, of 63 affiliates, there were 27 Accumulators, 27 Facilitators and 9 Utilizers. Thus, as predicted, while there are very few firms in the sample which have adopted an 'American-style' HRM strategy, most affiliates have adopted either a traditional Japanese (Accumulator) or a hybrid (Facilitator) approach.

Sample characteristics by HRM strategy type

As shown in Table 10.2, there is almost an equal proportion of manufacturing and non-manufacturing affiliates across each of the three HRM strategy types. On average, Accumulators have been operating in the USA for the longest period (20.32 years) while Facilitators have the shortest average tenure (12.71 years). Although Accumulators, Facilitators and Utilizers differ in the length of their overall tenure in the USA, there is wide variation within each strategy type and there is almost no difference in the average age of the affiliates in the sample (10–11 years old) across the three HRM strategy types.

In terms of ownership, when the affiliate was first established in the USA the parent firms of the Accumulators in the sample owned an average of 95 per cent of the capital, Facilitator parents owned 93 per cent, and Utilizer parents owned 86 per cent. Currently, the Japanese parent firms of Accumulators own an average of 93 per cent, Facilitators own an average of 98 per cent and all of the Utilizers are 100 per cent owned by their parent firms. While it appears that Utilizers have undergone a dramatic shift in ownership position over time, it should be kept in mind that the total number of Utilizers in the sample is small and, hence, these figures are easily influenced by the actions of just one or two firms.

As noted above, the majority of affiliates were established as greenfield operations. Among the three types of affiliates, Accumulators have the greatest percentage of greenfield affiliates (78.3 per cent) while Utilizers have the lowest proportion of greenfield affiliates (71.4 per cent). Again, although the differences between the three categories of firms are not large, it is interesting to note that those firms which have the

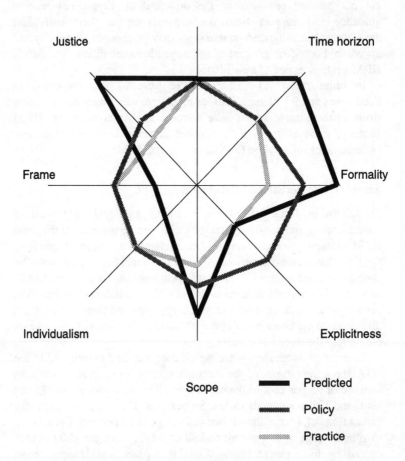

Figure 10.2 Predicted results, actual policies and actual practices for
Accumulators on the eight HRM dimensions

most 'Japanese-style' HRM strategy (Accumulators) have the greatest
proportion of greenfield investments while those firms with the most
'American-style' HRM strategy (Utilizers) have the lowest proportion of
greenfield sites. Although we cannot determine causality from this study,
these results may reflect the fact that Accumulators establish affiliates as
greenfield operations in order to more easily transfer 'Japanese-style'
HRM overseas, whereas Utilizers, because they have a more American

Table 10.2 Descriptive statistics on the three HRM strategy types, n = 63

	Total sample mean	Accumulators mean	Facilitators mean	Utilizers mean
Total sales of MNC worldwide (x 1,000)	$5,648,000 (15,244,000)[a]	$3,650,875 (11,182,500)	$9,103,105 (20,900,786)	$2,771,714 (3,044,409)
Total number of employees in MNC worldwide	16,500 (52,800)	3,338 (4,612)	32,100 (78,050)	9,082 (10,366)
Total number of MNC employees in US	700 (2,000)	424.29 (1,319.5)	1,014.30 (2,699.24)	574 (1,089.16)
MNC's years of experience in US	15.86 (17.18)	20.32 (20.85)	12.71 (15.24)	14.22 (9.47)
Number in manufacturing	29	12	12	5
non-manufacturing	34	15	15	4
Total sales of affiliate (x 1,000)	$128,763.89 (214,793.95)	$130,072.73 (128,921.13)	$99,900.00 (182,584.41)	$241,340.00 (428,694.62)
Number of employees in affiliate	256.20 (577.06)	166.75 (254.16)	230.00 (511.11)	660.14 (1,243.61)
Age of affiliate (years)	10.43 (8.06)	10.79 (7.96)	10.24 (8.80)	10.83 (6.65)
Capital held by parent when established	92.79% (18.87)	94.8% (14.93)	92.86% (21.40)	85.57% (24.64)
Capital of parent now	96.15% (11.1)	92.97% (14.93)	98.21 (6.70)	100% (0)
Type of investment Greenfield	75.5%	78.3%	73.1%	71.4%
Acquisition	14.0%	13.0%	15.4%	14.3%
Joint venture	10.5%	8.7%	11.5%	14.3%
Number of Japanese managers in affiliate	6.36 (4.18)	8.9 (4.6)	5.2 (3.0)	4.4 (3.8)
Percentage of Japanese managers of all affiliate managers	36% (0.47)	51% (0.68)	30% (0.225)	8% (0.04)

Note: [a] Numbers in parentheses are standard deviations.

approach, may be relatively less concerned with control. This interpretation is consistent with a previous study of control in Japanese affiliates in the USA (Kujawa 1985). It may also be the case that firms which do acquire existing firms or joint ventures may be unable to implement a 'Japanese-style' HRM strategy because of the presence of existing personnel, policies and systems which are difficult to change, and therefore turn to a more 'American-style' approach.

In terms of size, Accumulators employ fewer people in their American operations (424 employees) than either Utilizers (574) or Facilitators (1,014 employees). At the affiliates themselves, Accumulators again have the fewest average number of employees (167), while Utilizers have the most (660). However, there is wide variation in size among the firms in each of the strategy types, as shown by the standard deviations in Table 10.2.

Perhaps the most striking differences to be found among the three types is the size of the Japanese presence in the American affiliate. There are, on average, two to three Japanese expatriates in the top three management levels in all three types of firms. However, breaking out the sample by HRM strategy type, Accumulators, despite their relatively smaller size, have significantly more Japanese expatriates (an average of six) in management levels below the top three levels in the affiliate than either Utilizers (2.57) or Facilitators (2.96). In terms of the percentage of Japanese expatriate managers to all managers at the affiliate, the differences are even more striking. While an average of only 8 per cent of all managers in Utilizers are Japanese, 30 per cent of Facilitator managers are Japanese and 51 per cent of all Accumulator managers are Japanese.

Those firms with the most 'American-style' approach to HRM strategy have the smallest proportion of Japanese managers while those affiliates with the most 'Japanese-style' approach have the greatest proportion of Japanese managers. These results are consistent with the observations of a number of writers who have argued that in order to transfer 'Japanese-style' management overseas, a high concentration of expatriates is necessary since these individuals act as transfer agents from the Japanese headquarters to the overseas affiliate (e.g. Tsurumi 1976; Yoshino 1976). These findings support the proposition that firms attempting to implement Japanese HRM systems in their overseas affiliates exert tighter control over the HRM function.

Results for larger affiliates

Because follow-up interviews at a number of the sample companies revealed that very small affiliates generally take an *ad hoc* approach to HRM policies, we excluded all those affiliates with under ten employees when conducting the analyses of HRM policies and practices presented below. Descriptive statistics for this smaller sample are presented in Table 10.3. As shown in this table, there are statistically significant differences (using *t* tests between the three strategy groups) in the number of total MNC employees worldwide between Accumulators and Facilitators and between Facilitators and Utilizers. There are also significant differences on the percentage of capital owned by the Japanese parent between Utilizers (mean = 100 per cent) and Accumulators (mean = 91 per cent). In addition, there are significant differences between Accumulators and Facilitators and between Accumulators and Utilizers on the number of Japanese managers in the affiliate as well as between Facilitators and Utilizers and between Utilizers and Accumulators on the percentage of Japanese managers to total managers in the affiliate. These differences are consistent with those described above for the total sample of firms (including those affiliates with under ten employees). There are no statistically significant differences between the three HRM strategy types on any of the other descriptive characteristics presented in Table 10.3.

HRM POLICIES

In order to measure HRM policies on the eight dimensions of participation, time horizon, formality, explicitness, scope, individualism, frame and justice, we asked respondents to indicate where their HRM policies were located on a double-anchored seven-point scale. For example, in order to measure explicitness in compensation policy, we asked respondents to indicate whether the policies at their affiliate were closer to the statement 'Compensation policies are clearly stated and widely communicated within the firm' or the statement 'Compensation policies are not clearly stated nor widely communicated within the firm'.

For each of the eight HRM dimensions, we averaged respondents' scores across the five HRM functions to determine an overall measure. We then split the sample according to HRM strategy and calculated the average scores on each of the eight dimensions for the three HRM strategy types. These results are presented in Table 10.4. As shown in the table, Accumulators score highest of the three groups on the participation,

Table 10.3 Descriptive statistics on the three HRM strategy types (n=49) [a]

	Accumulators mean (n = 21)	Facilitators mean (n = 22)	Utilizers mean (n = 6)
Total sales of MNC worldwide (×1,000)	$1,703,833.33 (3,088,796.61)[b]	$10,169,647.06*[c] (21,908,137.14)	$3,877,000.0 (2,925,388.01)
Total number of employees in MNC worldwide	3,912.06 (5,209.18)	39,997.21* (87,009.21)	13,175.00 (11,933.69)
Total number of MNC employees in USA	461.42 (1,507.45)	1,375.50 (3,090.10)	805.17 (7.52)
MNC's years of experience in USA	22.66 (23.16)	13.95 (16.67)	14.67 (9.85)
Number in manufacturing	10	11	3
non-manufacturing	11	11	3
Total sales of affiliate (×1,000)	130,072.73 (128,921.13)	99,900.00 (182,584.41)	241,340.00 (428,694.62)
Number of employees in affiliate	190.19 (263.95)	271.09 (547.26)	769.17 (1325.16)
Age of affiliate (in years)	12.06 (8.05)	9.58 (8.13)	12.20 (6.42)
Capital held by parent when established	94.8% (13.74)	95.5% (12.62)	90.0% (22.36)
Capital of parent now	90.9% (17.0)	98.2% (7.52)	100%* (0)
Type of investment Greenfield	79.0%	71.4%	80.0%
Acquisition	10.5%	14.3%	0
Joint venture	10.5%	14.3%	20.0%
Number of Japanese managers in affiliate	9.14 (4.6)	5.2 (3.0)	6.2* (3.8)
Percentage of Japanese managers of all affiliate managers	31% (0.27)	24%* (0.15)	6%* (0.01)

Notes: [a] All affiliates with under ten employees have been deleted from the sample.
[b] Numbers in parentheses are standard deviations.
[c] Differences between the strategy types are significant. An asterisk after the Utilizers column indicates a significant difference between Utilizers and Accumulators.

Table 10.4 HRM policy profile: average scores on the eight HRM dimensions for the three HRM strategy types

	Accumulator	*Facilitator*	*Utilizer*
Participation	3.97	3.60	3.17*[a]
Time horizon	3.82*	3.51*	3.03**
Formality	4.56	4.35	4.08
Explicitness	3.99	3.84	4.40
Scope	3.89	3.53	3.55
Individualism	3.51	3.24	3.24
Frame	3.66	3.85	3.55
Justice	3.52	3.36	3.16

Notes: *, $p < 0.10$; **, $p < 0.05$.
  [a] Asterisks indicate level of significance on a *t* test of differences between means for the item means to the immediate left and right. Asterisks at the end of a row indicate significant differences between Utilizers and Accumulators on that item.

time horizon, formality, scope, individualism and justice dimensions. Utilizers score highest on explicitness and lowest on participation, time horizon, formality, frame and justice while Facilitators score lowest on explicitness and scope and highest on frame. Using a difference in means test (*t* test) between each of the three HRM strategy types, we found significant differences between Accumulators and Utilizers on the participation dimension. Compared with Utilizers (mean = 3.17), Accumulators are characterized by significantly higher levels of participation (mean = 3.97) when averaging across the five HRM functions of planning, staffing, compensation, appraisal and training and development. These results for Utilizers *vis-à-vis* Accumulators are as predicted. However, Accumulators in the sample actually have higher levels of participation than the Facilitators, contrary to our prediction, although the differences are not significant.

In addition, there are significant differences between all three groups on the time horizon dimension, with Accumulators having the longest average time horizon across HRM functions (mean = 3.82) and Utilizers having the shortest (mean = 3.03), as expected. None of the other differences between the three groups are significant, although an examination of Table 10.4 shows that most of the differences between the groups are in the expected direction.

Although we would predict that the eight dimensions should be consistent across the five HRM functional areas, we examined each of these areas separately, again comparing mean scores on each dimension for the Accumulators, Utilizers and Facilitators in our sample. The results

Table 10.5 HRM policy profile: scores on the eight HRM dimensions for the three HRM strategy types by HRM function

	Accumulator	*Facilitator*	*Utilizer*
Planning			
Participation	4.50*[a]	3.62	4.00
Time horizon	3.60	3.86*	2.50*
Formality	4.10	4.09	3.33
Explicitness	4.80**	3.95	4.67
Scope	4.20	3.82**	2.50***
Individualism	3.55	3.59	3.67
Frame	3.45	3.73**	2.00**
Justice	2.88	3.32	3.25
Staffing			
Participation	4.45	4.50	4.67
Time horizon	3.75	3.77	4.17
Formality	3.85	3.91	4.60
Explicitness	4.75	4.09	4.80
Scope	3.45	3.27	3.60
Individualism	4.11*	3.55	3.20
Frame	3.45	3.68	3.50
Justice	3.45	3.45	2.75
Compensation			
Participation	3.00	2.55	2.00
Time horizon	4.77	4.29	4.67
Formality	6.21**	5.45	5.33
Explicitness	2.32	3.23	3.00
Scope	5.00	4.27	4.40
Individualism	3.39	3.23	3.00
Frame	3.94	4.29**	2.60*
Justice	4.22	3.86	4.17
Appraisal			
Participation	3.63	3.86*	2.50
Time horizon	3.21	3.00*	2.17*
Formality	5.16	4.95	5.00
Explicitness	3.00*	3.86	3.50
Scope	2.68	3.27	3.00
Individualism	2.74	2.95	2.67
Frame	3.32	3.59	3.50
Justice	2.68	2.91	3.60
Training			
Participation	4.00	3.63	2.667*
Time horizon	3.21	2.91**	1.67***
Formality	3.47	3.32**	2.00**
Explicitness	5.05**	4.05**	5.83
Scope	4.00***	3.00*	2.17***
Individualism	3.26	2.86	2.83
Frame	3.79	3.95	4.00
Justice	4.42***	3.27	3.80

Notes: *, *p* < 0.10; **, *p* < 0.05; ***, *p* < 0.01.

[a] Asterisks indicate level of significance on a *t* test of differences between means for the item means to the immediate left and right. Asterisks at the end of a row indicate significant differences between Utilizers and Accumulators on that item.

for each of the HRM functions of planning, staffing, compensation, appraisal and training and development are presented in Table 10.5.

Overall, we found that our predictions are generally supported by the results, although there are a number of differences according to HRM functions. For example, there is only one significant difference between the three groups in staffing – between Facilitators and Accumulators on the individualism dimension. On the other hand, there are a large number of differences between the three strategy types in training policies. In this area, Accumulators have significantly higher levels of participation (mean = 4.0) than Utilizers (mean = 2.67). In addition, both Accumulators (mean = 3.21) and Facilitators (mean = 2.91) have significantly longer-term orientations than do Utilizers (mean = 1.67). There are also significant training policy differences between the three strategy types in terms of formality, explicitness, scope and justice, all consistent with our predictions.

Reflecting on the fundamental differences between the three HRM strategies, these different findings across the HRM dimensions are not particularly surprising. In our typology of Utilizers, Facilitators and Accumulators, the three strategies are most clearly differentiated according to their approaches toward training and development. It is important to note, however, that it is not merely the amount of training but also the type and purpose of such training which distinguishes between the three HRM strategies.

HRM PRACTICES

While policies indicate the planned intention of HRM activities or the direction that an organization wishes to move, HRM practices reflect the implementation of these plans. Parallel to the policy questions described above, we measured the eight HRM dimensions for practices in each HRM functional area. In order to reduce response bias and to distinguish between HRM policy and HRM practice, we asked respondents to indicate the percentage of managers to which a particular statement applied (Schuler and Jackson 1987).

Again we averaged the responses for each of the dimensions across the HRM functional areas to arrive at a profile of practices for each of the three HRM strategy types (Table 10.6). As predicted, Accumulators scored highest of the three groups on time horizon and scope, although they also unexpectedly scored highest on individualism as well. Also as predicted, Facilitators scored highest on participation, although they also scored highest on formality, explicitness, frame and justice.

Table 10.6 HRM practice profile: scores on the eight HRM dimensions
for the three HRM strategy types by HRM functions

	Accumulator (%)	Facilitator (%)	Utilizer (%)
Participation	57.4	60.3	49.4
Time Horizon	52.2	49.9	38.8
Formality	42.3	53.6*a	31.9
Explicitness	30.4	34.7	23.4
Scope	45.2	44.3	34.1
Individualism	51.2	49.9	43.1
Frame	50.6	53.3*	32.2
Justice	39.6	40.8*	25.3

Notes: *, $p < 0.10$; **, $p < 0.05$; ***, $p < 0.01$.
   [a] Asterisks indicate level of significance on a *t*-test of differences
   between mean for the items means to the immediate left and right.
   Asterisks at the end of a row indicate significant differences between
   Utilizers and Accumulators on that item.

Utilizers scored lowest on all eight dimensions. Whereas the results on
participation, time horizon, scope and justice were as predicted, the
Utilizers' scores were opposite to those predicted for the dimensions of
explicitness, frame and individualism. *t* tests show that the only
statistically significant differences across the functions are between
Utilizers and Facilitators on formality, frame and justice; with
Facilitators' practices being more formal, more externally oriented and
more egalitarian than those of Utilizers.

Looking more specifically at the differences between Accumulators,
Utilizers, and Facilitators on the various HRM functional practices, we
find that, parallel to the results for HRM policies, there is significant
variation between the three strategy types depending on HRM functional
area (Table 10.7). For example, in the area of compensation, Facilitators
have a significantly longer-term orientation (mean = 62.5 per cent) than
do Accumulators (mean = 36.9 per cent), contrary to our prediction. In
terms of justice, Accumulators have a significantly greater equity
orientation (mean = 59.2 per cent) than do Utilizers (mean = 86.3 per
cent), while Utilizers are significantly more equality oriented than are
Facilitators (mean = 64.2 per cent).

In order to compare policies and practices to our original predictions
regarding the rank ordering of the three strategy groups on each of the
eight dimensions, we transformed the original mean scores to *z* scores.
These scores, along with our original predictions for each dimension, are
presented in Table 10.8. In addition, the contrasts between predicted

Table 10.7 HRM practice profile: scores on the eight HRM dimensions for the three HRM strategy types by HRM function.

	Accumulator (%)	Facilitator (%)	Utilizer (%)
Staffing			
Participation	27.1	24.6	26.3
Time horizon	69.3	61.3	35.0
Formality	52.9	40.4	63.8
Explicitness	11.4*a	34.6	21.3
Scope	53.6	72.7	62.5
Individualism	30.0	39.6	33.8
Frame	62.1	56.4	63.8
Justice	33.6	35.0	13.8
Compensation			
Participation	61.5	45.7	40.0
Time horizon	36.9*	62.5	55.0
Formality	43.8	66.4	50.0
Explicitness	32.3	31.4**	0.0**
Scope	39.2	41.9	27.5
Individualism	49.2	47.3	52.5
Frame	52.3	56.9	27.5
Justice	59.2	64.2**	86.3*
Appraisal			
Participation	52.1	37.3**	85.0*
Time horizon	56.4	46.1	40.0
Formality	42.1	35.0*	75.0
Explicitness	45.0	36.2	40.0
Scope	67.9	67.5	82.5
Individualism	55.7	44.6	62.5
Frame	54.3	39.6	15.0*
Justice	45.7	46.7	36.3
Training			
Participation	48.2	62.1	68.8
Time horizon	72.5**	42.5	65.0
Formality	22.1	18.8	16.3
Explicitness	23.6	19.2	12.5
Scope	67.1	71.9	53.8
Individualism	33.6	51.8*	16.3
Frame	59.3	72.9	50.0
Justice	54.3	61.4	62.5

Notes: *, $p < 0.10$, **; $p < 0.05$; ***, = $p < 0.01$.
    a Asterisks indicate level of significance on a *t* test of differences between mean for the item means to the immediate left and right. Asterisks at the end of a row indicate significant differences between Utilizers and Accumulators on that item.

Table 10.8 Expected versus actual results (using *z* scores)

Dimension	HRM strategy		
	Accumulator	*Facilitator*	*Utilizer*
Participation			
Expected rank	Middle	Highest	Lowest
Policy mean	0.278[a]	−0.103	−0.546
Practice mean	−0.005[a]	0.134	−0.388
Time horizon			
Expected rank	Highest	Middle	Lowest
Policy mean	0.397	−0.095	−0.857
Practice mean	0.144	0.024	−0.556
Formality			
Expected rank	Highest	Lowest	Middle
Policy mean	0.155	−0.049	−0.311
Practice mean	−0.172	0.424	−0.721
Explicitness			
Expected rank	Lowest	Middle	Highest
Policy mean	0.031	−0.124	0.454
Practice mean	−0.044	0.161	−0.379
Scope			
Expected rank	Highest	Middle	Lowest
Policy mean	0.259	−0.185	−0.160
Practice mean	0.126	0.067	−0.593
Individualism			
Expected rank	Lowest	Middle	Highest
Policy mean	0.300	−0.150	−0.283
Practice mean	0.118	0.027	−0.447
Frame			
Expected rank	Lowest (internal)	Middle	Highest (external)
Policy mean	−0.048	0.181	−0.554
Practice mean	0.077	0.207	−0.815
Justice			
Expected rank	Highest (equality)	Middle	Lowest (equity)
Policy mean	0.129	−0.129	0.177
Practice mean	0.081	0.144	−0.665

Note: [a] Actual means have been converted to *z* scores for both policy and practice means.

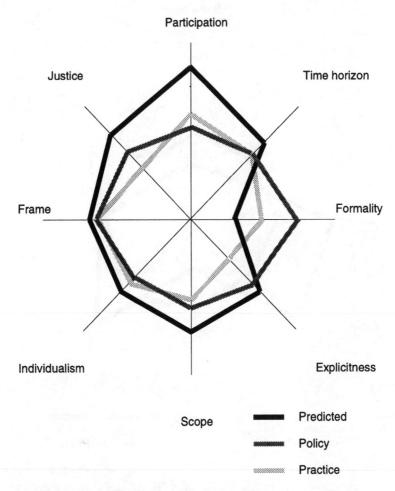

Figure 10.3 Predicted results, actual policies and actual practices for Facilitators on the eight HRM dimensions

results, actual policies and actual practices are presented graphically in Figures 10.2, 10.3 and 10.4 for each of the three HRM strategy types (Figure 10.2 is for Accumulators, Figure 10.3 for Facilitators, and Figure 10.4 for Utilizers). What is notable about these results is that Utilizers consistently score lower than the mean on every dimension in their HRM practices. In addition, Utilizers score consistently lower than the sample mean on HRM policies on all of the eight dimensions except for justice (contrary to our prediction) and explicitness (consistent with our prediction).

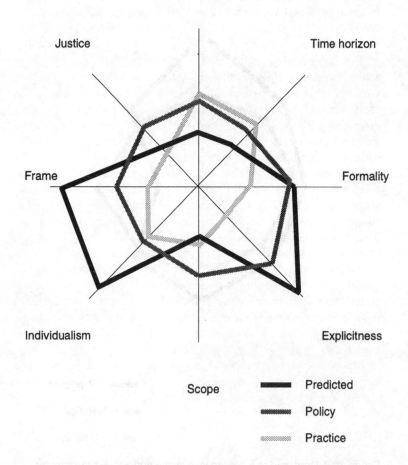

Figure 10.4 Predicted results, actual policies and actual practices for Utilizers on the eight HRM dimensions

DISCUSSION

Examining the differences between the firms in our sample in terms of actual HRM practices, we find very few differences between Accumulators, Facilitators and Utilizers on the eight HRM dimensions. While there are 27 significant differences between the strategy types on HRM *policies*, there are only a total of 11 significant differences between the three strategy types on *practices*. Thus, firms are differentiated on a number of dimensions in terms of policy, but differ little when it comes to actual practice. Executives in each firm believe that they are pursuing distinctive HRM strategies, yet they are not implementing them in distinctive ways.

This is not to suggest that the outcomes at these affiliates are necessarily the same, nor that the differing policies are unimportant. Policies, after all, represent a goal to pursue or a standard to strive for. The cross-sectional nature of this study prevents us from adequately determining the direction in which practices are moving. We cannot know from the results of this study whether practices are moving toward the espoused policies or away from them.

Turning now to the eight dimensions used to measure HRM practices and policies in this study, four dimensions – participation, time horizon, scope and justice – most clearly differentiate between the three types of strategies. In terms of HRM functions, the areas of training and planning policies clearly exhibit the most differences between the three HRM strategies. These results suggest that the planning and training functions are most influenced by a firm's particular HRM strategy, while staffing, appraisal and compensation may be more strongly influenced by external factors or by factors common to all of the firms in our sample. Certainly many practices in these three areas are tightly constrained by government regulations concerning employment, labour relations and wage and benefit packages.

In addition, our field interviews indicate that one reason for a common approach to recruiting and compensation across the firms in our sample, regardless of HRM strategy, is that many Japanese companies have a difficult time recruiting top-level managers and retaining American managers at every level in the organization. When employees quit, American managers tend to blame the company while the Japanese managers tend to blame the American employees for the failed relationship. A vicious cycle has therefore developed in many Japanese affiliates where American executives leave the firm, Japanese firms refuse to invest in their employees and Americans turn over because their firms do not invest in them.

One of the most obvious findings from this research study is the presence of a very small number of Utilizers. This may be an artifact of the sample, which consists of firms with a stated interest in HRM issues. It is possible that Utilizers were self-selected out of the original sample because they do not place a high priority on HRM. On the other hand, the small number of Utilizers may indicate that Japanese firms, even when they do adopt American policies and practices, do not 'go native', but retain some aspects of their 'Japanese-style' management approach. It is also possible that there are few Utilizers because foreign affiliates are, by definition, an extension of the parent's operations. As such, they incorporate firm-specific knowledge which cannot be acquired easily from local labour markets nor easily marketed to other firms. Given these constraints, the resource deployment approach embraced by a Utilizer strategy is difficult to employ effectively. Finally, it is also possible that the three types of firms are not evenly distributed in any sample, American or foreign. Resolution of this question must await further research.

While there are few Utilizers in the sample, over 40 per cent of the Japanese affiliates have adopted a Facilitator HRM strategy. The Facilitator differs fundamentally from both the Utilizer and the Accumulator in its emphasis on individual responsibility and choice in the development of human capital. Unlike the Accumulator, where the development of human potential is focused on the evolving needs of the organization, the Facilitator emphasizes and respects the preferences of the individual in development decisions.

Writers on Japanese management practices (Dore 1973; Rohlen, 1974; Abegglen and Stalk 1985; Hatvany and Pucik 1981; Lincoln and Kalleberg 1990) have stressed the point that Japanese organizations are skilful at aligning the interests of the workers with those of the organization. In their comparative study of control and commitment in Japanese and American companies, Lincoln and Kalleberg (1990) argue that Japanese companies pursue a form of welfare corporatism. This is characterized by what might be called an organization-wide community. Employees hold citizenship in the community (company) and take an active part in the management and guidance of its affairs. In exchange, the organization looks out for and takes care of its citizens.

Not unlike a community in the civic sense, there is an attempt to balance between the interests of the individual and the interests of the community. In Japan, however, the balance has traditionally been tilted in favour of company interests over individual interests. The alignment of individual and organizational goals occurs after employees are hired through the modification of workers' expectations with regard to short- and long-term rewards as well as expectations of long-term career development within the organization. In the USA, however, many Japanese firms apparently find it either necessary or advantageous to adapt the traditional Japanese approach to fit the local environment and to attract and retain local workers. Research on differences between Japan and the USA in terms of collectivism versus individualism (Hofstede 1984; Triandis 1986) has repeatedly found significant differences between the two, with Americans being more individualistic than Japanese. In the American affiliates of Japanese firms, where workers, blue-collar and white-collar alike, tend to focus more on short-term rewards and do not harbour expectations of long-term affiliation with the firm, many companies have adopted a Facilitator strategy and are attempting to retain and develop human capital by providing incentives which allow for greater individual freedom than would an Accumulator strategy.

From interviews with a number of human resource managers we found that many of the adaptations Facilitators have had to make have not been made willingly. These Japanese companies may have been forced, by cultural differences, to cater more to individual employee demands than they customarily do in Japan, since a traditional (Accumulator) Japanese approach does not readily accommodate individual employee needs and leads to difficulties in hiring and retaining able American employees.

At the same time, the large number of Facilitators in our sample may be reflective of current changes in Japanese management in general. In order to accommodate changes in individual preferences, the changing demographic makeup of the Japanese workforce and international competitive conditions, Japanese firms may be in the process of gradually shifting from an Accumulator to a Facilitator approach not only for their foreign employees but for their Japanese personnel in Japan as well.

Although many Western writers implicitly assume that Japanese-style management is both homogeneous and constant, policies and practices in Japanese firms clearly evolve over time. Further research is needed to determine whether Japanese change their HRM strategy when they come to the USA or whether the results signal an evolutionary trend in the development of Japanese management in general, whether there are industry or firm-specific effects which we have not been able to document in the present study and how much the American environment itself influences these processes.

The results of this study indicate that contrary to popular belief, not all Japanese companies adopt the same approach to HRM strategy. However, the results also indicate that when it comes to the actual implementation of practices that the Japanese firms in our sample do exhibit a number of consistent patterns. Nevertheless, interviews at a number of the sample firms indicate that these similarities in practices are not due to innate 'cultural factors' but to external environmental constraints. The results from this study also supply empirical verification of the often-stated but untested assumption that there is a strong association between the transfer of 'Japanese-style' management overseas and the presence of expatriates in the overseas affiliate. The presence of Japanese expatriates is associated with a more traditional Japanese approach to HRM. Companies with an Accumulator strategy tend to send more Japanese expatriates overseas to staff management positions in their affiliates. However, the actual role of the expatriates in the creation and/or maintenance of a particular HRM strategy in Japanese overseas affiliates cannot be determined from our data and requires further study.

Although many Japanese firms have adapted to the American environment, the results from this study indicate that few Japanese affiliates in the USA have 'gone local' or completely adopted the proto-typically American HRM strategy of the Utilizer. Those that have done so have relied almost exclusively on American personnel managers and have given them complete discretion over HRM policies and practices at the affiliate. On the other hand, the Facilitators in our sample are attempting to find a middle ground, trying to take the best from both worlds, Japanese and American. Whether this hybrid approach to HRM translates into higher individual and/or firm performance is an empirical question to be explored in the future.

Effective HRM policies and practices, particularly of American white-collar workers, is a key concern of Japanese firms. Japanese MNCs cannot compete in the global market-place without effectively mobilizing these resources through the implementation of HRM policies and practices which fit the needs of the organization, its employees and the external constraints imposed by the firm's environment. Technological prowess, close supplier relationships, just-in-time inventory controls, quality circles and all of the other mechanisms which have been highlighted as keys to Japanese success are meaningless without the human resources to implement them.

ACKNOWLEDGEMENTS

An earlier version of this paper was presented at the 1992 annual meeting of the Association for Japanese Business Studies in Denver, Colorado. We would like to sincerely thank James Kennelly for his assistance in conducting the data analyses presented in this paper. Portions of this study were funded by KPMG Peat Marwick, the Stern School of Business, New York University, and the Graduate School of Business, Columbia University.

REFERENCES

Abegglen, J. (1958) *The Japanese Factory*, New York: Free Press.

Abegglen, J. and Stalk, G. (1985) *Kaisha, the Japanese Corporation*, New York: Basic Books.

Beechler, S. and Yang, Z. (1992) 'The transfer for Japanese-style management overseas: contingencies, constraints, and competencies in Japanese-owned firms in the USA', Working Paper, Center for Japanese Economy and Business, Columbia University.

Boyacigiller, N. (1991) 'Staffing in a foreign land: a multi-level study of Japanese multinationals with operations in the USA', Paper presented at the First International Conference of the Western Academy of Management, Shizuoka, Japan.

Carroll, S. (1991) 'New HRM roles, responsibilities, and structures', in R.S. Schuler (ed.) *Managing HR in the Information Age*, Washington, DC: SHRM, pp. 204–22.

Cascio, W. (1991) *Costing Human Resources: The Financial Impact of Behavior in Organizations*, 3rd edn, Boston, MA: PWS-Kent.

DeNero, Henry (1990) 'Creating the "hyphenated" corporation', *The McKinsey Quarterly*, 4: 153–74.

Dore, R. (1973) *British Factory–Japanese Factory*, Berkeley, CA: University of California Press.

Dyer, L. (1984) 'Studying human resources management and planning', *Research in Personnel and Human Resources Management*, 3: 1–30.

Hatvany, N. and Pucik, V. (1981) 'An integrated management system: lessons from the Japanese experience', *Academy of Management Review*, 6: 469–80.

Hofstede, G. (1984) *Culture's Consequences: International Differences in Work Related Values*, Beverly Hills, CA: Sage Publications.

JETRO (1991) '1991 JETRO', *White Paper on Foreign Direct Investment*, Tokyo: Japan External Trade Organization.

Kagono, T., Nonaka, I., Sakakibara K. and Okumura, A. (1985) *Strategic vs. Evolutionary Management: A U.S.–Japan Comparison of Strategy and Organization*, New York: North-Holland.

Lincoln, J. and Kalleberg, A. (1990) *Culture, Control, and Commitment*, New York: Cambridge University Press.

Ouchi, W. (1981) *Theory Z*, New York: Addison-Wesley.

Pascale, R.T. and Athos, A. (1981) *The Art of Japanese Management*, New York: Simon and Schuster.

Pucik, V., Hanada, M. and Fifield, G. (1989) *Management Culture and the Effectiveness of Local Executives in Japanese-Owned U.S. Corporations*, New York: Egon Zehnder International.

Rohlen, T. (1974) *For Harmony and Strength*, Berkeley, CA: University of California Press.

Schuler, R.S. (1988) 'Systematic human resources management', Working Paper, New York University, Stern School of Business.

Schuler, R.S. and Jackson, S.E. (1987) 'Organizational strategy and organization level as determinants of HRM practice', *Human Resource Planning*, 10: 441–55.

Taylor, W. (1989) *Managing Across Cultures: Human Resources Issues in Japanese Companies in the U.S*, New York: The Japan Society.

Triandis, H. (1986) 'Collectivism vs. individualism: a reconceptualization of a basic concept in cross-cultural psychology', in C. Bagley and G. Verma (eds) *Personality, Cognition and Values: Cross-cultural Perspectives of Childhood and Adolescence*, London: Macmillan, pp. 301–30.

Tsurumi, Y. (1976) *The Japanese are Coming: A Multinational Interaction of Firms and Politics*, Cambridge, MA: Ballinger Publishing.

Van de Ven, A. and Drazin, R. (1985) 'The concept of fit in contingency theory', *Research in Organizational Behavior*, 7: 333–65.

Wright, G. (forthcoming) 'Strategic human resources management', *Annual Review of the Journal of Management*.

Yoshino, M. (1976) *Japan's Multinational Enterprises*, Cambridge, MA: Harvard University Press.

Chapter 11

The transfer of human resource management systems overseas
An exploratory study of Japanese and American maquiladoras

Schon Beechler and Sully Taylor

ABSTRACT

The field of international management has, until recently, largely ignored how human resource management (HRM) systems in overseas subsidiaries are designed and how design impacts performance. In addition, there is virtually no research comparing the HRM systems in Japanese and in Western affiliates.

In an attempt to begin to address this important issue, this chapter presents the results of a study of Japanese and American maquiladoras (in-bond assembly plants) in Mexico. The research builds on two streams of recent work in the international management field – the first on international HRM systems and the second on strategic roles of business units in multinational corporations (MNCs).

This chapter examines the relative influence of parent company strategy, strategic role of the affiliate, parent company administrative heritage and host country environment on the HRM systems in eight maquiladoras, four Japanese and four American, located in Tijuana, Mexico. Using a contingency framework, this chapter also describes the fits between each maquiladora's HRM system and its internal and external environments. Finally, it identifies the resulting impact of these fits on performance, both at the individual employee level and at the affiliate level.

INTRODUCTION

As the final decade of the twentieth century unfolds, global economic players from industrialized and newly industrializing countries alike dominate the world's economic landscape. Perhaps one of the most visible and formidable changes to this landscape has been the sudden arrival and powerful presence of Japanese multinational firms.

Although most Japanese firms did not begin internationalizing their operations until after the Second World War, Japanese MNCs have evolved through a number of stages of overseas involvement since the end of the Second World War. From the 1950s until the mid-1960s, Japanese MNCs were mainly exporters of finished goods from Japan. Overseas investments were made primarily in order to obtain raw materials, such as coal, timber etc. Then, as the Japanese economic miracle took off in the 1960s and labour costs began to rise, manufacturers were forced to look overseas for cheaper labour to help reduce costs in order to sustain sales of Japanese goods. Japanese MNCs moved from an export-oriented stage of overseas involvement to a second stage of investment in labour-intensive assembly operations, primarily in South-east Asia.

In addition to building assembly plants in South-east Asia, Japanese MNCs began to establish sales offices in the USA and Europe in this second stage in order to increase product sales in these large and important markets. This pattern of Japanese overseas investment continued until the late 1970s when the anaemic economic performance of the Western countries resulted in increasing political pressure and threats of protectionism against Japanese exports unless Japanese firms agreed to establish production plants in these countries. These changes resulted in a shift in Japanese corporate strategy and the transition to a third stage of Japanese overseas involvement – localization of production. Transferring production from Japanese to overseas sites served not only the interests of Westerners but also those of Japanese MNCs since these firms were simultaneously experiencing ever-higher manufacturing costs at home, particularly after the yen revaluation which resulted from the Plaza Accord of 1986.

Political pressures and the creation of regional economic blocks, as well as scarce and expensive labour at home, continue to drive Japanese foreign direct investments in a number of regions, including the USA and Europe. One important area to receive keen attention from Japanese firms has been the Mexican maquiladora industry, which offers low labour costs and easy access to the American market. At the same time, however, the maquiladora industry presents a number of complex and difficult challenges for managers of these firms. Here we report the results of intensive research into eight maquiladoras, four Japanese and four American, and focus on the HRM challenges facing these firms.

THE MAQUILADORA INDUSTRY

Maquiladoras are in-bond assembly plants located inside Mexico, usually along the border with the USA, the most important market for Japan. These plants have several significant advantages from the Japanese point of view. Manufacturers are allowed to send raw materials, parts or equipment into Mexico duty-free, as long as the finished products are exported. There are no local content requirements on maquiladora goods manufactured for export and manufacturers must pay import duty on only the value added to the product in Mexico (Teagarden *et al.* 1992). The low tariffs and low cost of Mexican labour, averaging approximately $1.63 per hour (*Businessweek*, 12 November 1990), along with a relatively high literacy rate and a plentiful and young workforce, are attractive to MNCs in industries such as electronics, woodworking, garments and automobiles where there is severe global price competition. These factors allow Japanese MNCs to avoid the full cost of locating production in the USA while still reaping most of the benefits. Moreover, because the goods are produced in Mexico, they are not counted against Japan's total allocation in those product classes which are subject to import quotas.

From a handful of assembly plants in the mid-1960s, maquiladoras now number over 1,900, employ over 500,000 workers and provide Mexico with its second largest source of income. Although almost all of the investments in the maquiladora industry before 1986 were made by American firms, in recent years the positive factors cited above have led to major Japanese investment in the maquiladoras. It is estimated that there are currently 200 Japanese maquiladoras (Teagarden *et al.* 1992), and although Japanese firms make up only one-ninth of the total number of firms, because of their relatively larger size, Japanese maquiladoras represent approximately 15 per cent of total employment in the maquiladoras (Scott and Oseghale 1990).

The Mexican maquiladora industry represents not just a present but also a future potential benefit to Japanese MNCs. With the passage of the North American Free Trade Agreement, an investment in Mexico will continue to provide labour cost advantages for the medium term while opening up the Canadian market. There is also the possible addition of South American countries, such as Chile, to the Agreement, which would expand the potential market for output from the maquiladoras. In the interim, these maquiladoras can serve as listening posts for the booming South American economies, as well as provide crucial experience in managing Latin-Americans.

The maquiladora industry of Mexico is therefore an important and increasingly strategic low-wage assembly platform for a growing number of firms from higher-wage countries, such as the USA, Germany and Japan, which face increased price competition from manufacturers from Thailand, Malaysia and other low-wage countries. In addition, the maquiladora industry presents an opportunity for foreign firms with operations in Mexico to expand and grow with the increasing economic development and integration of the region.

However, although Mexico may provide a safe haven from the spiralling wage costs at home and a strategic opportunity for the future, MNCs must contend with numerous obstacles to efficient production, including the management of the local workforce. The maquiladoras can represent a difficult and hostile environment where labour turnover, particularly along the border, is extremely high and labour–management relations in the past have been distant. In addition, many workers in the maquiladoras are from remote agricultural villages and have no prior industrial experience or skills. Workers often hold negative stereotypes about foreigners (e.g. Americans) and have little knowledge about Asia, including Japan, or Asian management.

Within this environmental context, there are essentially two approaches which MNCs can adopt in managing their maquiladora labour force: (a) adapt to the local practices, or (b) transfer the parent company's HRM system overseas. Each approach has strengths and weaknesses, as shown by a number of writers (e.g. Adler 1991; Milliman *et al.* 1991). Although a number of authors in international business have examined the transfer of management policies and practices overseas, there has been very little empirical research which looks at *why* firms choose either to export or to adapt to the local environment. In addition, in spite of the importance of both Japanese and American investment in the maquiladora industry, there is a paucity of research on the management of these firms (Taylor *et al.* 1991).

The research reported in this chapter begins to address this gap in our knowledge. In the following section we present a theoretical framework. We then present results from our research, explicitly addressing the theoretical propositions presented in the theoretical discussion. In addition to exploring the general characteristics of the HRM systems of each of the eight maquiladoras, we also address the issue of why a particular firm does or does not transfer its parent company policies and practices overseas and whether affiliate and individual performance are affected.

THEORETICAL FRAMEWORK

Organizations gain and sustain competitive advantage by capitalizing on their strengths – their distinctive competencies (Selznick 1953). There are two basic types of distinctive competencies in organizations: technological know-how and managerial know-how (Caves 1982). Technological know-how consists of research and development (R&D) and production while managerial know-how consists of finance, marketing and HRM. The last of these, HRM, has only recently been thought of as a managerial competence. There is increasing recognition, however, that HRM is an area that can contribute greatly to a firm's competitiveness (Pucik 1985; Evans 1986; Napier 1990; Butler *et al*. 1990; Schneider 1990; Ulrich and Lake 1990; Beechler *et al*. 1993).

There are three different components of an HRM system – philosophy, policies and practices. HRM *philosophy* is the prevailing beliefs and attitudes held by management concerning human nature and the nature of the employment relationship (Beechler *et al*. 1993). HRM *policies* can be thought of as decision rules: procedures that organization members are expected to follow. *Practices* are less formal than policies and can be thought of as the actual decisions taken by organization members. Practices thus reflect those policies that are actually carried out (Beechler *et al*. 1993).

For example, many large Japanese MNCs have a *philosophy* of 'lifetime employment' *vis-à-vis* their core workers, and institute certain HRM *policies* which provide employment security from the time the employee is hired until retirement, even though that employment may be in a subsidiary firm (Inohara 1990). Supporting HRM *policies* include selection procedures that focus on the personality fit of the candidate with the firm rather than immediate skills, and the promotion of internal candidates to open positions. The actual selection procedures (tests, interview and selection criteria, for example) as well as actual promotion decisions, on the other hand, represent *practices*.

The HRM system includes the functions of recruitment, selection, appraisal, compensation, training and career development. These functions represent an important source of distinctive competence because they influence the firm's ability to attract, motivate and retain the kinds of workers it needs – its overall HRM success (Schneider and Schmitt 1986). The greater the firm's reliance on its human resources as a source of competitive advantage, the more important HRM success will be to the overall success of the firm as a whole.

Although HRM has been explicitly recognized as a key competency by a few authors writing about domestic operations, most prior work on distinctive competencies in MNCs has focused on the utilization of the MNC's technological competencies by its foreign subsidiaries (e.g. Ghoshal and Bartlett 1988). However, both technological and managerial know-how can be transferred overseas (Caves 1982). Thus, the transfer and/or the local development of HRM systems in overseas affiliates can represent a key competence for MNCs.

In developing propositions about the transfer of HRM overseas, we use contingency assumptions to make predictions concerning the design of the affiliate's HRM system, given certain specified contingencies. Although there are a number of different approaches in contingency theory, we adopt a systems approach as it is the most comprehensive and also recognizes that the design of an organizational system must meet two often conflicting criteria: the outside contingencies facing the firm and the need to be internally consistent (Van de Ven and Drazin 1985). Thus, a systems approach allows us to acknowledge the conflicting demands on MNC systems which have been highlighted by a number of recent authors writing about MNCs (e.g. Doz 1986; Bartlett 1986; Bartlett and Ghoshal 1989; Rosenzweig and Singh 1991).

There are two often conflicting demands on the overseas affiliate: demands for internal consistency with the rest of the firm and demands for external consistency with the local environment (Adler 1991; Milliman *et al.* 1991; Rosenzweig and Singh 1991). Since clashes between the external and internal environments can inhibit organizational functioning at every level and in every functional area within the firm, management must resolve these conflicting demands in order to reach their organizational objectives. In designing and implementing an HRM system for an overseas affiliate, management must attempt to resolve these tensions to meet organizational, local environment and internal consistency demands.

In designing the HRM system for an overseas affiliate, the parent company may attempt to create HRM philosophies, policies or practices that reflect local values (high external consistency), attempt to transfer the parent firm's corporate HRM system overseas (high internal consistency) or to develop and implement a worldwide HRM system which combines both the characteristics of the parent company's HRM system and those of its overseas affiliates around the world (high internal consistency and moderate external consistency) (Bartlett and Ghoshal 1989). Although it is important to acknowledge these three possibilities theoretically, because we have not gathered data at headquarters or other subsidiaries of the MNCs in our sample, we cannot address the third possibility, the transfer of affiliate policies and practices to the rest of the MNC, but focus our attention here on the question of whether the MNC transfers parent company practices and policies overseas or adopts local practices and policies.

PARENT COMPANY CHARACTERISTICS

There are two primary categories of variables which influence the design of an overseas affiliate's HRM system: parent company characteristics and local environmental characteristics. The first of these, parent company characteristics, includes the overall strategy of the firm, the level of interdependence between the parent company and the affiliate, and the MNC's administrative history.

MNC strategy

At the business level, MNCs can orient themselves with regard to cost versus differentiation strategies (Porter 1986). A firm that follows a strategy of cost leadership seeks to achieve competitive advantage by being the least-cost producer of a product. Porter (1986) notes that a cost leadership strategy requires a firm to focus on functional policies. Under a cost leadership strategy, internal operations of the firm are driven by efficiency considerations. A cost strategy leads MNCs to establish tight cost controls, require frequent reports, enforce strict rules and establish incentives based on quantitative methods.

By contrast, when a firm adopts a differentiation strategy, it seeks competitive advantage by providing unique value to a product (Porter 1986). Firms are less concerned with cost and more concerned with identifying what special value they are able to add. A differentiation strategy forces a firm to develop an external focus, to be intimately aware of what its customers desire. This strategy requires an emphasis on co-ordination, incentives based on qualitative methods, and the maintenance of quality and technological leadership.

Those MNCs that are seeking to differentiate their products on a global basis are concerned that their product characteristics of interest to consumers be salient across the markets they serve. In order to follow a differentiation strategy, the firm depends on the involvement and commitment of the people involved in production in order to create a product with salient characteristics and will therefore be likely to transfer key successful HRM policies and practices from the headquarters to its overseas affiliate to sustain its competitive advantage.

Compared with firms following a differentiation strategy, MNCs following a low-cost strategy are more concerned with output measures, particularly productivity (Porter 1986). These firms are therefore more concerned that the affiliate keeps the cost of human resources as low as possible rather than managing people through a common set of HRM practices and policies. Thus, all else equal, firms following a differentiation strategy will be more likely than firms following a low-cost strategy to transfer a parent company HRM system to their overseas affiliates:

Proposition 1: MNCs following a differentiation strategy will be more likely to transfer the HRM system of the parent company to their overseas affiliates than will MNCs following a cost strategy.

Although business-level strategy can help predict whether MNCs will transfer their HRM system overseas, it is also necessary to examine strategy at the level since there are conflicting pulls between internal and external environmental forces on the affiliate's HRM system. For example, although MNCs can be characterized as following either a multidomestic or global strategy at the corporate level (Porter 1986) or a low-cost or differentiation strategy at the business level (Porter 1986), affiliates within a single MNC, and even within a single business line, may play different roles within a particular strategy (Gupta and Govindarajan 1991).

A number of typologies characterizing different roles for overseas affiliates have been proposed in the literature (e.g. Bartlett and Ghoshal 1989). One important dimension which is expected to influence the level of consistency of HRM systems is the degree of interdependence between the activities of the parent company and the particular overseas affiliate. Interdependence is determined by both the volume and the direction of resource flows between organizational sub-units (Gupta and Govindarajan 1991). Although interdependence is no doubt greater in firms following a global strategy than a multidomestic one (Bartlett and Ghoshal 1989), within a single MNC there are different levels of interdependence between the parent and its various overseas affiliates (Gupta and Govindarajan 1991).

The nature of the resource flows between the parent company and its overseas affiliates is important in understanding the transfer of HRM overseas because resource flows determine the need for co-ordination and control mechanisms to manage the resulting interdependence (Pfeffer and Salancik 1978). Although ownership patterns and financial controls have been the focus of most research in this area, the HRM system presents an important means to manage the interdependence between the overseas affiliate and the parent firm. The parent firm relies on individuals, in addition to policies and practices, to ensure that needed human resources are hired, developed and compensated so that the employees' behaviour will lead to the results desired by the firm in order to implement its strategy. The higher the level of interdependence between the parent firm and the overseas affiliate, the greater the likelihood that the parent firm will transfer its HRM system overseas to its affiliate, since, generally speaking, both co-ordination and control functions are facilitated by standardization.

Proposition 2: The higher the interdependence between the parent company and the overseas affiliate, the more likely it is that the parent company will transfer its HRM system to its overseas affiliate.

Administrative heritage

Another important characteristic of the parent firm is its administrative heritage (Bartlett and Ghoshal 1989). The administrative heritage of an MNC is the combination of the 'configuration of assets, distribution of responsibilities, dominant management style, and ingrained organizational values' that an MNC has built up over time (Bartlett and Ghoshal 1989: 41). The MNC's administrative heritage is the outcome of a combination of factors, including the company founder's ideology and beliefs, the company's history both at home and abroad, the composition of top management etc.

An MNC's HRM system is both influenced by and influences the administrative heritage of the firm. The firm's current HRM policies and practices are partially a product of the firm's history – organizational learning from past successes and failures – as well as a reflection of organizational norms, values and goals, which are themselves reflective of the societal norms and values internalized by the founders and by generations of employees. Although MNCs may face similar environmental constraints, use similar technologies and have equivalent experience in international operations, the companies' HRM competencies, because they are reflective of the firm's administrative heritage and unique past, are to some extent firm specific (Bartlett and Ghoshal 1989).

Although administrative heritage represents a complex system of values, structures and processes, one important component of the MNC's administrative heritage which will influence the transfer of HRM systems to foreign affiliates is the firm's overseas experience, both in terms of the length of time it has had overseas operations and its past successes or failures in the management of overseas affiliates.

MNCs with extensive experience overseas acquire information about the environments in which they do business. They learn through trial and error how to manage in different environments if they have effectively learned from their experiences. This process provides management with first-hand knowledge of differences between host and home country practices and norms, information concerning which parent company HRM policies and practices can be exported overseas and which cannot be used, as well as information on how to implement those HRM policies and practices most effectively, given the local environment. This leads us to predict the following proposition.

Proposition 3: The greater the MNC's experience in successfully transferring its HRM systems overseas, the more likely it is that the parent firm will transfer its HRM system to its overseas affiliates.

Although it plays a key role, prior experience is not the only important dimension of administrative heritage influencing the transfer of the parent company HRM policies and practices overseas. Another important component of the administrative heritage of a firm is the strength of its corporate philosophy and management's belief that the MNC's overseas subsidiaries should adopt the parent company's management philosophy. At Procter & Gamble, for example, the belief of the management at headquarters in the company's way of doing things was so strong that each overseas subsidiary was set up as a miniature replica of the US corporation (Bartlett and Ghoshal 1989: 38). Procter & Gamble believed that the parent's HRM system represented a distinctive competence that gave the firm a competitive edge *vis-à-vis* its competitors.

Obviously such management beliefs on the part of parent company's management can lead an MNC to establish overseas HRM policies and practices which are similar to those in the parent company. This leads to the following proposition.

Proposition 4: The stronger the parent company management's belief that the firm's HRM system represents a distinctive competency, the more likely it is that the parent firm will transfer its HRM system to its overseas affiliates.

HOST COUNTRY CHARACTERISTICS

In addition to MNC characteristics, the characteristics of the host country are of obvious importance in determining the overseas affiliate's HRM system. Such factors as the labour market conditions, as well as the legal, political and social environment, will influence what HRM philosophy, policies and practices are feasible or even allowable within a given environmental context. Subsidiaries operating in China, for example, face considerable difficulty in trying to incorporate parent company HRM practices and policies based on capitalistic assumptions into their systems (Von Glinow and Teagarden 1990). In general, the more similar the host country and the home country characteristics, the easier it is for firms to transfer their HRM systems overseas.

Although environments are multi-dimensional, for the purposes of this study we focused our attention on only one of these dimensions – the cultural dimension of the environment. One of the most well-known and accepted definitions of this cultural dimension of the environment has been formulated by Hofstede (1984).

In a study of 160,000 IBM managers in over 60 countries, Hofstede (1984) found that cultures vary on four primary dimensions:

> individualism/collectivism, power distance, uncertainty avoidance, and masculinity/femininity. Individualism implies that people define themselves as individuals and organize into loosely knit social frameworks. On the other hand, collectivism implies that people define themselves in terms of their group membership and organize into tight social networks. Power distance measures the extent to which less powerful members of society accept the unequal distribution of power while uncertainty avoidance measures the extent to which people in a society feel threatened by ambiguous situations and the extent to which they try to avoid these situations. Finally, masculinity is defined as the extent to which the dominant values in society emphasize assertiveness and the acquisition of money and things, while downplaying relationships among people. Femininity, on the other hand, emphasizes relationships among people, concern for others, and the overall quality of life.
>
> (Hofstede 1984)

Comparing Mexico, Japan and the USA, Hofstede's research shows that Japanese are moderately high on power distance, moderate on individualism, very high on uncertainty avoidance and high on masculinity. Mexicans are very high on power distance, moderately low on individualism, moderately high on uncertainty avoidance and moderately high on masculinity. Americans are moderately low on power distance, high on individualism, moderately low on uncertainty avoidance and moderately high on masculinity. Looking across all four dimensions, there is greater cultural distance between the USA and Mexico than between Japan and Mexico, according to Hofstede's data (1984).

The smaller the cultural distance between the parent firm's home country and the affiliate's local environment, the fewer potential difficulties in transferring the parent company's HRM philosophy, policies and practices to its overseas affiliates, since the underlying values which form the foundation of the HRM system are similar across the two countries. This leads to the following proposition.

Proposition 5: Japanese firms, because of the smaller cultural distance between Japan and Mexico, will be more likely than American firms to transfer the parent's HRM system to their overseas affiliates.

OUTCOME MEASURES: HRM AND OVERSEAS AFFILIATE PERFORMANCE

The predictions outlined above focus on fits between the characteristics of the firm and the host country environment, but we have not yet considered the outcomes these fits have on the performance of the overseas affiliate. Using a systems approach we make the general prediction given in the following proposition.

Proposition 6: When the HRM system of the overseas affiliate fits with the characteristics of the MNC and its local environment, the affiliate will enjoy higher levels of performance than when the HRM system does not fit with these internal and external environments.

RESEARCH METHODOLOGY

The firms chosen for inclusion in this study are all maquiladoras located in Tijuana, Mexico. While Americans own the vast majority of maqui-ladoras in Mexico, approximately 80 per cent, Japan's investment in these facilities has been growing rapidly in recent years. Of approximately 200 Japanese maquiladoras and 1,400 American maquiladoras operating in Mexico today (Scott and Oseghale 1990), approximately 650 are located in Tijuana.

Eight Tijuana maquiladoras, four American and four Japanese, were examined in this study. Because this research was meant to be exploratory in nature, this sample provided a range of cases which could be studied in enough depth to discern both common patterns and significant differences. All but one of the maquiladoras is involved in electronics manufacturing. The exception, an American firm, is involved in miscellaneous manufacturing operations. By including both American and Japanese maquiladoras we are able to compare the international HRM strategies of firms from countries with different cultural distances from Mexico, and with different traditions regarding the management of human resources. However, the study also focused on within-nationality as well as between-nationality differences to examine the impact of administrative heritage and parent-company–affiliate interdependence on the overseas affiliate's HRM system.

To test the propositions above, intensive face-to-face interviews at the eight maquiladoras, supplemented by written questionnaires, were used since a multi-method approach is appropriate in the theory-building stage (Jick 1984). Because the theoretical framework presented in this paper is a synthesis and extension of previous work in several areas (strategy, HRM, international management), the case approach was used to provide a richer understanding of the applicability of the framework and the propositions derived from it.

Case studies were carried out at each of the eight sample maquiladoras through semi-structured interviews with each of the following persons: the managing director, the HRM director, two line managers and three line operators. In some of the companies, a number of additional interviews were conducted with managerial personnel. In addition to the face-to-face interviews, the following materials were requested from each of the maquiladoras: an organization chart, copies of performance appraisal forms, a description of the maquiladora's selection procedures and criteria, copies of selection tests, the new employee handbook, a description of compensation system and benefits, and data on turnover during the last three years.

Written questionnaires were also developed for two groups of employees: top managers and line operators. For the top managers, a questionnaire focusing on strategy, headquarters–affiliate interdependence, affiliate performance and other variables of interest was developed by the authors. The questionnaire was first pilot-tested in Mexico and then distributed to all managing directors and HRM directors at each maquiladora in the sample, all of whom returned completed questionnaires.

In addition, questionnaires were distributed to either all or a subset of the line workers, the decision being made by the sample company, in seven of the eight maquiladoras in the study in order to measure employee satisfaction, commitment and employees' perceptions of the differences between their maquiladora's HRM system and local Mexican practices.

The researchers took questionnaires for all line workers to the head of personnel in each maquiladora, who then passed them out to employees. Workers were told that their responses were confidential and would not be available to anyone in their company. They were instructed to deposit their completed questionnaires in a box set up in the company cafeteria. This box was picked up one week after questionnaire distribution by a Mexican research associate. Managers at the one firm that did not participate in the operator questionnaire portion of the study felt that it was not appropriate to do so since there were some labour–management problems at the time of data collection. Approximately 1,300 operator questionnaires were left at the seven maquiladoras by the researchers and a total of 444 usable questionnaires were returned. Of these 444 respondents, 382 were operators and 52 were supervisors. On average, the operators at the maquiladoras had been with their firms for 22 months and supervisors for an average of 41 months. The average age was 24 years for operators and 30 years for supervisors.

Compared with the total population of workers in these firms, questionnaire respondents had been employed somewhat longer than average and are also somewhat older than the non-respondents. In addition, although figures on literacy are not available from the companies, it is logical to assume that respondents have a higher rate of literacy than the non-respondents in the study.

RESEARCH RESULTS AND DISCUSSION

Basic descriptive information on the size, date of establishment and other characteristics of the sample firms is presented in Table 11.1. From Table 11.1 we see that the Japanese firms are, on average, larger in size and were established later than the American firms in the sample. This is consistent with trends of investment by these two countries in the maquiladoras: there were almost no Japanese firms in the maquiladora industry in Mexico until after 1986. Although Japanese investment in Mexico still remains at a relatively low level overall, those companies which have invested, including all of our sample firms, have made major investments. In terms of employment, for example, the Japanese maquiladoras in our sample are all large operations, with between 700 and 2,000 employees.

On the other hand, American firms typically established small shelter operations in Mexico during the 1970s and then, if operations were

Table 11.1 Maquiladora characteristics

Firm	Parent nationality	Year maquiladora was established	Total number of employees in maquiladora	Nationality of maquiladora president/ director	Number of American/ Japanese dispatchees	Type of product assembled
J1	Japanese	1982	2,000	Mexican	28	Consumer electronics
J2	Japanese	1980	1,250	Japanese	25	Consumer electronics
J3	Japanese	1985	1,600	Mexican	36	Consumer electronics
J4	Japanese	1986	700	Japanese	5	Consumer electronics
A1	American	1983	550	Mexican	0	Consumer electronics
A2	American	1985 (1960)[a]	97	American	3	Electronics
A3	American	1988 (1977)[a]	500	American	25	Electronics
A4	American	1983 (1979)[a]	1,200	American	10	Consumer goods

Note: [a] Actual year operations were established in Tijuana (as a shelter operation).

successful, converted them into wholly owned affiliates after a number of years of operating experience. Shelters are locally owned maquiladoras with which firms contract to manufacture products, thus avoiding taking on the direct investment and management themselves. All of the American companies in our sample first established shelter operations in Tijuana in the 1970s and then, in the mid- to late 1980s, converted them into wholly owned maquiladoras. However, many of these American-owned firms are relatively small compared with their Japanese counterparts, with employment ranging from 97 to 1,200 employees.

Looking at the total number of expatriates currently stationed in each of the maquiladoras, three of the four Japanese firms have 25 or more expatriates while only one American firm has 25 or more expatriates. Controlling for differences in size, we find that the proportion of expatriates to total employees in Japanese maquiladoras ranges from 0.07 per cent to 2.3 per cent, and in the American maquiladoras in the sample the proportion ranges from 0 per cent to 5 per cent. According to interviews with managers at the maquiladoras, these figures have remained relatively constant over time after the initial start-up period (when a large number of expatriates were dispatched to set up the plants).

We also see from Table 11.1 that two of the Japanese maquiladoras are headed by a local national while two are headed by Japanese. In the American firms in the sample, three of the four maquiladoras are headed by an American.

Although there are some differences in staffing patterns between the Japanese and the American firms in the sample, interviews revealed that the nature of the expatriates and their roles in the organization vary greatly across companies, particularly when comparing the American with the Japanese maquiladoras.

The American firms in the sample have traditionally tended to use 'ringers' – Americans with no experience working for the parent firm who are hired in Mexico to run the plant. For example, firm A2, which has a very paternalistic orientation toward its workers, has been managed by a series of ringers since its establishment. The current managing director has no parent company experience but managers from the parent company frequently visit the maquiladora and are in constant contact with the managing director concerning all major decisions, and even many minor ones. Without using company-trained expatriates, the parent company has had moderate success in transferring HRM policies and practices to its maquiladora. Firm A4, on the other hand, has not used ringers in the management of its maquiladora but it has dramatically altered the kind of expatriate it sends overseas after a disastrous performance in 1990. Until 1991, the parent company relied on American expatriates from the head office who had proved themselves in the domestic US operation. In June 1991, however, the firm replaced the top American at the maquiladora with a new American director who is more internationally experienced and culturally aware than his predecessors. This new director is actively attempting to transfer policies and practices, including those in HRM, from the parent company to the maquiladora but is adapting his style of implementation to fit with the local Mexican culture and environment.

This new managing director, unlike his predecessor and other Americans at the plant, was told by his American boss that to get the Tijuana assignment he would have to learn Spanish. He enrolled in a two-month intensive Spanish-language programme in the USA at company expense and since moving to Mexico has studied daily with a tutor. While we were visiting the plant, the managing director gave his first formal presentation to his Mexican staff – in Spanish. It is clear that although this firm still uses expatriates for its top maquiladora management positions, it is now attempting to train and assign managers who are capable of adapting parent company HRM practices and policies to fit with the local environment.

Although the Japanese firms in the sample do not tend to use ringers to run their maquiladoras, both J1 and J3 have hired Mexican managers with extensive experience in the maquiladora industry to run their operations. The primary differences between these individuals and those Mexican executives whom we interviewed in the American firms are that: (a) the Japanese firms hire only Mexicans with maquiladora experience, not other nationalities, such as Americans; (b) in the American firms ringers run the local operations after receiving approval via fax or telephone or mail from the head office in the USA, whereas in the Japanese firms the Mexican managers work closely on the spot with top-level Japanese expatriates and decisions are made after much face-to-face discussion and negotiation; (c) ringers in the American maquiladoras are expected to move on after a certain period of time and have no long-term job security with the firm, whereas the Mexican top managers in the Japanese firms are expected to stay with the maquiladora.

Those firms which hire ringers but do not make them a permanent part of the organization are, in essence, limiting the amount of organizational learning which occurs while these executives are with the firm. Because ringers are outsiders who are expected to move onto another firm after they have successfully managed the maquiladora through a certain stage in its development, the knowledge and skills of these individuals do not become part of the organization's administrative heritage. Organizational learning can only occur in a partial fashion, often long distance, through conversations between company employees at the headquarters and the locally hired executives. Even in those Japanese companies which integrate Mexican executives into the local organization, Mexicans are never rotated back to the headquarters, and so their knowledge and skills do not build expertise at the head office.

However, the situation at some companies is changing. For example, until June 1991, A3 was run by a long-term ringer who specialized in maquiladora management. In June, however, the parent company, in an effort to more closely integrate the Mexican operations into the American operations and to respond to severe industry changes, dispatched a young but very successful 'company man' to head up the maquiladora. This maquiladora is currently in the midst of a fundamental shift in terms of both strategy and HRM system. At the same time, the parent company views its own HRM system as a liability rather than a competence and is searching for other models, neither parent company nor local Mexican, to use in this change effort. The parent company is hoping to learn from the experiences of both its related company affiliates and its overseas affiliates, and to implement 'best practices' from its far-flung operations in MNC headquarters. It is attempting to profit from knowledge, skills and expertise developed around the world and therefore has begun a process of change so that the organizational learning process is not unidirectional but bi-directional – both to and from the overseas affiliates.

It is also interesting to note that the Japanese firms which have hired local top managers and integrated them into the local organization have relatively higher levels of performance *vis-à-vis* the Japanese maquiladoras headed by Japanese nationals and all but one of the American maquiladoras in the sample. It is unclear, however, whether placing Mexicans into top executive positions within the maquiladoras has increased subsidiary performance or whether high levels of performance have given the firms the confidence to replace expatriates with local managers.

Turning now to the propositions presented earlier in this chapter, we hypothesized in Proposition 1 that MNCs following a differentiation strategy will be more likely to transfer the HRM system of the parent company to their overseas affiliates than will MNCs following a cost strategy. Table 11.2 shows that three of the four Japanese firms in the sample are predominantly following a cost strategy while two of the American firms are following a cost strategy and two are following a differentiation strategy. It is important to point out here that although a number of maquiladoras in our sample are pursuing a differentiation strategy, interviews with the managing directors revealed that cost is still a major factor affecting all of their operations. All of the firms in our study are engaged in global industries and face severe cost pressure from competitors from lower-wage countries.

We see from Table 11.2 that, contrary to our prediction in Proposition 1, there does not seem to be a relationship between the MNC's strategy and the transfer of HRM overseas. J3 is the only Japanese firm with a differentiation strategy and, contrary to our prediction, this firm has a relatively low level of HRM transfer from the parent to the maquiladora. J1, J2 and J3 are all following a cost strategy and have high levels of HRM transfer. For the Japanese firms in our sample, it appears that firms following a cost strategy are, contrary to our prediction, more likely to transfer the firm's HRM system overseas than those Japanese firms following a differentiation strategy. Interviews with top managers confirm that Japanese managers in the high-transfer firms believe that using HRM systems developed in Japan contribute to lower costs.

Among the American firms, on the other hand, firms A1 and A4 are following a cost strategy and have medium to low transfers whereas firms A2 and A3 are following a differentiation strategy and also have medium to low HRM transfers. For the American maquiladoras in our sample, MNC strategy does not seem to have an impact on the transfer of the parent's HRM system overseas.

Proposition 2 stated that the higher the interdependence between the parent company and the overseas affiliate, the more likely the parent company will be to transfer its HRM system to its overseas affiliate. The nature of our sample would lead us to assume, on the basis of maquiladora size alone, that the American MNCs should be far less dependent on their operations than are the Japanese MNCs. However, in questionnaires filled out by top management, all respondents indicated that interdependence is high, except in the case of firm A2, where interdependence is low (see Table 11.2). This maquiladora currently has only 97 employees, down from over 200 employees less than one year ago. Although this firm has been operating in Mexico for over 31 years, the current American recession has significantly reduced the need for overseas assembly and operations have been largely centralized at the parent company.

In addition, in all of the firms except A2, managers stated in interviews that the level of interdependence between their parent company and the maquiladora was high and was likely to increase in the future. For example, both J1 and J2 were adding new product lines from the USA to their maquiladora operations during our field visit in August 1991. It was clear from interviews that these new product lines would serve to increase further the level of interdependence not only between the Japanese parent firms and their maquiladoras, but also between the Japanese firms' American affiliates and the maquiladoras.

Although none of the American firms was in the process of adding additional production, interviews at the two largest American maquiladoras revealed that global rationalization, brought on by severe economic conditions, particularly in the USA, was increasing. As part of this rationalization process, integrating mechanisms were being implemented not only between the parent firm and the maquiladora, but also between the maquiladora and other overseas operations, in order to reduce duplication and lower costs. Even in the smaller American maquiladoras the managing directors told us that their maquiladoras depended almost exclusively on the parent company for production inputs, technology, and management systems while the parent company was highly dependent on the maquiladoras for finished products for the American market.

Table 11.2 Parent company characteristics, maquiladora characteristics and performance results

Firm	MNC strategic focus	Level of parent-affiliate inter-dependence	Number of years experience in Mexico	HRM transfer success	Belief that parent HRM is a competence	Level of HRM adaptation to Mexico	Level of HRM transfer from parent	Employee satisfaction[a]	Employee commitment[b]	Employee turnover (average per cent per month)	Overall maquiladora performance
J1	Cost	High	9	Moderate	High	Low	High	3.18	4.55	07	Moderate
J2	Cost	High	11	Moderate	High	Low	High	—[c]	—[c]	10	Moderate
J3	Differentiation	High	6	Moderate	Low	Moderate	Low	4.02	5.48	09	High
J4	Cost	High	5	Moderate	High	Low	High	3.21	4.17	NA	Moderate
A1	Cost	High	19	Low	Low	High	Moderate	3.66	4.83	16	High
A2	Differentiation	Low	31	Moderate	Moderate	Moderate	Moderate	3.50	4.49	07	Moderate
A3	Differentiation	High	14	Low	Low	Low	Low	3.39	4.67	06	Moderate to high
A4	Cost	High	12	Low	Low	Moderate	Low	3.68	4.82	15	Moderate to high

Notes: [a] Satisfaction was measured in questionnaires to supervisors and operators and was measured on a five-point Likert scale. The higher the number, the higher the level of employee satisfaction.
[b] Commitment was measured in questionnaires to supervisors and operators and was measured on a seven-point Likert scale. The higher the number, the higher the level of employee commitment to the maquiladora.
[c] Questionnaires were not distributed in this maquiladora.

Because all but one of the managing directors stated that their firms are highly integrated, we cannot directly address Proposition 2. However, it is clear that interdependence is not a factor in this sample in determining whether HRM is transferred overseas from the parent company or not – some firms with high levels of interdependence transfer their systems while others adapt to the local norms. Thus, for these firms, interdependence does not differentiate between firms which transfer HRM systems overseas and those which adapt to local practices, contrary to our prediction.

Turning now to a firm's past experience, Proposition 3 states that the greater the MNC's past experience in successfully transferring its HRM systems overseas, the more likely the parent firm will be to transfer its HRM system to its overseas affiliates. The four Japanese parent firms in our sample all have extensive international experience in a wide range of countries. The American firms, on the other hand, are mixed. All of the American parent firms, except for A1, do have a number of overseas affiliates around the world. However, these American overseas operations are generally on a smaller scale than those of their Japanese counterparts.

Despite the differences between the Japanese and the American firms in the sample, our interviews with top managers in the maquiladoras indicate that previous international experience in general is not a particularly important factor in determining whether top management at the parent company attempts to transfer its HRM practices and policies overseas. Experience in Mexico, on the other hand, does seem to have some impact, with the American firms more likely to make dramatic adaptations in the face of transfer failure and the Japanese firms more likely to make gradual adaptations.

In general, we found that for the American firms in the sample, past negative experiences in transferring the parent company system overseas led to an emphasis on local adaptation, which was reflected both in company policies and practices as well as management philosophy. For example, firm A1 is a fairly small firm and has only one overseas operation. Its negative experiences in trying to transfer the American parent company's HRM system to Mexico a number of years ago led to its current policy of adopting local HRM policies and practices. This maquiladora currently does not have a single expatriate in its Tijuana plant and the Mexican managing director is insistent that the firm be run as a Mexican company.

For the Japanese companies, on the other hand, past negative experiences have led some firms (J3, and to some extent J1) to adapt to

Mexican practice while for other firms (J2 and J4) past negative experiences have led to greater efforts to transfer the parent company's system overseas. As discussed in further detail below, it appears that when management believes that the parent company's HRM system represents a distinctive competency, they persist in their attempts to transfer HRM overseas, even in the face of failure. Thus, international experience does not have a consistent effect on transfer of the MNC's HRM system to its maquiladoras.

Although it plays a key role, prior experience is not the only important dimension of administrative heritage influencing the transfer of the parent company HRM policies and practices overseas. Another important component of the administrative heritage of a firm is the strength of its corporate philosophy and the management's belief that the MNC's overseas affiliates should adopt the parent company's management philosophy.

From Table 11.2 we see that there is strong support for the proposition that the stronger the parent company management's belief that the firm's HRM system represents a distinctive competency, the more likely the parent firm will be to transfer its HRM system to its overseas affiliates. In fact, of all of the factors which we examined in this study, including previous experience, corporate strategy, nationality of the parent firm etc., the belief that HRM represents a distinctive competitive advantage for the MNC came out again and again in our interviews as the most important reason why a firm did or did not attempt to transfer its parent company's HRM system overseas. Whether transfer has been successful in the past or not, top management's belief that the parent company's HRM system is a distinctive competency appears to drive the transfer of the parent company system overseas.

This finding does not merely represent firm differences in success of transfer, for there are firms in the sample which have not been successful using home country HRM policies and practices overseas yet continue to try to apply them. Firm J2, for example, has over 11 years of experience in Tijuana, yet because it cannot make Japanese policies and practices work effectively, managers complained that the local workforce was the source of all of their problems, not the firm's management style or practices. At J1, workers were keenly aware of the strong, consistent desire of the Japanese managers to operate the maquiladora as though it were located in Japan. One line worker commented that: 'If it were left up to them [the Japanese managers], everyone would work like a Japanese. They wish we were Japanese. They have Japanese rules.' This employee's view was shared in interviews with other workers who indicated that the HRM system in this plant was becoming *more* Japanese over time.

In addition to firm-specific characteristics, we proposed in Proposition 5 that Japanese firms in general, because of the smaller cultural distance between Japan and Mexico, will be more likely than American firms to transfer the parent company's HRM system to its overseas affiliates.

While three of the four Japanese firms score low on adaptation to Mexican HRM policies and practices, three of the four score high on their level of HRM transfer from the parent company. At the same time, three of the four American firms have medium to high levels of adaptation while two have moderate levels of transfer and two of the maquiladoras have low levels of HRM transfer from the parent company. The results thus support our prediction, although our interviews uncovered an interesting caveat to these results.

While we originally assumed that absolute differences in cultural distance would be consistent with perceived cultural differences, we consistently found in our interviews with Mexican managers and operators that the Mexican perception is that Japanese and Mexican cultures are much further apart than are American and Mexican cultures. At the same time, a number of Japanese managers were quick to point out similarities between Japanese and Mexican cultural values.

Actual cultural distance may help in predicting whether an MNC attempts to transfer its HRM policies and practices overseas. At the same time, it may be that 'perceived' cultural distance, regardless of 'actual' cultural distance, may be the more important factor in predicting how local employees will react to those policies and practices. Interviews revealed that Mexican managers and operators attributed most of their dissatisfaction with Japanese policies and practices to 'cultural differences'. Although we did not measure respondents' perception of cultural distance directly in this study, it may be a lack of familiarity, rather than cultural distance *per se*, which is most important in determining local employees' reactions to the transferred management system.

Finally, Proposition 6 predicts that when the HRM system of an overseas affiliate fits with the characteristics of the MNC and its local environment, the affiliate will enjoy higher levels of performance than when the HRM system does not fit with these internal and external environments. Looking first at the individual performance measures of organizational commitment and satisfaction of employees in the Japanese and American maquiladoras in the sample, we see from Table 11.3 that, on the whole, Mexican workers in American maquiladoras are

Table 11.3 Results of *t* tests for differences on measures of satisfaction, commitment and similarity between Japanese and American maquiladoras

	Satisfaction	Commitment	Similarity to Mexican practice
Japanese firms	3.25***	4.58*	4.05***
American firms	3.60	4.74	4.56

Notes: *, $p < 0.10$; ***, $p < 0.00$
Results are from questionnaires distributed to supervisors and operators in seven of the eight sample maquiladoras.Total number of respondents, 444.

significantly more satisfied and committed to their firms than are Mexican workers in Japanese maquiladoras.

At the same time, there is a significant difference between respondents in Japanese and American firms in how similar they perceive their companies to be to Mexican firms in general (see Table 11.3). Overall, Mexicans in American firms believe that their companies are more 'Mexican' than do respondents in Japanese maquiladoras. Comparing individual firms, however, a Japanese firm, J3, enjoys the highest levels of employee commitment and satisfaction and employees at this maquiladora perceive it to be fairly 'Mexican' in management approach. These results indicate that it is not the nationality of the maquiladora which is important, but certain management practices employed by individual Japanese firms which result in low levels of employee satisfaction and commitment among Mexican workers. Although it is impossible to determine causality in this study, our interviews lead us to believe that these results indicate that the transfer of Japanese HRM practices to the maquiladora, in the face of large perceived cultural differences, negatively impacts on the satisfaction and commitment of Mexican employees.

However, the lower levels of satisfaction and commitment of the Mexican workers in all of the Japanese firms except for J3 do not appear to be associated with higher levels of turnover in the Japanese firms in our sample (see Table 11.2). From a manager's point of view, the important question may be whether the lower satisfaction in most of the Japanese maquiladoras impacts on job performance. Prior research in the USA indicates that the relationship is not always that strong (e.g. Mobley 1982), and in our data, there is no obvious relationship between maquiladora performance as reported by the managers and satisfaction or commitment of the operators. Interviews with the operators themselves, however, indicated that their lower satisfaction levels are associated with low morale and a sense of resentment toward the Japanese managers in the maquiladoras.

In terms of affiliate-level performance, which was measured in written questionnaires and interviews with maquiladora managers, we find that overall, most of the maquiladoras are performing at a level consistent with their local competitors, while two of the firms, one Japanese (J3) and one American (A1), are performing well above average.

Out of all of the firms in the sample, J3 seems to be enjoying the highest performance in relation to the performance of other maquiladoras, other subsidiaries of the parent firm and *vis-à-vis* headquarters' expectations for the maquiladora. J3 also enjoys the highest levels of employee satisfaction and commitment among the eight firms in the sample, has adapted its HRM practices and policies to local norms to a moderate extent and has not transferred its Japanese HRM system overseas but has attempted to use a number of practices and policies in Mexico which were developed in its American subsidiary. Although J3 has only had six years of experience in Mexico, the parent company does have extensive international experience in a large number of countries. In addition, although managers we interviewed at J3 do not believe that the parent company's HRM system is a source of distinctive competence *per se*, they do believe in an internationalized HRM system. This hybrid maquiladora, combining characteristics of Japanese, American and Mexican systems, has thus far been relatively successful in terms of both employee and maquiladora-level performance.

A2, the other high performing maquiladora in our sample, has much longer experience in Mexico – 19 years. Although its performance is high, this maquiladora may well go out of business as operations are consolidated in the USA. Although it is less expensive to produce the company's products in Tijuana, because this firm has a 'family' corporate culture, the top management is letting the Mexican workforce decline through attrition in order to maintain employment in the USA. The future of this maquiladora depends not on its relative success in Tijuana but on how well the American economy does in the next 12 months.

SUMMARY AND CONCLUSIONS

Taking the results together, there are significant differences between the American and Japanese maquiladoras in our sample in a number of areas. First, while none of the managers at the American maquiladoras believed strongly that the parent company's HRM system was a distinctive competence, managers at three of the four Japanese maquiladoras did. Furthermore, as stated above, a belief in the parent's HRM competence seems related to high levels of HRM transfer from the parent company to the maquiladora. This finding certainly confirms the numerous reports of the ethnocentric approach of Japanese firms to their overseas operations (e.g. Fucini and Fucini 1990), in which there is an attempt to mould the overseas subsidiary into as close a replica of the home plants as possible, at least with regard to management practices. It is telling that the workers in the Japanese maquiladoras which used such an approach were less satisfied and committed than those working for American firms.

It is neither the pure American nor the pure Japanese approach which is most successful in the Tijuana maquiladora context but the hybrid organization of J3 which has achieved relative success in balancing both internal and external consistency demands. This firm enjoys high levels of employee commitment and satisfaction, as well as a high level of sub-unit performance. Although we cannot rule out the possibility that other factors not measured in this study are responsible for these results, interviews with J3 managers, workers and competitors all point to the hybrid HRM system as the key to its success in Mexico.

For the Japanese firms in the study, with the exception of J3, lower levels of individual and maquiladora performance may be outweighed by the cost savings of operating in Mexico in the short run. However, as more and more companies continue to invest in Mexico, there will be greater competition at the firm level and greater competition for the loyalties of the local workforce. Those firms which, through appropriate HRM policies and practices, are better able to attract and retain the local workforce will gain a competitive advantage over those firms which cannot. This is not to say that firms should forgo internal consistency in favour of external consistency but that, in the long run, competitive conditions will require high levels of both internal and external consistency which will allow the MNC to simultaneously integrate and differentiate its operations around the world, and therefore meet the demands of a globalized economy (Bartlett and Ghoshal 1989; Ghadar and Adler 1989).

At the same time, those firms which hire local executives for the long term and integrate them into the organization, will facilitate organizational learning and the creation of an administrative heritage which reflects the values and norms of both the home country and the host country. Organizational learning, whether it occurs in Mexico, Indonesia or Spain, will facilitate the globalization of MNCs and move corporations out of the third phase of internationalization and into the fourth phase.

In this new stage, the focus of Japanese corporate strategy will shift away from the localization of production to an emphasis on balancing localization and global integration (Bartlett and Ghoshal 1989). A complex and sophisticated HRM system which can effectively utilize the human resources in the organization, regardless of their nationality, and create not only global products but global mind sets, will be an essential competency for the transnationals while leading the way into the twenty-first century.

ACKNOWLEDGEMENTS

We would like gratefully to acknowledge the assistance of Debbie Adams at Portland State University and Lic. G. Enrique Nunez Hurtado, Director of Education at Centro de Ensenanza Tecnica y Superior, Tijuana, Mexico. This research was supported by the Management Institute at Columbia Business School and Corporate Associates Summer Research Fund at Portland State University Business School.

REFERENCES

Adler, N. (1991) *International Dimensions of Organizational Behavior*, 2nd edn, Boston, MA: PWS-Kent.
Bartlett, C. (1986) 'Building and managing the transnational: the new organizational challenge', in M. Porter (ed.) *Competition in Global Industries*, Cambridge, MA: Harvard University Press, pp. 367–404.
Bartlett, C. and Ghoshal, S. (1989) *Managing Across Borders*, Boston, MA: Harvard University Press.
Beechler, B., Bird, A. and Raghuram, S. (1993) 'Linking business strategy and human resource management practices in multinational corporations: a theoretical framework', in S.B. Prasad and R.B. Peterson (eds) *Advances in International Comparative Management*, Greenwich, CT: JAI Press, vol. 8, pp. 199–216.
Businessweek (1990) 'Mexico: a new economic era', 12 November: 102–13.
Butler, J., Ferris, G. and Napier, N. (1990) *Strategy and Human Resources*, Cincinnati, OH: South-Western Publishing Co.
Caves, R. (1982) *Multinational Enterprise and Economic Analysis*, London: Cambridge University Press.
Doz, Y. (1986) *Strategic Management in Multinational Companies*, Oxford: Pergamon Press.
Evans, P. (1986) 'The strategic outcomes of human resources management'. *Human Resource Management*, 25 (1), Spring: 149–67.
Fucini, J.J. and Fucini, S. (1990) *Working for the Japanese*, New York: Free Press.
Ghadar, F. and Adler, N. (1989) 'Management culture and accelerated product life cycle', *Human Resource Planning*, 12 (1): 37–42.

Ghoshal, S. and Bartlett, C. (1988) 'Creation, adoption, and diffusion of innovations by subsidiaries of multinational corporations', *Journal of International Business Studies*, 19 (3), Fall: 365–88.

Gupta, A.K. and Govindarajan, V. (1991) 'Knowledge flows and the structure of control within multinational corporations', *Academy of Management Review*, 16 (4): 768–92.

Hofstede, G. (1984) *Culture's Consequences: International Differences in Work Related Values*, Beverly Hills, CA: Sage.

Inohara, H. (1990) *Human Resource Development in Japanese Companies*, Tokyo: Asian Productivity Organization.

Jick, T. (1984) 'Mixing qualitative and quantitative methods: triangulation in action', in T. Bateman and G. Ferris (eds) *Methods and Analysis in Organizational Research*, Reston, VA: Reston Publishing.

Milliman, J., Von Glinow, M.A. and Nathan, M. (1991) 'Organizational life cycles and strategic international human resource management in multinational companies: implications for congruence theory', *Academy of Management Review*, 16 (2): 318–39.

Mobley, W.H. (1982) *Employee Turnover: Causes, Consequences, and Control*, Reading, MA: Addison-Wesley.

Napier, N. (1990) 'Strategy, human resources management, and organizational outcomes: coming out from between the cracks', in G. Ferris, K. Rowland, and M. Buckley (eds) *Human Resources Management: Perspectives and Issues*, Boston, MA: Allyn and Bacon, pp. 16–22.

Pfeffer, J. and Salancik, G. (1978) *The External Control of Organizations: A Resource Dependence Perspective*, New York: Harper and Row.

Porter, M.E. (1986) 'Competition in global industries: a conceptual framework', in M. Porter (ed.) *Competition in Global Industries*, Cambridge, MA: Harvard University Press, pp. 15–60.

Pucik, V. (1985) 'Strategic human resource management in a multinational firm', in H.V. Wortzel and L.H. Wortzel (eds) *Strategic Management of Multinational Corporations*, New York: Wiley, pp. 424–34.

Rosenzweig, P.M. and Singh, J.V. (1991) 'Organizational environments and multinational enterprise', *Academy of Management Review*, 16 (2): 340–61.

Schneider, S. (1990) 'National vs. corporate culture: implications for human resource management', in M. Mendenhall and G. Oddou (eds) *International Human Resources Management*, Boston, MA: PWS-Kent, pp. 13–27.

Schneider, B. and Schmitt, N. (1986) *Staffing Organizations*, Glenview, IL: Scott, Foresman.

Scott, C. and Oseghale, B. (1990) 'Japanese maquiladoras: threat to the border industrialization programme', *American Business Review*, January: 55–60.

Selznick, P. (1953) *TVA and the Grass Roots: A Study of Politics and Organization*, Berkeley, CA: University of California Press.

Taylor, S., Beechler, S. and Moxon, D. (1991) 'The transfer of HRM competence to Japanese and American maquiladoras: a research proposal', Paper presented at the Association of Japanese Business Studies Meeting, Honolulu, Hawaii.

Teagarden, M., Butler, M. and Von Glinow, M.A. (1992) 'Mexico's maquiladora industry: where strategic human resource management makes a difference', *Organizational Dynamics*, 20 (3), Winter: 34–47.

Ulrich, D. and Lake, D. (1990) *Organizational Capability*, New York: Wiley.
Van de Ven, A. and Drazin, R. (1985) 'The concept of fit in contingency theory', *Research in Organizational Behavior*, 7: 333–65.
Von Glinow, M.A. and Teagarden, M. (1990) 'The transfer of HRM technology in Sino–U.S. co-operative ventures: problems and solutions', in M. Mendenhall and G. Oddou (eds) *International Human Resources Management*, Boston, MA: PWS-Kent, pp. 301–25.

Chapter 12

The core workforce – peripheral workforce dichotomy and the transfer of Japanese management practices

Vagelis Dedoussis

ABSTRACT

The internationalization of Japanese sub-contracting networks, accompanied by the reproduction of Japan's industrial dualism across national borders, produces conditions for the emergence of the core workforce–peripheral workforce dichotomy at the level of the Japanese multinational corporation. We assess human resources management (HRM) practices in overseas Japanese firms against the peripheral model of Japanese management. The findings suggest that HRM practices in overseas Japanese firms deviate substantially from the pattern of management practices which are known to prevail among core employees in Japan. Furthermore, the findings suggest that the size of the firm as well as the type of the workforce are key variables in the practice of HRM in overseas Japanese firms.

INTRODUCTION

During the past 15 years or so issues related to the transfer of management and work organization practices from Japan to other countries have been extensively debated in the literature on Japanese management (Kraar 1975; Ichimura 1981; White and Trevor 1983; Kobayashi 1985; Fukuda 1988; Dedoussis 1990). There are several reasons behind the interest in the transfer and application of Japanese management and organizational practices to other countries: first, Japan's indisputable economic success in the post-Second World War period which has often been linked to the prevalence of certain management systems and practices among the country's enterprises; second, the rapid internationalization of Japanese enterprises underlined by the establishment of full-scale production facilities and the introduction of innovative management methods to host countries (Kujawa 1986; Shibagaki *et al.* 1989); third, the adoption of management systems and practices associated with Japanese management by many Western corporations (Pascale and Athos 1981; Ouchi 1982; Oliver and Wilkinson 1988), which has stimulated much interest in the viability of Japanese management in the context of another country; and finally, the belief held by many academics and management practitioners alike, that Japanese management is characterized by superior and progressive forms of organizing and controlling labour has certainly been a major factor behind the interest in its transfer and application to other countries.

The literature on Japanese management has tended to focus on 'core'[1] employees in the country's large-scale oligopolistic enterprises, who typically enjoy security of employment, a structured career path, high wages and a number of benefits such as heavily subsidized housing. Consistent with this trend in the literature is the adoption of a unified model of Japanese management and the implicit assumption about its applicability among all segments of the workforce in Japanese firms. The unified model has been extensively used in the growing literature on the transfer of Japanese management practices from parent companies in Japan to overseas subsidiaries. Thus, most studies on the transfer of Japanese management have tended to compare management practices in overseas subsidiaries with practices defining the relationship between core employees and large-scale enterprises in the home country. The differences in management practices between parent companies in Japan and overseas subsidiaries have been, almost invariably, attributed to the influence of various socio-cultural factors. In this way the culturalist argument for the incompatibility of Japanese management with the socio-cultural context of host countries has dominated the literature (Yoshino 1976; Iida 1985; Fukuda 1988).

However, empirical evidence in the literature on the transfer of Japanese management (White and Trevor 1983; Takamiya and Thurley 1985; Kujawa 1986; Dedoussis 1987; Oliver and Wilkinson 1988; Shibagaki *et al.* 1989) suggests that the practice of HRM in Japanese firms overseas shows substantial differences from the above-mentioned unified model of Japanese management which applies to core employees in large-scale parent corporations. For example, remuneration of the local workforce is based on prevailing market rates with little consideration of employee seniority (Ishida 1986; Pang and Oliver 1988; Yu and Wilkinson 1989), while bonus payments are practically absent (Kujawa 1983; Abo 1988). Furthermore, the welfare system is poorly developed (Thurley 1983), while security of employment for local employees is directly related to the market performance of subsidiaries (Dedoussis

1991). Additionally, there is limited involvement of local mid-level managers in the decision-making process (Jain and Ohtsu 1983). The above are in sharp contrast with the development of seniority-based remuneration, including substantial bi-annual bonuses, company-sponsored welfare systems, considerable security of employment for regular employees and wide involvement of mid-level managers in the 'bottom-up' type of decision making featuring in the standard, core model of Japanese management.

In light of the differences mentioned above, it may be suggested that the relationship between local employees and overseas Japanese firms is defined by a different model of management. This model is characterized by the limited internalization of labour markets, which is especially evident in the case of smaller size firms and white-collar employees. The limited internalization of labour markets may be partly attributed to the small size of many overseas Japanese firms. Thus, the behaviour of smaller size overseas firms is consistent with the home country pattern where typical 'Japanese' management practices can be developed by large-scale enterprises only. On the other hand, the limited internalization of labour markets for white-collar employees reflects the under-utilization of their skills and expertise in Japanese multinational corporations (Heidrick and Struggles 1990; Dobbie 1991). That is, there is very little need for the implementation of internal labour market procedures among local white-collar employees as these employees are hired in order to perform specific tasks and not as generalists like their counterparts in Japan's large-scale enterprises (Dedoussis 1990).

The limited internalization of labour markets in overseas Japanese firms does not, however, preclude the introduction of certain HRM practices which can offer distinct advantages to the organization. For instance, job rotation, internal training and loose demarcations, practices commonly associated with the standard model of Japanese management defining the relationship between core employees and large-scale enterprises, are found in many larger Japanese manufacturing subsidiaries overseas (Wickens 1987; Watanabe 1989; Wilkinson et al. 1989). This suggests that management aims at the optimum utilization of the overseas workforce without, however, the introduction of certain high-cost practices, such as seniority wages, company welfarism and tenured employment, which would increase costs and reduce organizational flexibility.

We examine HRM practices in eight Japanese manufacturing firms in Australia from the viewpoint of the core workforce–peripheral workforce dichotomy. The examination is undertaken in the context of major changes with far-reaching implications already under way in aspects of HRM and industrial relations practices in several Western countries and the widespread perception that Australian and Western industry would benefit by the introduction of Japanese management practices.

REVIEW OF THE LITERATURE ON THE TRANSFER OF JAPANESE MANAGEMENT

The strong belief in the uniqueness of the Japanese firm, which is often viewed as a unit concerned primarily with the maintenance of the welfare of its members and secondarily only with economic functions and the pursuit of profit (Tsuda 1979: 25; Suzuki 1984: 65), has led several scholars to suggest that its culturally specific management style cannot be easily transplanted into the operations of Japanese subsidiaries operating in other countries. Central to this position is the argument that Japanese management cannot be transferred overseas while ignoring the meanings and values that underline it (Hayashi 1986: 38) as well as the particular context of countries where Japanese subsidiaries are established (Fukuda 1987: 80; Briggs 1988: 28). Therefore, the transfer of Japanese management is often seen either as a question of modifying and adapting substantially its HRM practices in order to suit socio-cultural conditions in host countries (Sato 1981: VI; Dillon 1983: 77; Johnson 1988: 35) or as rather futile since nothing especially 'Japanese' is allegedly found among overseas Japanese firms (Newell 1984: 243). Notwithstanding the scepticism with which the possibility for the transfer of HRM practices from parent companies to overseas subsidiaries has been viewed by scholars arguing for the culturally bound nature of Japanese management, there exists abundant empirical evidence suggesting that a number of HRM practices commonly associated with Japanese management have actually found their way into the operations of overseas Japanese firms. Several broad conclusions can be drawn after reviewing the major sources on the transfer of HRM practices from parent companies in Japan to overseas subsidiaries (Ichimura 1981; Yamada 1981; White and Trevor 1983; Kobayashi 1985; Takamiya and Thurley 1985; Kujawa 1986; Abo 1988; Fukuda 1988; Ishida 1989; Shibagaki et al. 1989; Dedoussis 1991).

The first conclusion is that the transfer of HRM practices does not appear to be influenced to any appreciable extent by the location of the subsidiary and the socio-cultural context of the host country. The evidence in the literature suggests that there is no significant variation in the practice of HRM in Japanese subsidiaries established in developed

West European and North American countries on the one hand (Takamiya and Thurley 1985; Kujawa 1986; Shibagaki *et al*. 1989) and in less developed Asian countries on the other hand (Jain 1987; Ishida 1989). The uniformity in the transfer of management practices across countries of various physical proximity and cultural affinity to Japan undermines the culturalist argument for the rejection of the Japanese model by the allegedly alien socio-cultural environment of host countries. That is, if the socio-cultural environment of host countries was the crucial factor determining the transfer of Japanese management, as claimed by culturalists, the introduction of at least several HRM practices should have been more prevalent in the case of Japanese subsidiaries established in a number of Asian countries than in the case of subsidiaries operating in West Europe and North America. This is because, apart from the closer physical proximity, cultural affinity with Japan is said to be closer in the case of the former region than in the latter region (Fukuda 1988). Yet, there is no evidence that the transfer of HRM practices has taken place in substantially different ways across countries with diverse socio-cultural context and distance from Japan.

The transfer of HRM practices also appears to depend upon the industrial sector and the type of the workforce of the subsidiary. For instance, the direct recruitment of young school leavers with little consideration of their skills and expertise takes place among blue-collar workers in manufacturing subsidiaries (Pang and Oliver 1988: 17–18; Wilkinson *et al*. 1989: 18). In this case adaptability and ability to work in teams are the crucial factors determining the employment of blue-collar candidates (Dicle *et al*. 1988: 335–6; Fucini and Fucini 1990). On the other hand, however, mature-age candidates are hired on the basis of their specialist knowledge and expertise in white-collar positions by subsidiaries in the service industry (Jain and Ohtsu 1983: 108; White and Trevor 1983: 101). In general, very few of the 'Japanese' HRM practices are known to apply among locally recruited white-collar employees in overseas subsidiaries (White and Trevor 1983; Kujawa 1986; Weiermair 1990; Dedoussis 1991).

A further conclusion is that the size of the subsidiary appears to be the most significant factor influencing the transfer of HRM practices. For instance, there is less scope for internal training and job rotation in smaller size subsidiaries while both practices are usually found in large-scale overseas operations (Hayashi 1986; Park *et al*. 1990; Dedoussis 1991). Furthermore, the generally poor state of welfare benefits for the local workforce has been, at least partly, attributed to the small size of many overseas Japanese subsidiaries (Lin 1984). The findings of various studies on the transfer of HRM practices from parent companies in Japan to overseas operations undermine the suggestion made elsewhere (Abo 1988) that smaller size subsidiaries are likely to be managed in a more 'Japanese' way. On the contrary, it appears that, in general, the introduction of practices associated with Japanese management has been far more prevalent among larger rather than smaller subsidiaries (Putti and Chong 1986; Fukuda 1988; Dedoussis 1990).

The evidence in the literature on the transfer of Japanese management practices suggests the existence of a divide between manufacturing and non-manufacturing subsidiaries as well as between smaller and larger size subsidiaries. In general, it appears that Japanese HRM practices have been introduced to a greater extent into large-scale subsidiaries and subsidiaries in the manufacturing industry than into smaller size subsidiaries and subsidiaries in the service industry (White and Trevor 1983; Kujawa 1986; Dedoussis 1991). However, in view of the scarcity of studies focusing on smaller size subsidiaries and subsidiaries in the service sector, the conclusions drawn above should be treated with care.

THE PERIPHERAL MODEL OF JAPANESE MANAGEMENT

In the light of the conclusions drawn from the review of the major sources on the transfer of Japanese management it may be suggested that the relationship between local employees and overseas Japanese subsidiaries is defined by the peripheral model of Japanese management. Underlying the peripheral model is the lack of long-term commitment to host countries by Japanese multinational corporations. As is well known (Nakatani 1982; Dore 1986; Uekusa 1987), Japanese large-scale enterprises hive-off labour-intensive activities to numerous subsidiaries, affiliated firms and sub-contractors, which are often organized in tightly knit sub-contracting networks known as *keiretsu* (*Kigyo Keiretsu Yoran* 1991). In the context of the continuing globalization of production and the overseas expansion of the Japanese *keiretsu* it may be anticipated that production activities in host countries will continue to be carried out as long as conditions remain favourable from the viewpoint of parent companies. This, however, means that the commitment of the subsidiary firm to the host country and to local employees is likely to be significantly weaker compared with the commitment of the parent corporation to its regular, core workforce in the home country.[2] In the latter case commitment is expected to be stronger as corporate management decisions of Japanese firms are said to be subject to the dual control of ownership and employees' interests (Aoki 1990).

The lack of long-term commitment to host countries, where labour-intensive activities are typically carried out through the establishment of subsidiaries, necessitates the decentralization of HRM. In this way the management of heterogeneous segments of the workforce in multinational corporations becomes easier, while a relatively undifferentiated employment structure can be maintained in parent companies. In other words, the decentralization of HRM, which follows the more extensive use of sub-contractors and the establishment of subsidiaries, may abate some of the difficulties associated with the management of a workforce comprising heterogeneous groups of employees in large-scale corporations (Aoki 1987: 285). The decentralization of HRM leads, however, to the exclusion of the local workforce from management strategies, such as the development of an internal labour market, which are known to underline the standard model of Japanese management applying to the core segment of the workforce (Hatvany and Pucik 1981). This, in turn, suggests that HRM practices among locally recruited employees in overseas Japanese firms will differ significantly from HRM practices which are known to prevail among core personnel in Japan's large-scale enterprises.

The differences in HRM practices between Japanese firms in the home country and overseas, as briefly mentioned in the introduction, reflect differences in the nature of parent companies and overseas subsidiaries. That is, parent companies are subject to the dual control of ownership and the interests of core employees (Aoki 1990), as mentioned previously. However, the interests of local employees cannot be expected to exercise any substantial influence in corporate management decisions in the case of overseas subsidiaries in light of the absence of long-term commitment to host countries. Thus, overseas subsidiaries may be considered profit maximizers rather than entities seeking the realization of the interests of both owner and employees on a long-term basis. It may, therefore, be expected that HRM in overseas subsidiaries will be underlined by the introduction of low-cost practices which can offer distinct and immediate advantages to the organization. On the other hand, high-cost practices featuring in the standard, core model of Japanese management, such as tenured employment, structured career and seniority-based remuneration, which aim at ensuring the presence of a loyal and committed workforce, necessary for the realization of high, long-term profits, need not be introduced to any great extent into overseas subsidiaries. It may, therefore, be suggested that the relationship between local employees and overseas Japanese firms is defined by the peripheral model of Japanese management which includes the following key practices.

1 Young employees with no previous work experience are directly recruited for shop floor positions in manufacturing firms. However, recruitment of white-collar workers is indirect and focuses on mature-age and experienced candidates. Recruitment of both blue-collar and white-collar personnel depends upon the demands of production.

2 The background of all candidates is thoroughly scrutinized. Adaptability and ability to work in teams are important selection criteria for blue-collar employees while specialist knowledge is highly valued in the case of white-collar employees.

3 Internal, on-the-job training is the dominant type of training for blue-collar employees in large-scale manufacturing firms. Internal training is emphasized in the initial stages of operations as well as whenever new technology is introduced. However, internal training is less developed among smaller size firms or white-collar employees who are hired as specialists.

4 Job rotation for blue-collar workers is widely practised in large-scale manufacturing firms while its scope is limited in smaller firms. Job rotation is less frequent among white-collar personnel.

5 Internal promotion is generally practised. However, internal promotion may be expected to lose its importance under conditions of rapid business expansion. Seniority plays an important role in internal promotion.

6 Flexible assignments and work allocated to groups are extensively practised among blue-collar employees in manufacturing firms. However, both practices are less evident among white-collar personnel.

7 Decision making by consensus and open lines of communications are common practices. However, as the decision-making process is dominated by Japanese managers, the actual involvement of local staff is minimal.

8 The range of welfare benefits provided to local employees is limited. This is especially the case in smaller size firms.

9 The seniority factor is not important in the remuneration system. Few allowances and a small amount of bonus are offered to local employees.

10 Small group activities, such as quality control circles and suggestion schemes, are either absent or poorly developed.

11 Induction programmes for locally recruited employees are absent.

12 Security of employment depends on the market performance of each

firm and is generally higher in large-scale firms and in firms experiencing growth. Reductions in employment levels may be expected to take place whenever adverse economic and business conditions prevail.

In the next section the above-outlined practices of the peripheral model of Japanese management, defining the relationship between local employees and overseas Japanese firms, will be tested against data from Japanese firms established in Australia.

THE AUSTRALIAN CASE STUDIES

A survey of HRM practices in eight Japanese manufacturing firms established in Victoria and New South Wales, Australia, was undertaken twice (in mid-1986 and in early 1990). The firms vary in size, the smallest (Hoya) has a workforce of 68 and is capitalized at A$0.3 million, while the biggest firm (Toyota) has 4,330 employees and is capitalized at A$142 million. As identified by industrial sector, two firms (Matsushita, Sanyo) produce consumer electronics, two firms (Canobolas, Lachlan) are in the wool scouring and top making industry, two firms (Nippon-denso, Toyota) are in the motor vehicle industry, Hoya manufactures optical lenses and NEC is a producer of telecommunications equipment. All firms have Japanese managing directors, while six firms are wholly owned subsidiaries of Japanese corporations (there is a limited amount of Australian equity in two of the firms). The case study method, involving interviews with senior Japanese and Australian managers, employees and representatives of unions, was employed in the research. A brief profile of the firms surveyed is presented in Table 12.1.

As may be seen from Table 12.1, five firms – Canobolas, Lachlan, NEC, Nippondenso and Toyota – have experienced improvements in market position as expressed by increased sales and improved profitability. Improvement in market position has been accompanied by increased employment levels at Lachlan, NEC, Nippondenso and Toyota, while the decrease in employment at Canobolas may be attributed primarily to the introduction of labour-saving equipment which resulted in a number of redundancies. On the other hand, a deterioration in market position and a decrease in employment levels have taken place at Hoya, Matsushita and Sanyo. It is therefore evident that employment levels are generally affected by the market position of each firm. However, the relationship between employment levels and market position is quite complex as it is affected by factors such as technological change.

Table 12.1 Profile of firms surveyed

Firms	Number of employees (1990)	Trend in number of employees (1986–90)	Trend in market position[a] (1986–90)	Paid up capital (A$ millions) (1990)
Small size (less than 100 employees)				
Canobolas	70	–8%	Improved	2.0
Hoya	68	–15%	Deteriorated	0.3
Lachlan	96	+25%	Improved	0.5
Medium size (100–500 employees)				
Matsushita	147	–2%	Deteriorated	2.5
Sanyo	254	–27%	Deteriorated	15.0
Large size (over 500 employees)				
NEC	1,483	+65%	Improved	28.0
Nippondenso	540	+54%	Improved	4.0
Toyota	4,330	+780%	Improved	142.0

Note: [a] The trend in market position was assessed using data for profitability and sales turnover.

Nevertheless, it is possible to distinguish between firms which, as a result of rapid growth in employment, have become large-scale organizations and those firms which have remained small sized with either stable or reduced employment. The former group includes NEC, Nippondenso and Toyota, while the five remaining firms fall into the latter group (Lachlan is included in the latter group despite a 25 per cent increase in employment between 1986 and 1990. The company is still a small-scale organization.) The significance of the distinction between large size and small size firms becomes clear when the status of the personnel department and the position of the personnel manager are examined (Table 12.2).

As may be seen from the table, personnel departments do not exist among the three smaller size firms, Canobolas, Hoya and Lachlan. Personnel issues in these firms tend to be treated in a rather casual manner as exemplified by the appointment of a part-time employee in charge of personnel at Hoya and the assignment of personnel responsibilities to the maintenance supervisor at Lachlan. This suggests peripherality of the personnel function in the three smaller firms. Furthermore, both the status of the personnel department and the position of the personnel manager have been adversely affected among firms which have experienced deterioration in market position and reduction in employment levels. For

Table 12.2 Status of personnel department and position of personnel manager

Firms	Status of personnel department	Responsibility for personnel matters	Reporting relationship to
Canobolas	No personnel department	Plant manager	Managing director
Hoya	No personnel department	Assistant to administration manager	Administration manager
Lachlan	No personnel department	Maintenance supervisor	Managing director
Matsushita	Combined with general affairs department	Personnel and general affairs manager	Managing director
NEC	Separate division	Assistant general manager	Managing director
Nippondenso	Separate department	Personnel manager	Managing director
Sanyo	No personnel department	Assistant to general manager finance	General manager finance
Toyota	Separate division	Manager finance	Director finance

instance, personnel responsibilities were assigned to the factory manager following the redundancy of the personnel supervisor at Sanyo's factory. After the closure of the company's production facilities in Australia and the loss of more than 120 jobs, the personnel department became part of the finance department. The restructuring was accompanied by the redundancy of the personnel manager whose duties were taken over by an assistant to the general manager of the finance department. Similarly, Canobolas' personnel manager was retrenched in early 1981 following the implementation of rationalization programmes when the company was experiencing adverse market conditions.

In contrast to the experience of the firms mentioned above, separate personnel departments exist in the three bigger firms, NEC, Nippondenso and Toyota. It may therefore be suggested that the importance of the personnel function increases in larger firms which have experienced an improvement in market position and a growth in employment level. On the other hand, however, the personnel function becomes less important in smaller firms and whenever adverse market conditions prevail and the level of employment decreases.

In the light of the preceding discussion it is unsurprising that, while formal personnel policies are absent in the three smaller firms, Canobolas, Hoya and Lachlan, they exist among larger firms such as Matsushita, NEC, Nippondenso, Sanyo and Toyota. However, the size of the firm alone cannot fully explain the existence/absence of formal personnel policies. For example, formal personnel policies were absent at Nippondenso and Toyota when first cited in 1986, although employment levels, standing at the time at 345 and 490 employees respectively, were by no means small. On the other hand, it may be suggested that the existence of formal personnel policies at Matsushita and Sanyo relates more to the legacy of the past size of the two firms, which used to have 220 and 670 employees respectively in 1981, than to their size when surveyed in 1986 and 1990. It therefore appears that, apart from firm size, managerial strategies of parent companies regarding the utilization and development of human resources may be another factor influencing the establishment of formal personnel policies in the Australian subsidiaries.

Following the presentation of the profile of the firms surveyed and discussion of the relationship between size and importance of the personnel function, the examination of specific HRM practices will now take place. The practices are examined in the order in which they were listed in the peripheral model of Japanese management above.

Recruitment

Mid-career recruitment, focusing on the 35–40 age group, is the dominant type of recruitment for blue-collar and white-collar positions in most firms. Formal educational qualifications are largely unimportant with the exception of candidates for managerial positions in larger firms, while previous work experience is highly valued. Blue-collar employees are recruited directly in all firms. This is also the case for white-collar staff in the three smaller size firms. However, there is varied reliance on professional agencies for the recruitment of managers in larger firms. For example, Nippondenso and Sanyo make use of professional expertise rather frequently. On the other hand, evidence of internalized labour markets was found at NEC and Toyota as the policy of the two firms is to give preference to internal recruitment as far as possible. Recruitment at NEC focuses on the 25–35 age group, which sets this firm apart from the rest as mentioned above. With the exception of NEC and Toyota, where limited scale periodic recruitment has been introduced in anticipation of continuing business expansion, recruitment in other firms depends upon the immediate demands of production.

Selection

The ability to perform specific jobs is almost the sole selection criterion in smaller size firms. On the other hand, adaptability and teamwork ability are important criteria in the selection of blue-collar workers in larger firms (NEC, Toyota). Previous work experience in the same or a similar type of industry and position is important among larger firms. The background of candidates is extensively scrutinized in all firms by means of reference checks with previous employers and referees while more than half of the firms place much emphasis on the 'prospect for commitment' of their recruits.

Internal training

Internal, on-the-job training is more developed in larger rather than smaller size firms. Training focuses almost exclusively on blue-collar employees while managers and administrative staff receive very little or no training at all. All firms reported the establishment of on-the-job training programmes in the initial stages of operations in Australia. Thereafter, the provision of training depends upon the introduction of new technology and changes in production methods. The frequent introduction of new technology at NEC has been accompanied by the establishment of a wide range of training programmes, conducted at the company's operations in Melbourne as well as in Japan. Almost 40 per cent of NEC's employees have received training in Japan. This is the highest percentage among all firms, followed by Toyota where 12 per cent of the workforce has participated in training programmes at the Japanese headquarters. NEC and Toyota reported the highest percentage of salaries/wages spent on training among all firms surveyed.

Job rotation

Job rotation is restricted and conducted in an unplanned manner in the three smaller firms (Canobolas, Hoya, Lachlan) where relevant formal policies are absent. By contrast, job rotation takes place in a planned manner in larger firms where formal policies have been established, although its frequency varies depending largely upon the demands of production in each firm. Larger firms reported that their policies on job rotation are clearly explained to prospective employees during the selection process. This is done in order to minimize possible employee resistance to job rotation in the future. There is practically no job rotation for white-collar employees in any firm with the partial exception of NEC where a small number of younger employees are rotated at approximately two-year intervals.

Internal promotion

Policies specifying reliance on internal promotion for vacancies on the shop floor exist in almost all firms. Larger size firms (Matsushita, NEC, Nippondenso, Sanyo and Toyota) rely mostly on internal promotion for white-collar vacancies, while a dual policy of relying both on internal promotion and on external recruitment for administrative and managerial vacancies is followed by the three smaller firms. However, policies on internal promotion, especially for white-collar employees, are compromised whenever there is a substantial increase in employment levels. For instance, the percentage of internal promotions to total promotions for white-collar employees is quite low in firms such as NEC, Nippondenso and Toyota, reflecting the significant increase in employment in these firms. On the other hand, higher rates of internal promotion are found at Matsushita where the employment level has more or less stabilized. Internally promoted employees have an above average length of service record in almost all firms; however, the existence of any causal relationship between length of service and promotion was denied by management.

Flexible assignments and work groups

The absence of job descriptions in most firms is accompanied by emphasis on the performance of tasks as required by the demands of production. For example, at Nippondenso and Toyota, where the just-in-time production system is in operation, employees are assigned to posts according to the demand for semi-finished products from the next workstation. Even at Matsushita and Sanyo, the only firms where job descriptions exist, functional demarcations are not strictly adhered to, as employees are required to perform a variety of duties depending upon the production schedule. The absence or very loose application of job descriptions is associated with higher wage rates for employees, who are prepared and have the potential to become multi-skilled, and the simplification of job classifications. Higher wage rates are offered in order to ensure the development of a flexible workforce while job classifications have been radically reduced in some cases. For instance, the ten broad groups with a total of 42 job classifications which existed at Toyota in 1986 had been replaced by three broad skill levels including eight pay points by 1990. Work groups are present in four of the larger firms, i.e. Matsushita, NEC, Nippondenso and Toyota, while tasks are allocated to individuals in smaller firms. However, there was no evidence suggesting that either the multi-skilling or the allocation of work to groups had been attempted among white-collar personnel.

Decision making and communications

The fairly extensive presence of Australian managers in most firms[3] relates little to their actual authority and involvement in the decision-making process. Australian managers deal mostly with the day-to-day implementation of decisions which are often made without much input from them. The actual responsibility for decision making is in the hands of Japanese managers and advisors, the latter having in most firms direct access to Japanese managing directors. The presence of expatriate advisors in five firms places significant constraints upon the authority of Australian managers as the former have the authority to block or even reverse the decisions of the latter. This is the case even among firms such as Matsushita and Sanyo, where Japanese managers claimed that the participatory, bottom-up style of decision making is practised widely. Proposals submitted by Australian managers for consideration by management committees, which in half of the firms meet rather infrequently, are generally restricted in their scope and refer mostly to operational aspects of decision making. The establishment of manage-ment philosophy and formal lines of communications, including regular pre- and after-work meetings and addresses by senior managers, is more developed in larger firms, however, the overall flow of communications tends to be one-way, i.e. top-down, in most firms.

Welfare benefits

Welfare and fringe benefits provided by the three smaller firms (Canobolas, Hoya and Lachlan) are very limited. By contrast, a far more extensive range of benefits, including subsidized education, subsidized meals, staff purchasing schemes and free refreshments at lunch time, is offered by larger firms. It may be noted that the provision of benefits in a number of firms has taken place on the initiative of management rather than after requests by unions. As a result, withdrawal of some benefits has taken place rather easily without opposition by the unions. High-cost benefits, such as non-contributory superannuation and low-interest loans, are not offered by more than one or two firms (NEC, Toyota).

Remuneration

Most firms follow the 'bottom-line' approach in remuneration as wages do not exceed wages offered by competitors and other companies established in the same locality. Furthermore, seniority is almost irrelevant in remuneration, while bonus payments are either absent or made up of rather small amounts. Various allowances offered by the firms do not generally exceed the legally required levels. Partial deviation from the above pattern was found at NEC and Toyota where the two firms offer above-award-level wages which in the case of NEC are approximately 5 per cent higher than the competitors' average. Small seniority increments, not exceeding 2 per cent of commencing wages for regular shop floor employees, were found at Hoya, NEC and Toyota, while the existence of a productivity-linked bonus system was reported at Lachlan and Matsushita. On the other hand, it appears that the remuneration packages offered to a few Australian managers who were recruited to senior positions in several larger firms (NEC, Nippondenso and Toyota) are high compared with remuneration they used to receive from their former employers.

Small group activities

Small group activities including quality control circles and suggestion schemes were in operation at NEC, Nippondenso and Toyota, although all firms had attempted to introduce such activities in the past. The failure of most firms to establish viable small group activities may be attributed to a number of factors, such as poor planning and implementation, lack of support by local managers and supervisors, especially during busy production periods, as well as lack of understanding of the very nature of these activities. It may be noted, however, that even in the three firms mentioned above small group activities are characterized by low employee participation rates (12 per cent for Nippondenso and 18 per cent for Toyota), a low number of suggestions per employee (1–2 suggestions per year) and a short life span (not exceeding two years for quality control circles).

Induction

Narrowly focused induction programmes which last for about two or three days and aim at the familiarization of newly recruited employees with work-related issues were found in the five medium-sized and larger firms (Matsushita, NEC, Nippondenso, Sanyo, Toyota). Matsushita is the only exception to this pattern as its induction programme includes issues related to corporate philosophy and objectives as well. Matsushita and Toyota are the only firms making use of an induction manual.

Security of employment

Security of employment is generally higher among larger rather than smaller size firms. This is evidenced by the existence of formal policies allowing the hiring of non-regular employees only in emergency and unusual situations (NEC and Toyota) as well as by the generally low percentage of non-regular employees, i.e. casual and temporary employees, in larger firms (non-regular employees are 0.3 per cent of the workforce at NEC, 2 per cent at Toyota and 6 per cent at Nippondenso). On the other hand, 13 per cent and 16 per cent of the workforce are employed as non-regulars at Lachlan and Canobolas respectively. Furthermore, market position is another factor exercising significant influence upon security of employment. Employment levels have increased in firms such as NEC, Nippondenso and Toyota which have enjoyed improvement in their market position while the opposite has taken place at Hoya and Sanyo. Significantly, all the evidence available suggests that no retrenchments have ever taken place at NEC, Nippondenso and Toyota since their operations commenced in Australia.[4] When required to reduce employment, most firms have resorted to retrenchments, while in only two cases (Hoya and Lachlan) were employment levels reduced by the combination of retrenchments and natural attrition.

UNDERSTANDING THE TRANSFER OF JAPANESE MANAGEMENT

The findings suggest that the size of the firm is a crucial variable in the practice of HRM. In general, 'Japanese' practices are more evident among larger rather than smaller size firms. Furthermore, there are clear differences between blue-collar and white-collar employees with respect to certain aspects of HRM such as training, job rotation and work groups.

The findings of the present study are generally consistent with the findings of other studies (White and Trevor 1983; Sethi *et al*. 1984; Takamiya and Thurley 1985; Kujawa 1986; Fukuda 1988; Oliver and Wilkinson 1988; Shibagaki *et al*. 1989; Abo 1990) on overseas Japanese firms taking into consideration, whenever possible, the size of the overseas subsidiary as well as the type of the workforce, blue collars or white collars. However, it appears that a few differences in HRM practices exist between Japanese firms established in Australia and Japanese firms operating in other countries. The differences are summarized below.

The recruitment of experienced, mature-age blue-collar employees takes place in the Australian subsidiaries. This is in contrast with recruitment practices among Japanese subsidiaries in other countries which are known to focus on young candidates with no previous work experience (Taira 1980: 390; Thurley 1983: 124; Kono 1984–5: 36; Morris 1988; Wilkinson *et al*. 1989: 18). While white-collar employees are recruited directly by most of the firms surveyed, Japanese subsidiaries established elsewhere are known to recruit white-collar employees indirectly (Jain and Ohtsu 1983: 108; White and Trevor 1983: 101). Seniority was found to play an important role in internal promotion among Japanese firms in Australia, as evidenced by the above average length of service record of internally promoted employees. By contrast, the findings of other studies suggest that seniority is less important in promotion (Kujawa 1986: 156; Pang and Oliver 1988: 18). Finally, there was no evidence for the existence of 'open door' policies allowing employees direct access to senior management as suggested elsewhere (Kraar 1975: 121). Although lines of communications are open in the larger size firms surveyed, the flow of communications is from the top down and the involvement of local employees in the much-vaunted consultative decision-making system is minimal.

It is extremely difficult to explain the few differences in recruitment, promotion and communications between the firms surveyed and Japanese companies established in other countries without taking into account several factors such as size and sector of firms examined, the nature of the local labour market and HRM practices in parent corporations in Japan. However, in most cases details on these factors are not provided in the literature on the transfer of Japanese management. This in turn imposes limitations in drawing conclusions regarding differences between the firms surveyed and Japanese firms in other countries.

Occasionally, it is possible to compare aspects of HRM in subsidiaries of the same parent corporation operating in different countries. For example, recruitment at Toyota plants in the USA and Canada focuses on high-school graduates in their early thirties with no record of work in the automobile industry (Wilkinson *et al.* 1989). On the other hand, experienced employees in their late thirties are recruited by Toyota in Australia. It may, however, be noted that while Toyota's plants in North America have been established in areas without vehicle assembly tradition, Toyota Australia operates on the outskirts of Melbourne where several other automobile makers are also established. This may suggest that Toyota Australia takes advantage of locally available skills by recruiting experienced personnel, a practice that is not possible in Toyota plants in North America. In the above example, differences in recruitment practices may be attributed to the nature of local labour markets. Nevertheless, it must be pointed out that the overall pattern of HRM practices at Toyota plants in North America does not appear to be substantially different compared with Toyota Australia.

The test of the peripheral model of Japanese management against data from the Australian case studies, in conjunction with the conclusions drawn earlier after reviewing the literature, suggests that HRM in overseas Japanese firms is practised in a uniform way across national borders taking into account the size of the firm, industrial sector and the type of workforce. This in turn undermines the culturalist argument regarding the alleged exclusiveness of Japanese management and its incompatibility with different socio-cultural conditions in countries where subsidiaries of Japanese corporations have been established. The few differences in HRM practices between the firms surveyed in Australia and Japanese firms in other countries noted above can most probably be attributed to factors such as size, industrial sector and local labour market conditions.

Issues related to the transfer of Japanese management practices have not, so far, been considered in the literature from the perspective of the core workforce–peripheral workforce dichotomy. We have sought to argue that the core workforce–peripheral workforce dichotomy, which operates at the interfirm and intrafirm levels in Japan, provides a framework within which issues related to the transfer of Japanese management can be explained in a persuasive way. The starting point for the development of this framework is the internationalization of Japanese businesses. Japanese sub-contracting networks, dominated by commercial and industrial trust, have been expanding their activities on a global scale. It has been argued, however, that the on-going internationalization of production strengthens even further the international division of labour (Enderwick 1984) and produces conditions for the emergence of the core workforce–peripheral workforce dichotomy at the level of the multinational corporation.

Evidence in the literature suggests the existence of a dual employment system, underlined by the core–periphery dichotomy, in Japanese multinational corporations (Ozawa 1979: 212; Yamada 1981: 1–30; Thurley 1983: 124; Kobayashi 1985: 239–40; Negandhi *et al.* 1985: 101). Thus, employment conditions for home country personnel in Japanese multinationals are determined by internal labour market procedures as these apply to core employees in parent companies. However, local employees are hired under a different set of employment conditions with little, if any, attempt to incorporate them into the internal labour market (Heidrick and Struggles 1990; Dobbie 1991). It is suggested that the adoption of different employment conditions for local employees aims at increasing the flexibility of the multinational corporation in the light of rigidities associated with the operation of internal labour markets. Additionally, the deployment of layers of non-core employees at the global level helps to safeguard the interests of the privileged segment of the core workforce which is essential for the realization of high, long-term profits.

The protection of the interests of core employees is an important consideration in the operations of Japanese firms. Aoki (1990) has proposed that corporate management decisions of Japanese firms are subject to the dual control of financial (ownership) interests and employees' interests, rather than to unilateral control, in the interests of ownership. This view contrasts sharply with the neoclassical view identifying the firm with the profit-maximizing entrepreneur or the stockholder in the modern context (Aoki 1984, 1987). Along similar lines it has been argued that Japanese firms choose the amount of both output and labour and capital inputs in order to maximize income for employees together with the payment of a fixed share of profits to shareholders (Komiya 1989). This contrasts with the notion of the stockholder-controlled firm which seeks the maximization of its stock value under the competitive wage system (Aoki 1990).

Among the several features of firms that are dually controlled by owners and employees, certain points are especially important in the context of the present discussion. First, the dually controlled firm tends to pursue a higher growth rate in investment decision making than the stockholder-controlled firm facing the same level of employees' current earnings. This happens because the dually controlled firm takes into account employees' extra benefits from the growth of the firm in the form of enhanced future promotion possibilities. Second, the dually controlled firm provides a higher degree of job security compared with the stockholder-controlled firm. This is possible by the regulation of employment levels in the dually controlled firm. Third, labour-intensive activities are spun-off to sub-contractors and subsidiaries, where wages are relatively lower. These features help the dually controlled firm to protect the interests of its incumbent employees (Aoki 1990).

It is generally acknowledged that the extent and intensity of the interfirm division of labour, which is made possible under the *keiretsu* system of industrial structure, are more pronounced in Japan than in other capitalist societies (Dore 1973: 39–40; Clark 1979: 62–3, 233–4; Shinohara 1982: 7–78). One of the main motives behind the increasing use of sub-contractors and spinning-off activities to subsidiaries, in Japan and overseas, relates to the attempt by management in larger companies to trim the workforce and keep employees as homogeneous as possible in terms of employment conditions, career and so forth (Aoki 1987: 285). Thus, the use of sub-contractors and the establishment of subsidiaries reflect the need for a 'leaner and meaner' organizational structure of large-scale Japanese enterprises (Whitehill 1991: 274) in the face of lower growth rates in the domestic economy, increasing competition in world markets and cost-containment policies adopted by management. However, the establishment of subsidiaries and the development of sub-contracting relationships makes easier the practice of HRM at the enterprise level. This is because the decentralization of HRM, which follows the more extensive use of sub-contractors and the establishment of subsidiaries, may abate some of the difficulties associated with the management of a workforce comprising heterogeneous groups of employees in large integrated firms (Aoki 1987: 285). In this way a relatively undifferentiated employment structure can be maintained in large-scale corporations (Aoki 1984: 29).

In conjunction with management's attempts to streamline operations and keep the core workforce as homogeneous as possible, the continuing expansion of the periphery is bound to take place. This is because the periphery, comprising smaller size sub-contractors and subsidiaries integrated in the *keiretsu* system of industrial structure, provides much of the flexibility necessary for large firms to overcome business downturns and achieve steady, long-term growth. This means that the well-known divide between core employees–large firms and peripheral employees–smaller firms will be maintained and most probably will become even more pronounced. Thus, a direct result of the increasing use of sub-contractors and spinning-off production activities to subsidiaries will be the strengthening of the core workforce–peripheral workforce dichotomy.

The internationalization of Japanese businesses, involving the transfer of economic and production activities previously carried out in Japan, is bound to lead to the reproduction of Japan's industrial dualism across national borders. This will take place in the following ways. First, by means of direct Japanese investment in selected industries and sectors of the economy in host countries. Japanese investment, however, will intensify the unbalanced international division of labour through the decentralization of manufacturing operations across countries as the vertical division of production in Japan is replaced by sub-contracting at the international level. Put differently, features of Japan's industrial dualism will become present at the international level as international sub-contracting becomes the new pattern of production. Second, Japanese enterprises in host countries will attempt to integrate smaller local suppliers and sub-contractors in international production networks dominated by Japanese corporations. Direct Japanese investment overseas, which is effectively a form of spinning-off production activities to the global level, in conjunction with the integration of local firms into international sub-contracting networks, will, however, provide additional layers of periphery supporting the employment conditions of the privileged segment of core employees in parent companies.

As the internationalization of Japanese businesses and the reproduction of Japan's industrial structure at the global level progress, appropriate managerial strategies and HRM practices for segments of the global workforce in multinational enterprises have to be developed. In the light of the well-known existence of different managerial strategies and HRM practices underlining Japanese management in the context of the home country, it may be suggested that the practice of Japanese management at the international level will be characterized by the intense segmentation of labour. That is, the core workforce–peripheral workforce dichotomy, featuring at the inter-enterprise level in Japan, is bound to be reproduced at the level of the Japanese multinational corporation. The reproduction of this dichotomy, arising from the reproduction of Japan's industrial structure across national borders, may be called the 'Japanization' of HRM.

CONCLUSION

The internationalization of Japanese enterprises has produced much interest in the practice of Japanese management in host countries where subsidiaries of Japanese multinational corporations have been established. However, the almost exclusive association of Japanese management with the relationship between core employees and large-scale corporations presents a major problem in the study of the practice of HRM in overseas Japanese firms. That is, the practice of HRM in Japanese firms operating in foreign countries is, in most cases, approached in the literature as an issue of whether the practices defining the relationship between core employees and large-scale corporations in Japan are present or not in overseas subsidiaries. In conjunction with the strong influence of the culturalist approach (Yoshino 1976; Iida 1985; Fukuda 1988), which considers Japanese management the particular product of a unique society and culture, the practice of HRM in overseas Japanese subsidiaries is often defined as a question of the rejection or acceptance of exclusively Japanese practices by the socio-cultural context of host countries.

However, if Japanese management is considered from a wider perspective, which takes into account the diversity in HRM practices among segments of the workforce and firms of different size and sector in the home country as well as the major factor producing such diversity, namely the widespread use of sub-contracting affiliations under the *keiretsu* system of industrial structure, the issue of the practice of HRM in overseas Japanese firms is transformed. That is, the practice of HRM in overseas Japanese firms may be seen as essentially an issue of devising and implementing strategies and practices which can help the Japanese multinational corporation achieve the most efficient and effective utilization and control of its globally deployed workforce. Considered from this perspective, the practice of HRM in overseas Japanese firms should not be expected to result in any significant expansion of the core workforce. Rather, the practice of HRM among overseas Japanese firms may be expected to produce conditions leading to the peripheralization of the local workforce in the context of the Japanese multinational corporation. This will be due to the globalization of production and the integration of local firms into Japanese sub-contracting networks operating at the global level.

The internationalization of Japanese *keiretsu* networks, whereby many smaller affiliated and sub-contracting companies follow the main producer in overseas expansion (Saso 1990: 188), generates conditions for the reproduction of features of Japan's industrial dualism across national borders. This is because many Japanese firms operating abroad are not independent but form part of an overseas expansion network dominated by large-scale manufacturing and general trading companies. These, typically smaller size, firms are effectively forced into a position similar to that of sub-contracting firms in Japan, the only difference being that in the case of the former sub-contracting takes place on a global rather than national scale (Tsurumi 1989: 150). Thus, the reproduction of Japan's structured dualism beyond the borders of the home country will inevitably lead to the emergence of the core workforce–peripheral workforce dichotomy at the international level.

The practice of HRM in overseas Japanese firms is underlined by the fragmented transfer of the home-country practices. The evidence in the literature suggests that management practices offering distinct advantages to the organization have been generally transferred in the case of larger firms. On the other hand, however, management practices incurring significant financial costs, for instance seniority-based remuneration and the provision of extensive welfare benefits, do not feature in overseas Japanese firms. It may therefore be suggested that the transfer of Japanese management practices is basically an issue of introducing practices which will make possible the most efficient and effective utilization and control of the overseas workforce. The effective and efficient utilization and control of the overseas workforce relate to the costs involved with the introduction of specific management practices and to the benefits that may be anticipated following the introduction of these practices.

The existence of certain HRM practices, such as internal training, job rotation and internal promotion for blue-collar employees in larger Japanese firms in Australia, was noted earlier. This points to the higher internalization of labour markets in larger rather than smaller firms. However, the absence of many other, relatively high cost, practices featuring in Japanese management, for instance tenured employment, seniority-based advancement and the provision of extensive welfare benefits, suggests that the internalization of labour markets for blue-collar employees in larger Japanese firms in Australia is far more restricted than in large-scale enterprises in Japan. Thus, the existence of certain 'Japanese' practices in the firms surveyed appears to reflect the management's response to particular problems, e.g. shortage and retention of skilled labour, rather than an attempt to have employment practices for Australian blue-collar employees determined by internal labour market procedures on a systematic basis. The findings on blue-collar employees are consistent with findings of other studies suggesting a much higher 'Japanization' of management practices among this segment of the workforce than white-collar employees (White and Trevor 1983; Weiermair 1990).

The limited internalization of labour markets for blue-collar employees as well as the exclusion of white-collar personnel from internal labour market procedures in overseas Japanese firms can be understood in the context of the dually controlled firm, i.e. the firm controlled by owners and employees, proposed by Aoki (1990). Consideration of the interests of incumbent employees in the dually controlled firm dictates against the centralization of HRM whereby uniform managerial strategies would apply to all segments of the global workforce in Japanese multinational corporations. Thus, the maintenance of a relatively undifferentiated employment structure in the parent company safeguarding the interests of core employees can be made possible only by the adoption of different managerial strategies for other segments of the global workforce.

In light of the above, it is suggested that the existence of the dual employment system in overseas Japanese firms (Thurley 1983; Kobayashi 1985; Heidrick and Struggles 1990) aims at protecting the interests of core employees by keeping this group as homogeneous as possible. Thus, employment conditions for home-country personnel on overseas secondment are determined by internal labour market procedures. On the other hand, however, employment conditions for local white-collar employees are 'localized', effectively placing this group outside the scope of the internal labour market. The exclusion of local white-collar employees from internal labour markets operating in Japanese multinational corporations has often been attributed to the different socio-cultural background and high turnover rates of local personnel (Yoshino 1976). Nevertheless, the decentralization of employment conditions for local white-collar personnel is made necessary by the very nature of the dually controlled firm which protects the interests of incumbent core employees. This can help explain the existence of employment practices underlined by the unimportance of seniority in remuneration and promotion, the absence of tenured employment and the reliance on the external labour market for the recruitment of white-collar staff for specific tasks in overseas Japanese firms. It is therefore evident that the standard, unified model of Japanese management is unsuitable for the examination of management practices prevailing among local white-collar personnel.

The practice of HRM among blue-collar employees in overseas Japanese firms is affected by the dichotomy in employment practices between core Japanese personnel and local white-collar employees as this is made necessary by the nature of the dually controlled firm. That is, this dichotomy makes impossible the wider application of internal labour market procedures among local blue-collar employees. This is because of the need to maintain the prerogatives of local management and its authority over the workforce. In a different case, if blue-collar employees were to become part of the internal labour market, their management would become extremely difficult, if not impossible, considering that local managers are excluded from internal labour markets in Japanese multinationals. As noted previously, limited 'Japanization' of HRM has taken place among blue-collar employees in overseas Japanese firms. This can be attributed to distinct advantages offered by the introduction of specific practices such as internal training, job rotation and allocation of work to groups. However, the internalization of labour markets for blue-collar employees can be only restricted and unsystematic given the exclusion of local managers from internal labour market procedures.

The preceding discussion suggests that the core workforce–peripheral workforce dichotomy, underlining the practice of Japanese management in the home country, is reproduced in overseas Japanese firms. This is the combined outcome of the internationalization of Japanese sub-contracting networks dominated by large-scale corporations and the exercise of control by employees in the dually controlled firm. The localization of HRM in Japanese multinational corporations translates into the exclusion of local employees from internal labour markets, notwithstanding the transfer of some Japanese practices among blue-collar employees. Put differently, the deployment of layers of peripheral employees on the global level, which follows the reproduction of Japan's industrial dualism across national borders, helps to protect the interests of core employees by maintaining a relatively undifferentiated employment structure in parent companies.

The evidence from the Australian case studies points to the absence of HRM practices which are associated with the well-known model of Japanese management featuring among core employees in smaller size Japanese firms. This is an effect of size and is consistent with the practice of management in the home country where the development of distinct 'Japanese' practices is almost impossible for smaller size companies.

The absence of a solid theoretical framework in the rapidly growing literature on the transfer of Japanese management from parent companies to overseas subsidiaries is striking. The vast majority of studies are purely descriptive, while seldom has an attempt been made to explain issues related to the transfer of Japanese management practices. Unfortunately, the dominance of the culturalist position has been a major stumbling block in the development of new theoretical perspectives. Thus, explanations have conveniently been built around the position that the allegedly alien socio-cultural environment of host countries allows limited, at best, transfer of the Japanese model. In light of the discussion in this paper it may be suggested that future research in the following areas will make significant contributions towards understanding issues related to the transfer of Japanese management.

There is an obvious need for more research on white-collar employees and non-manufacturing Japanese subsidiaries. We have highlighted the absence of Japanese practices among local white-collar employees in overseas Japanese firms and have offered a possible interpretation of this phenomenon. However, more research is required in this area in the context of the emerging internationalization of Japan's tertiary industries.

Much emphasis has been placed in the literature on the applicability of the Japanese model of management to overseas subsidiaries of Japanese corporations. However, we have argued that there are two models of Japanese management, one applying to core employees and another to peripheral employees. The application of the latter model among the local workforce should be the subject of future research. This is a more meaningful line of inquiry rather than trying to determine the extent that 'unique' management practices featuring in the 'uniform' Japanese model could be introduced into the allegedly alien socio-cultural environment of host countries.

There is an urgent need to break away from the narrow confines of the culturalist position and seek instead to develop new theoretical perspectives on the transfer of Japanese management. It has taken a long time since Abegglen's book appeared (1958) to establish that Japanese firms behave not in culturally bound mysterious and irrational ways, but in accordance with an economic logic as shaped by conditions specific to the country's capitalism. It has also taken time to realize that Japanese management is not the product of the country's unique tradition but the outcome of factors related to the country's economic conditions. This paper has sought to analyse issues related to the transfer of Japanese management from a novel perspective by making use of a model focusing on economic considerations. It is hoped that future research will make more valuable contributions.

NOTES

1 The term 'core' employees is borrowed particularly from Friedman (1977) and Paci (1981). The term core employees refers to employees who 'through their skill or their contribution to the exercise of managerial authority are considered essential by top managers to secure high long-run profits. . . . These employees collectively force top managers to regard them as essential. . . . Core employees enjoy a guaranteed status of employment and higher earnings compared with other segments of the workforce...' (Friedman 1977:

109–17; Paci 1981: 210–14). By contrast, the term 'peripheral' workforce or 'peripheral' employees used in this paper refers to employees who:

(a) perform work which can easily be carried out by the remaining workers;
(b) perform work which is not necessary for the output which top managers desire to be produced after demand has fallen;
(c) perform work for which replacement workers are readily available when top managers want them;
(d) will not cause disruption among the remaining workers when laid off because of lack of solidarity with them;
(e) do not contribute to the maintenance of managerial authority.

Generally speaking, the groups of workers top managers consider to be peripheral will be unskilled and semi-skilled manual workers (and skilled manual workers to a lesser extent) and lower level administrative staff (Friedman 1977: 110–11). Peripheral workers are 'the workers in small factories, artisan workers and industrial home-workers, who are not usually protected by unions' (Paci 1981: 211).

2 Given the relatively late entrance of Japanese capital onto the global scene and the short history of Japanese multinational corporations, the validity of the above premise cannot be fully ascertained at this stage. Nevertheless, the following two cases, both referring to Japanese firms in Australia, support the argument for the absence of long-term commitment to host countries by Japanese multinationals. Sanyo entered Australia on a joint venture with the British Guthrie in 1973. In 1978 Sanyo bought out Guthrie's share in the venture. In 1986, when first researched, Sanyo was shifting from mass production to small-batch production and imports of finished television sets. By 1988, i.e. 15 years after its entrance into Australia and only ten years after it had acquired full control of operations, Sanyo's domestic production ceased although the company still operates in Australia as an importer. In early 1992 the Australian business community was shocked by Nissan's decision to stop domestic production, resulting in the loss of several hundred jobs in the midst of Australia's worst recession for years. Nissan justified its pull out on the poor economic performance of its Australian subsidiary.

3 On the average, Australian managers make up 56 per cent of all managers.

4 This is based on information provided by management which was cross checked with unions and long-serving employees.

REFERENCES

Abegglen, J. (1958) *The Japanese Factory. Aspects of its Social Organization*, Glencoe, IL: Free Press.

Abo, T. (1988) *Nihon Kigyo no America Genchi Seisan (Local Production of Japanese Enterprises in the USA)*, Tokyo: Toyo Keizai Shimposha.

Abo, T. (1990) 'Overseas production activities of Nissan Motor Co', Paper presented to the *Symposium on Perspectives for Asian and European Enterprises in the 90's: Co-operation or Competition?* Japan–German Center, Berlin. Euro-Asia Management Studies Association, Berlin, 18 December.

Aoki, M. (1984) 'Aspects of the Japanese firm', in Masahiko Aoki (ed.) *The Economic Analysis of the Japanese Firm*, Amsterdam: Elsevier, pp. 3–43.

Aoki, M. (1987) 'Japanese firm in transition', in Kozo Yamamura and Yasukichi Yasuba (eds) *The Political Economy of Japan*, vol. 1, Stanford: Stanford University Press, pp. 263–88.

Aoki, M. (1990) 'Toward an economic model of the Japanese firm', *Journal of Economic Literature*, XXVIII, March: 1–27.

Briggs, P. (1988) 'The Japanese at work: illusions of the ideal', *Industrial Relations Journal*, 19 (1), Spring: 24–30.

Clark, R. (1979) *The Japanese Company*, London: Yale University Press.

Dedoussis, V. (1987) 'Management systems and practices in Japanese subsidiaries: Japanization or localization?', *Human Resource Management Australia*, 25 (1), March: 42–54.

Dedoussis, V. (1990) 'Japanese management transferred: the Australian experience', *The Otemon Bulletin for Australian Studies*, 16, December: 101–21.

Dedoussis, V. (1991) 'Human resource management practices in Japanese manufacturing firms in Australia, Ph.D. thesis, Division of Commerce and Administration, Griffith University, Nathan, Queensland, Australia, July.

Dicle, U. Dicle, A. and Alie, R. (1988) 'Human resource management practices in Japanese organizations in the USA', *Public Personnel Management*, 17 (3), Fall: 331–9.

Dillon, L. (1983) 'Adopting Japanese management: some cultural stumbling blocks', *Personnel*, 60 (4), July/August: 73–7.

Dobbie, M. (1991) 'Benefits and obligations of working for the Japanese', *Business Review Weekly*, 26 April: 54–6.

Dore, R. (1973) *British Factory–Japanese Factory*, Berkeley, CA: University of California Press.

Dore, R. (1986) *Flexible Rigidities*, London: Athlone Press.

Enderwick, P. (1984) 'The labour utilization practices of multinationals and obstacles to multinational collective bargaining', *Journal of Industrial Relations*, 26 (3), September: 345–64.

Friedman, A. (1977) *Industry and Labour: Class Struggle at Work and Monopoly Capitalism*, London: Macmillan.

Fucini, J. and Fucini, S. (1990) *Working for the Japanese*, New York: Macmillan.

Fukuda, J. (1987) 'The practice of Japanese-style management in South East Asia', *Journal of General Management*, 13 (1), Autumn: 69–81.

Fukuda, J. (1988) *Japanese-Style Management Transferred: The Experience of East Asia*, London: Routledge.

Hatvany, N. and Pucik, V. (1981) 'An integrated management system: lessons from the Japanese experience', *Academy of Management Review*, 6 (3): 469–80.

Hayashi, K. (1986) 'Crosscultural interface management: the case of Japanese firms abroad', *Japanese Economic Studies*, XV (1), Fall: 3–41.

Heidrick and Struggles (1990) *Zaidoku Nihon Kigyo ni Okeru Jugyoin no Jokyo Sono Bunseki to Tenbo* (*Employment Conditions in Japanese Companies in Germany. Analysis and Observations*), Gesellschaft fur Wirtschaftsforderung, Nordhrein-Westfalen, Dusseldorf, Germany, June.

Ichimura, S. (1981) 'Japanese firms in Asia', *Japanese Economic Studies*, X (1), Fall: 31–52.

Iida, T. (1985) 'The relationship between management settings and organizational problems in Australian-based Japanese subsidiaries', Ph.D. thesis, Department of Sociology, La Trobe University, Australia.

Ishida, H. (1986) 'Transferability of Japanese human resource management abroad', *Human Resource Management*, 25 (1) Spring: 103–20.

Ishida, H. (1989) 'Managemento Genchika Mondai' ('Problems in the localization of management'), *Nihon Rodo Kyokai Zasshi*, 31 (6), June: 28–35.

Jain, H. (1987) 'The Japanese system of HRM: transferability to the Indian industrial environment', *Asian Survey*, XXVII (9), September: 1023–35.

Jain, H. and Ohtsu, M. (1983) 'Viability of the Japanese industrial relations system in the international context: the case of Canada', *Proceedings of the Sixth World Congress of the International Industrial Relations Association*, Kyoto, Japan, 28–31 March, pp. 96–115.

Johnson, C. (1988) 'Japanese-style management in America', *California Management Review*, 30 (4), Summer: 34–45.

Kigyo Keiretsu Yoran (1991) A Survey of *Keiretsu*-affiliated Enterprises, Tokyo: Toyo Keizaisha.

Kobayashi, N. (1985) 'The patterns of management style developing in Japanese multinationals in the 1980's', in T. Takamiya and K. Thurley (eds) *Japan's Emerging Multinationals: An International Comparison of Policies and Practices*, Tokyo: University of Tokyo Press, pp. 229–64.

Komiya, R. (1989) 'Structural and behaviouristic characteristics of the Japanese Firm', in Ryutaro Komiya (ed.) *Gendai Chugoku Keizai: Nicchu no Hikaku Kosatsu*, (*The Contemporary Chinese Economy: A Comparative Study of China and Japan*), Tokyo: University of Tokyo Press, pp. 97–145.

Kono, T. (1984–5) 'An excerpt from strategy and structure of Japanese enterprises', *Japanese Economic Studies*, XIII (1–2), Fall–Winter: 3–195.

Kraar, L. (1975) 'The Japanese are coming-with their own style of management', *Fortune*, March: 116–64.

Kujawa, D. (1983) 'Technology strategy and industrial relations: case studies of Japanese multinationals in the United States', *Journal of International Business Studies*, 14 (3), Winter: 9–21.

Kujawa, D. (1986) *Japanese Multinationals in the United States: Case Studies*, New York: Praeger.

Lin, V. (1984) 'Productivity first: Japanese management methods in Singapore', *Bulletin of Concerned Asian Scholars*, 16 (4), October–December: 12–25.

Morris, J. (1988) *The Who, Why and Where of Japanese Manufacturing Investment in the U.K*, Cardiff : Cardiff Business School.

Nakatani, I. (1982) *The Role of Intermarket Keiretsu Groups in Japan*, Japan Pacific Economic Papers 97, Australian National University, Canberra, Australia.

Negandhi, A., Eshigi, G. and Yueu, E. (1985) 'The management practices of Japanese subsidiaries overseas', *California Management Review*, XXVII (4), Summer: 93–105.

Newell, W. (1984) 'Japanese factories in Australia: is there a Japanese style of management in Australia?', in Alan Rix and Ross Mouer (eds) *Japan's Impact on the World*, Japanese Studies Association of Australia, Brisbane: Griffith University, pp. 239–246.

Oliver, N. and Wilkinson, B. (1988) *The Japanization of British Industry*, London: Basil Blackwell.

Ouchi, W. (1982) *Theory Z: How American Business Can Meet the Japanese Challenge*, New York: Avon Books.

Ozawa, T. (1979) *Multinationalism Japanese-style: The Political Economy of Outward Dependency*, Princeton, NJ: Princeton University Press.

Paci, M. (1981) 'Class structure in Italian society', in D. Pinto (ed.) *Contemporary Italian Sociology*, London: Cambridge University Press.

Pang, K. and Oliver, N. (1988) 'Personnel strategy in eleven Japanese manufacturing companies in the UK', *Personnel Review*, 7 (3): 1–21.

Park, S.J., Gunther, D. and Osten, B. (1990) 'The second enquete on the practice of Japanese management in West Germany', Paper presented to the *Symposium on Perspective for Asian and European Enterprises in the 90's: Co-operation or Competition?*, Japan–German Center, Berlin. Euro-Asia Management Studies Association, Berlin, 17 December.

Pascale, R. and Athos, A. (1981) *The Art of Japanese Management: Applications for American Executives*, New York: Simon and Schuster.

Putti, J. and Chong, T. (1986) 'Human resource management practices of Japanese organizations', *Singapore Management Review*, 8 (2), July: 11–19.

Saso, M. (1990) *Women in the Japanese Workplace*, London: Hilary Shipman.

Sato, K. (1981) 'Can Japan export Japanese-style management?', Editor's introduction, *Japanese Economic Studies*, X (1), Fall: III–X.

Sethi, P., Namiki, N. and Swanson, C. (1984) *The False Promise of the Japanese Miracle: Illusions and Reality of the Japanese Management System*, Marshfield, MA: Pitman Publishing.

Shibagaki, K., Trevor, M. and Abo, T. (1989) *Japanese and European Management*, Tokyo: University of Tokyo Press.

Shinohara, M. (1982) *Industrial Growth, Trade and Dynamic Patterns in the Japanese Economy*, Tokyo: University of Tokyo Press.

Suzuki, N. (1984) 'Japanese-style management and its transferability', *Japanese Economic Studies*, XII (3), Spring: 64–79.

Taira, K. (1980) 'Colonialism in foreign subsidiaries: lessons from Japanese investment in Thailand', *Asian Survey*, XX (4), April: 373–98.

Takamiya, S. and Thurley, K. (eds) (1985) *Japan's Emerging Multinationals: An International Comparison of Policies and Practices*, Tokyo: University of Tokyo Press.

Thurley, K. (1983) 'How transferable is the Japanese industrial relations system? Some implications of a study of industrial relations and personnel policies of Japanese firms in Western Europe', *Proceedings of the Sixth World Congress of the International Industrial Relations Association*, Kyoto, Japan, 28–31 March: 117–31.

Tsuda, M. (1979) 'Japanese-style management: principle and system', *Japanese Economic Studies*, VII (4), Summer: 3–32.

Tsurumi, Y. (1989) 'Japan's challenge to the U.S. industrial policies and corporate strategies', in Jagdish Sheth and Golpira Eshghi (eds) *Global Strategic Management Perspectives*, Cincinnati, OH: South-Western Publishing, pp. 140–53.

Uekusa, M. (1987) 'Industrial organisation. The 1970's to the present', in K. Yamamura and Y. Yasuba, (eds) *The Political Economy of Japan*, vol. 1, Stanford: Stanford University Press, pp. 469–515.

Watanabe, N. (1989) 'Nikkei Jidosha Kigyo no Kaigai Shinshutsu to Ibunka kan Shokumu Kunren' ('Overseas operations of Japanese automobile companies and cross-cultural job training'), *Organizational Science*, 23 (2), November: 59–70.

Weiermair, K. (1990) 'On the transferability of management systems: the case of Japan', in P. Buckley, and J. Clegg (eds) *Multinational Enterprises in Less Developed Countries*, London: Macmillan, pp. 56–76.

White, M. and Trevor, M. (1983) *Under Japanese Management: The Experience of British Workers*, London: Heinemann Educational.

Whitehill, A. (1991) *Japanese Management: Tradition and Transition*, London: Routledge.

Wickens, P. (1987) *The Road to Nissan: Flexibility, Quality, Teamwork*, London: Macmillan.

Wilkinson, B., Morris, J. and Oliver, N. (1989) 'Japanizing the world: the case of Toyota', Paper presented to the *Asia Pacific Research in Organisational Studies Conference*, Australian National University, Canberra, Australia, 13–15 December.

Yamada, M. (1981) 'Japanese-style management in America: merits and difficulties', *Japanese Economic Studies*, X (1), Fall: 1–30.

Yoshino, M. (1976) *Japan's Multinational Enterprises*, Cambridge, MA: Harvard University Press.

Yu, C. and Wilkinson, B. (1989) *Pay and Appraisal in Japanese Companies in Britain*, Japanese Management Research Unit, Working Paper No. 8, Cardiff Business School.

Chapter 13

The challenges of globalization
The strategic role of local managers in Japanese-owned US subsidiaries

Vladimir Pucik

ABSTRACT

The current recession has underscored poor performance of many Japanese multinationals. It has been argued that one of the reasons may be the inadequate integration of local managers into the global management infrastructure of Japanese firms.

This study is based on a survey of top local executives in 32 Japanese affiliates in the USA. The study deals with three core questions related to the globalization of management: To what extent does the globalization of decision making influence performance of Japanese subsidiaries overseas? What is the linkage between involvement in decision making by local managers and subsidiary performance? And finally, what are the perceived benefits of genuine globalization?

The results show that high globalization of business activities is strongly correlated with the achievement of most performance objectives, but is negatively associated with most measures of job satisfaction. Key performance measures are also strongly associated with an increased input from local executives. Subsidiaries where local executives perceived a smaller globalization gap performed significantly better. There is no doubt that the severity of global competition will force Japanese multinationals to rethink their policies with respect to local management. They have no choice if they want to survive.

INTRODUCTION

After spending billions of dollars moving manufacturing plants to all corners of the world, and endowing numerous programmes in Japanology in the world's best institutions of learning, Japanese companies have just uncovered a disconcerting truth: their competitors do not love them.

Winning in global competition and being popular are clearly two different things.

Reacting to this sudden realization, some well-known Japanese industrialists, and in particular the Sony chairman, Akio Morita, called for a re-examination of the competitive strategies of Japanese firms. Morita argued that if the Japanese changed the way they compete in the global markets by putting less emphasis on growth and more emphasis on profits, not only would they be able to win the respect and affection of their competitors, but Japanese employees and shareholders would be better off (Morita 1992). The notion of 'harmonization' (*kyosei*) seems to replace 'internationalization' (*kokusai-ka*) as the new guiding light of corporate Japan.

In his specific recommendations, Mr Morita called for a reduction of working hours while raising both salaries and dividends, all of this funded from increased profit margins. These could be secured if the current market-share-driven business strategies were to be discarded in favour of strategies focused on product profitability. This should allow Japanese firms to pay higher salaries to their employees as well as give more attention and yen to community and environmental needs.

All these goals are commendable from the viewpoint of key corporate stakeholders, but the world's consumers would have to be willing to bear the costs in terms of higher prices for Japanese products. In a free market economy, this is unlikely to happen. In fact, fatter profits may come only through a further increase in the competitiveness of Japanese firms, thus leading to even sharper conflicts with firms in the host countries.

However, the merit of Morita's proposals is not an issue here, as the starting point of the debate should be the diagnosis of the underlying problem, not just a review of the proposed solutions. In this sense, the premise of this chapter is opposite to that of Morita; the strategic challenge to Japanese multinationals overseas is not that they are 'too competitive' *vis-à-vis* their local rivals, their problem is that they are not competitive enough.

In our view, the profit handicap of many Japanese multinationals is not caused by a misdirected management strategy emphasizing market share growth over profits, as argued by Morita and others. Rather, the low levels of profits may reflect the failure to globalize the corporate management to the degree that it has the capacity and ability to capture the appropriate returns from global operations. For too many Japanese firms the slogan 'think globally, act locally' is not a statement of corporate strategy, but a reflection of the current division of labour: the Japanese do the thinking, while the acting is left to the locals.

Resistance to the increasing Japanese presence overseas is driven by similar shortcomings of corporate management, namely the failure to integrate the local management into the global framework, thus providing the 'transplants' with at least some degree of immunity against resentment and rejection as, for example, the US firms were able to do in Europe since the era of 'the American challenge'. Not surprisingly, the resistance to the Japanese is again strongest in Europe, and it was upon return from Europe that Morita wrote his now famous essay. However, both sets of factors that put the Japanese global firms on the defensive have little to do with their drive to compete. Reducing the intensity of competition may therefore not be the appropriate response. To the contrary, the reality of the free-market mechanism is that Japanese multinationals, like firms in every other open economy, would find it difficult to survive without a sharp focus on competition. The vision of a 'kinder, gentler' Toyota, Matsushita or Fanuc is in the long run unrealistic.

Past economic history shows clearly that running away from competition undermines healthy corporate culture, breeds complacency and encourages short-term thinking. The absolute pursuit of cushier margins may perhaps lead to the same kind of competitive decline that many Western firms have been experiencing in the last two decades. It is doubtful, however, that such a competitive decline would make Japanese multinationals any more liked, although certainly they would be less feared.

FAILED GLOBALIZATION

From a broader perspective, Morita's pronouncements can, therefore, be viewed as an implicit admission that Japanese companies failed to globalize their competitive spirit. By and large they were not able to build up strong management teams of local executives who would internalize the concept of global competition. Not only does this sap the vitality of the overseas subsidiaries, but the lack of capability to compete globally will inevitably damage the parent company as well.

The recent deterioration of the competitive position of many Japanese global firms in the North American market put this issue into sharp relief. According to the MITI 1991 survey of Japanese companies with operations overseas and data released by the USA Department of Commerce, Japanese manufacturers experienced a sharp decline in profitability in both their manufacturing and sales operations. The US $1.5 billion surplus of local plants and sales operations in 1988 turned into a loss of US $1.3 billion by 1991, with even larger losses expected in 1992 (Yamada 1992).

While the overall business results may be influenced by external factors such as the recession in the USA, data for individual firms show similar deteriorating tendencies. Typical examples are the $500 million loss incurred in 1991 by Bridgestone in their so-far unsuccessful takeover of Firestone, the $100 million plus write-off by Kubota of a failed high-tech venture capital investment, and the well-known difficulties of Sony and Matsushita and their Japanese competitors in the consumer electronics business (Thorton 1992).

Some observers see examples of failed globalization especially in the area of sales and marketing management (e.g. DeNero 1990). It is being argued that the marketing strategies of Japanese firms often do not sufficiently take into account market differentiation. The poor fine-tuning of products limits the value added created in local operations. Slow and unresponsive decision making in this area is seen as a common weakness of Japanese global firms due to their heavy centralization and the dominance of head-office functional organizations (in most cases, manufacturing or sales).

Slow and centralized decision making is also blamed for a very spotty record in Japanese acquisitions overseas. Attractive deals have to be closed quickly, yet prudent analysis of business conditions inside the target firm is also essential. As Japanese firms are often not able to do this in a timely manner, they have developed a reputation not only for paying too much for their acquisitions, but also for accumulating problems rather than assets. This applies not only to the 'go-go' Japanese real estate companies rushing to the USA during the cheap-money era of the late 1980s, but also to such conservative Japanese firms as Matsushita (acquisition of MCA) and Bridgestone (acquisition of Firestone). It is being asserted repeatedly that these examples of failed globalization are due to the well-known propensity of Japanese firms to rely mainly on their own home-grown managers in directing their overseas investment activities. For example, according to surveys by MITI, less than 50 per cent of executive positions worldwide are filled by local nationals (MITI 1991). In service firms the ratio is even lower – less than 30 per cent are occupied by locals. In contrast, according to the preliminary data compiled by Japan's Labour Ministry, over 80 per cent of such positions are filled by Japanese in Western multinationals in Japan.

However, the challenge of an effective implementation of global competitive strategies goes much beyond the power, the numbers and the country of origin of the expatriate executives. As many US multinational firms have discovered to their dismay, merely replacing expatriates with locals does not solve the fundamental problem facing firms in a global environment: how to reconcile the seemingly conflicting demands of national responsiveness and global integration (Bartlett and Ghoshal 1989; Kobrin 1992).

The challenge of globalization is not in managing the trade-offs among these divergent needs, but in incorporating the conflicting strategic objectives into a new type of global competitive organization (Pucik 1992). Can Japanese firms manage this process? What role should be played by local executives in Japanese overseas affiliates that would optimize their contribution to the competitive strategies of the subsidiaries as well as that of their parent firms?

THE FOCUS OF INQUIRY

This paper reviews three core issues that reflect the globalization challenge confronting Japanese multinational companies today. They all relate to the decision-making roles and responsibilities of locally recruited managers and executives. However, in contrast to most of the traditional writing on Japanese-owned operations overseas, the emphasis of the discussion is not on the 'fairness' or 'good citizenship' of the Japanese firms in terms of their employment practices, but on the linkage of decision-making systems and management practices with company performance.

Such an approach is necessary because, in our view, the clear failure to increase the influence of local executives during the past decade is at least partly due to the fact that empowering local managers was seen by many Japanese firms only as a show of goodwill, rather than a necessity of business. Yet, it may not be possible to challenge this attitude without a better understanding of how organizational practices facing local executives and managers working for the Japanese, as well as their behaviour and attitudes, impact the key performance indicators.

The first issue to consider is the most general: to what extent does the globalization of decision making (i.e. making business decisions on the basis of a tightly co-ordinated global strategy) influence firm performance, such as profitability or market share. Also, what is the impact of global integration on the job satisfaction and morale of local managers? These questions are also addressed more specifically by examining the correlation between global integration in specific business functions (such as manufacturing or finance) and key performance variables.

The second set of issues focuses on the degree of involvement by local managers and executives in corporate decision making and its linkage with the performance of the firm.

This study examines the relationship between managerial involvement in various parts of the decision-making process and the key performance variables, and also analyses managerial preferences for changes in the decision-making mechanism in terms of a more effective globalization.

Finally, the third core area concerns the perceived benefits of genuine globalization. These are highlighted by comparing the current and optimal decision-making patterns in terms of the location of decision-making authority and the nationality of participants, and by linking these comparisons with indicators of subsidiary performance. Again, the two sets of decision-making patterns are analysed, disaggregated by specific functional areas.

The three critical groups of issues facing Japanese multinationals, as they deal with the demands of globalization, are reviewed in the context of a larger study that analysed the management culture and effectiveness of local managers and executives in major Japanese affiliates in the USA (Pucik et al. 1989). The data for this research came from an extensive survey of top-level American managers in 32 major Japanese-owned affiliates supplemented by in-depth interviews with local executives and senior Japanese expatriates.

The firms in the sample were mainly large and 'established' Japanese multinationals. Two-thirds of the firms studied were engaged in manufacturing, the rest were in finance and other services. Most of the firms were among the largest in their lines of business in Japan, including a number of market leaders, and also had extensive overseas business experience, the average presence in the USA being 18 years. However, several firms had already accumulated more than 30 years of US business experience.

A total of 132 questionnaires were distributed by mail to US executives who were at the time of the survey assigned to one of the top three management layers in the local affiliate. Eighty-two questionnaires were returned for a response rate of 61 per cent, which is relatively high for this kind of research. The complete demographic profile of the sample has been described fully elsewhere (Pucik et al. 1989). A further 51 executives were interviewed in person.

In addition, in order to understand better the perspective of the parent firms, a number of interviews were then conducted throughout 1990 and 1991 in the head office of the firms that participated in the survey. In a series of in-depth interviews, home-office executives in charge of 'globalization strategy' were interviewed in the form of a dialogue about the interpretation of results from the original survey.

THE INFLUENCE OF GLOBALIZATION

As proposed by Bartlett and Ghoshal (1989), the trend toward a 'transnational corporation' that balances global efficiency, multinational responsiveness and worldwide learning is the dominant organizational reaction to the forces of globalization. However, it was also proposed that Japanese firms may face a particularly difficult challenge managing the transition from a 'global' efficiency mode of operations to a multi-focal 'transnational mode' (Bartlett and Yoshihara 1989), because of their fundamental weakness in integrating local managers into the global organization.

To shed light on this issue, the degree of integration of specific business functions with the parent company in Japan was examined first, measuring to what extent a company was being managed on a global basis. Predictably, the responses varied by industry, company and function, but in general, the local senior managers reported a moderate but increasing level of business integration and globalization across the board. Their observations were confirmed during interviews with headquarters' staff in Japan.

Business planning and fund procurement were two functions that were most consistently managed from a global perspective. These results parallel an earlier research conducted by MITI (1991) that reported similar conclusions. Among manufacturing firms, a heavy emphasis was also placed on global co-ordination of the parts and components networks, in particular in the field of consumer electronics, where USA-based operations are highly dependent on the linkage to manu-facturing facilities in South-east Asia.

On the other hand, firms in the automobile industry expressed interest in a regional rather than global approach to purchasing co-ordination, capitalizing on the increasing presence of their affiliated suppliers in North America. In most cases, however, the so-called North American headquarters was still a semi-empty corporate shell, lacking power and resources to influence the decision making. Several US executives reporting to such a 'regional centre' expressed the frustration of being continuously outflanked by their Japanese 'subordinates' informally linked to their 'mother plants' in Japan.

Personnel management, management training, distribution and mar-keting were globalized the least. The weak global linkage of management training is particularly striking, given the key role assigned to management development in the process of global integration (Evans 1992). This makes it difficult to implement two key objectives of global human resource strategies: development of a common corporate culture as the 'glue' binding the network of subsidiaries, and career planning for high-potential managers from the local operations. Without a global direction and co-ordination, any such programmes are generally too scattered, unfocused and short-lived.

The weakness of the global 'cultural' glue came out clearly in our interviews with local American executives. Their knowledge of headquarters' strategies, policies, and culture was often minimal, even to the point that many of them could not agree about such basic business facts as their parent firms' sales volume and number of employees. While poor information flow from Japan was clearly an issue (most routine communications from the headquarters still come by fax in Japanese), the lack of concern for the 'big picture' on the part of some of the US managers was indeed striking.

Utilizing the data on globalization of specific business functions, an aggregate 'globalization index' was computed. To no surprise, subsidiaries involved in manufacturing were more integrated on a global basis than affiliates engaged only in distribution or finance. This reflected the well-known reliance of Japanese overseas subsidiaries on the Japanese parent and its manufacturing network for product design and critical components (EPA 1991). No major differences with respect to overall integration were observed within the manufacturing sector, as differences in co-ordination strategies among individual firms seem at this point larger than differences among sectors.

According to the data, the older manufacturing subsidiaries were more closely integrated with the parent firm than newer affiliates. Thus the 'late-globalization' hypothesis, namely that local affiliates will become more 'naturalized' over time (e.g. Kreinin 1989), just as happened with most US subsidiaries in Europe, is not supported. This probably reflects the fact that Japanese manufacturing firms who entered into the USA early are those that can benefit most from global integration and co-ordination.

In fact, some of the youngest Japanese-owned operations reported most autonomy. These were mainly firms recently acquired (however, the sample size is too small to lend itself to a statistical test). Until the onset of the 'bubble crisis', Japanese firms were mainly content to let their new acquisitions run as before, often even without integrating them to their existing US operations. However, because of resource scarcity at home, and some significant management failures in the USA, such a 'hands-off' strategy is now being reconsidered.

The competitive advantage gained from business globalization is

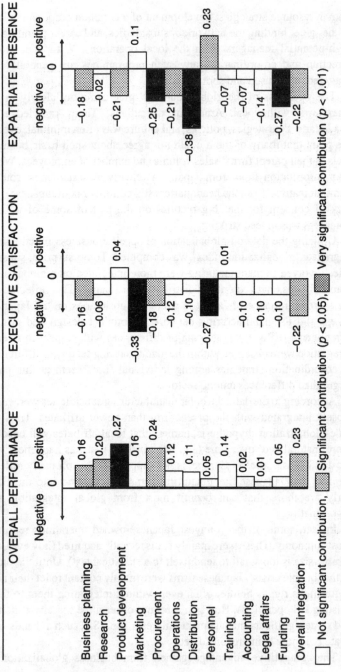

Figure 13.1 Integration, performance and satisfaction: correlation coefficients

clearly reflected in the survey data, as we observed a significant relationship between the degree of globalization (overall integration in Figure 13.1) and the overall performance of the subsidiary.

Also, with respect to specific performance objectives, a high degree of business globalization is, in particular, strongly correlated with market share and speed of new product development. However, no significant relationship between levels of profitability in the subsidiary and the degree of globalization was observed. It may be that, because of transfer pricing and other financial manoeuvres, the true level of profitability is impossible to estimate.

For specific business functions, the strongest positive impact on overall performance comes from the global integration of the product planning, product development, research and parts procurement areas. Other functions show no significant relationship to the level of performance. As expected, a positive relationship between the global integration of marketing strategies and subsidiary performance was observed.

At the same time, while globalization has in general a positive impact on performance, it is also associated with lower employee morale and diminished satisfaction with job autonomy and the managerial role. In particular, the globalization of marketing and personnel policies seems to have the most pronounced negative effect. While these factors may not be directly linked to poor business performance, they may in fact contribute to the conflicts between Japanese and US managers often reported in the business press. In other words, the results can be best described as a 'globalization paradox'. A high overall integration of business activities is strongly correlated with the achievement of most performance objectives, in particular with market share, new product development and conformance with budget. On the other hand, a high globalization is negatively associated with most measures of job satisfaction, such as satisfaction with job autonomy or scope of the managerial role.

The survey data illustrate an additional point that may impact the job satisfaction of local managers and executives: the degree of formal autonomy granted to the subsidiaries does not parallel a decrease in the presence of Japanese expatriates. To the contrary, global business integration and expatriate presence are negatively correlated. The weight of Japanese nationals among the top management team was consistently larger in subsidiaries where local managers reported weaker global integration. Only in the personnel area did the expatriate presence contribute to a tighter linkage with global policies and systems.

A large Japanese staff may indicate a corporate emphasis on 'cultural' control (Pucik and Katz 1986), allowing for more decentralization and less formal co-ordination between the headquarters in Japan and the US subsidiary than in more 'traditional' Japanese firms. In other words, the overseas operations can be integrated into the global network either through formal reporting and planning systems or through informal channels of communication controlled by Japanese expatriates.

The dilemma facing many US executives working for the Japanese is that they don't like the formal 'global' reporting system that, in their opinion, stifles the decision-making autonomy of the local operations, but find it equally hard to accept the extensive Japanese presence in an 'autonomous' subsidiary. However, from the Japanese headquarters' point of view, the policy choice is not so much focused on the role of local executives, but merely on what kind of 'ethnocentric' control would be the most appropriate. Without 'local' managers with a 'global' mind, alternative control systems, such as empowering local managers to represent corporate interests, are not feasible.

INVOLVEMENT IN DECISION MAKING

The generally negative impact of global integration on job satisfaction and morale among local executives can be analysed further by examining the degree of involvement of American executives and managers in making critical business decisions in contrast to the involvement of executives in the Japanese headquarters or Japanese staff dispatched to the USA. Fifteen such decision areas were identified ranging from the formulation of the subsidiary's middle-range plans and the development of new products to decisions concerning sales promotion methods and the compensation of local executives.

Ten different decision-making alternatives (organizational levels differentiated by national origin and location of decision makers) were specified on the survey form: from decisions made solely by senior executives in Japan to those delegated entirely to local managers in the subsidiary. Joint decision-making patterns were also an option. Based on the responses, the ten levels were then combined into six decision-making modes (Figure 13.2).

According to the survey participants, primary responsibility for most business decisions today still rests with Japanese. Out of all decision-making points examined, 47 per cent involved only Japanese staff, including 22 per cent where the decision-making responsibility was located exclusively in Japan. In contrast, American executives

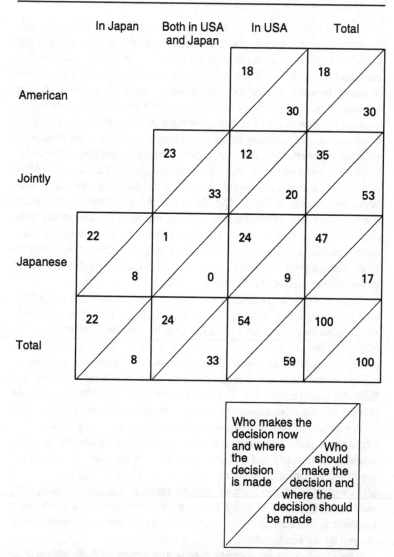

Figure 13.2 Decision location matrix (per cent)

maintained exclusive decision-making prerogatives in only 18 per cent of the cases. When the US managers were involved in headquarters' decision making, it was mostly together with their Japanese colleagues resident in the USA. Even then, local executives were not involved in more than 53 per cent of all decisions.

The functional areas where the local executives were most heavily involved are primarily in the marketing domain, e.g. product pricing, sales and profit targets and sales promotion. This again partly contradicts observations made by DeNero (1989) who attributed the low profitability of many Japanese-owned US operations to insufficient input of local marketing executives into the decision-making process. The survey data indicate that the cause of poor performance may not be the lack of local decision-making authority in the marketing area, but a weak linkage of short-term operational decisions with the strategic direction of the firm.

Interviews confirmed the observations from the survey. Most American executives asserted that strategic planning activities were performed mainly in Japan. The US side supplied schedules, forms and numbers, but was not integrated into the planning process at the head office. Only a few of the local executives that were interviewed had any clear understanding of what the corporate long-term plans and strategies were. Many appeared to have a limited time horizon defined by the length of the current budget cycle in the subsidiary.

Comments from a banking executive – 'I don't know if there is a five-year programme for building a long-term position. They probably have such a plan in Tokyo, but I have not seen it' – reflect a general feeling expressed by many other US managers. Clearly, the long-term focus, presented so often as one of the core values of Japanese management culture, does not assert itself in the overseas subsidiaries – at least not from the local perspective. The lack of input into the strategic planning process was therefore a common source of frustration for local management.

Predictably, local executives and managers are least involved in decisions concerning core research programmes in Japan and the establishment of new subsidiaries, factories and branches. However, the specific decision-making pattern varied not only by firm and function, but often within a firm. Paradoxes were frequent. In a securities firm, only very broad limits were set by Tokyo on risk exposure – a key strategic indicator in this business – but even routine space decisions needed to be cleared by the headquarters.

The actual strategic planning mechanism varies by firm, although in general a typical medium-term plan would be less specific in comparison with business plans most American executives were used to in their previous jobs. While some may view this as an advantage and an opportunity to take the initiative, the lack of specificity was often disturbing: 'Not really being on the inside and not knowing the real direction of the bank, we surrendered planning to Japan,' acknowledged another high-level American banker.

To complicate matters, the involvement of local executives in strategic planning was determined as much by the 'credibility' of individuals as by their formal position in the organizational hierarchy. Credibility with the Japanese was not, however, gained from a well-designed strategy of career development or from long-term appraisals of managerial performance, which most Japanese firms in the USA still lack. It was usually deeply personalized and dependent on a relatively unpredictable combination of 'soft' managerial traits and behaviours and on the sponsorship by influential Japanese.

In the survey, local executives were also asked to indicate where, based on their personal judgement, the individual business decisions should be made (see Figure 13.2). Not surprisingly, they would like to see more decisions delegated to the local management. However, because of the highly competitive environment, they also do not see a far-reaching decentralization as very desirable at this point in time. Joint decision making by transnational teams involving executives and staff at the Japanese parent firm, Japanese expatriates and the local management staff was by far the preferred pattern of decision making.

It should be pointed out that such a 'global' perspective is fairly unique among most local managers of multinational firms. For example, data collected in Japan show that local managers working for Western multinationals strongly believe that a unilateral decentralization of decision-making authority would be most desirable. The headquarters' influence is seen mainly as a negative factor in local performance (Pucik 1991). In contrast, most US managers working for the Japanese see global co-ordination as essential for maintaining the competitive ad- vantage. They just would like to take a greater part in this process.

The key question remains, however, whether the desired increased decision-making involvement of local executives would have a positive impact on the performance of Japanese subsidiaries. While absolute proof of such a 'what if' scenario is, of course, not feasible, it may be possible to estimate the direction of the impact of increased shared decision making by analysing the existing relationship between local management participation in the decision-making process and the subsidiary performance.

This can be done by computing correlations between several key performance measures (level of profits, market share, employee morale and overall performance relative to the industry), as reported by local managers, and the degree of their involvement in the decision making relevant to the specific business areas and functions. The key observations are presented in Figure 13.3.

Performance indicators

Decision areas	Level of profits	Market share	Employee morale	Overall performance
Plan formulation	0.20	0.39	0.32	0.31
New product development	0.26	0.17	0.26	0.18
Changes in design	0.21	0.19	0.15	0.14
Pricing	0.13	0.15	0.19	0.10
Sales promotions	0.03	−0.01	0.23	0.03
Profit margins	0.12	0.14	0.20	0.10
Executive promotions	0.07	0.16	0.21	0.11
Compensation	0.12	0.16	0.06	0.08
Overall involvement	0.11	0.17	0.17	0.11

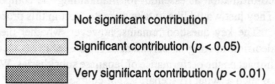

Not significant contribution

Significant contribution ($p < 0.05$)

Very significant contribution ($p < 0.01$)

Figure 13.3 Involvement in decision making and performance: correlation coefficients between performance measures and degree of involvement of local managers in decision making

The data suggest an across-the-board positive contribution derived from a localization of the decision-making authority to most performance measures. As can be expected, among all performance indicators, employee morale is most affected by the degree of involvement in key decision-making areas. However, what is most relevant to concerns expressed by Akio Morita, the profitability measure is strongly associated with an increased input from local executives on issues related to business planning and development of products for the US market.

Market share performance was positively influenced by the involvement of local managers in plan formulation, product design and development, and in decisions about promotions and compensation of local executives. The latter indicates substantial opportunities to improve the alignment of the reward and recognition systems with corporate business objectives. Again, local participation in the marketing domain (sales pricing, margins and sales promotions) did not come out as significant.

The involvement of local executives and managers in corporate strategy planning and new product development is consistently among the strongest indicators of subsidiary performance. In fact, these two variables are the only two impacting the overall performance level. From this perspective, the business logic supporting local participation in strategy formulation seems to be overwhelming.

GLOBALIZATION GAP AND CORPORATE PERFORMANCE

The latent benefits of increased participation by local executives in corporate strategy determination can be further illustrated by comparing the current and perceived optimal decision-making patterns and then correlating these comparisons with indicators of subsidiary performance. In order to do that, a 'globalization gap' index was computed from the two sets of responses regarding the location of decision-making responsibility, as the difference between where the key decisions are made today and where they should be optimally made, according to the survey respondents. The correlation of the 'gap index' with principal performance measures is presented in Figure 13.4.

In the majority of decision-making areas, as well as in the aggregate, the size of the 'globalization gap' was negatively correlated with most performance measures. Subsidiaries where local executives perceived a smaller globalization gap performed significantly better. In seven out of the eight key decision-making areas, the globalization gap had a negative impact on market share; in six out of seven key areas, it had a negative impact on the level of profits and overall performance. Not surprisingly, employee morale was adversely affected by the globalization gap in all decision-making areas.

Product development including design changes and the reward and recognition systems (promotions and compensation) were the two decision-making areas where the globalization gap had the most

Performance indicators

Decision areas	Level of profits	Market share	Employee morale	Overall performance
Plan formulation	–0.14	–0.23	–0.41	–0.21
New product development	–0.25	–0.24	–0.21	–0.25
Changes in design	–0.22	–0.27	–0.21	–0.26
Pricing	–0.21	–0.21	–0.29	–0.21
Sales promotions	–0.07	–0.02	–0.21	–0.05
Profit margins	–0.01	–0.19	–0.20	–0.09
Executive promotions	–0.19	–0.26	–0.32	–0.26
Compensation	–0.36	–0.30	–0.37	–0.36
Overall involvement	–0.24	–0.24	–0.34	–0.24

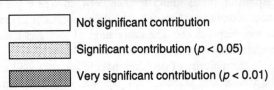

Not significant contribution

Significant contribution ($p < 0.05$)

Very significant contribution ($p < 0.01$)

Figure 13.4 Involvement in decision making and performance: impact of globalization gap on performance: correlation coefficients

consistently negative influence on subsidiary performance. Two of the marketing decision areas, product pricing and margin determination, were also shown as being sensitive to the size of the globalization gap. This may perhaps explain some of the observations listed by DeNero (1990).

While these results further reinforce the earlier findings about the relationship between the involvement of local managers in decision making and corporate performance, some caution in interpreting them is in order. It cannot be ruled out that the responses to the survey may contain a certain bias, as it is likely that the globalization gap is probably most apparent in low-performing firms. Poor business results are often a priori attributed by local executives to a lack of their influence and input into the decision-making process – in this data set, employee morale and globalization gap in plan formulation exhibit the highest correlation.

On the other hand, however, interviews with local executives again and again highlighted the general unhappiness of most American executives with their exclusion from the strategy formulation process. This was often attributed to the Japanese unwillingness to share strategic information because of their (often legitimate) fears that local managers may leave the firm and take the knowledge with them. Thus a vicious circle is created: local managers leave because they object to being excluded from the inner core, which then serves as a justification for the exclusion of their successors.

The formal reporting structure of many US affiliates further complicates the picture. Although many local manufacturing operations are nominally autonomous from product divisions in Japan, this is not always the case in reality. The 'behind the scenes' influence was quite frustrating to many US executives who felt locked out of the critical stages of the planning and decision-making processes. The frustration was often exacerbated by perceptions that many of the Japanese expatriates involved in these negotiations are primarily representatives of a particular factory or division who do not put much value in protecting the interests of the American subsidiary, and sometimes even of the global firm as a whole.

In this respect, many executives both in the USA and in Japan pointed out the critical 'bridging' role of Japanese expatriates. Their willingness and ability to share with local managers information on developments in the head office was an important factor influencing the perception of local executives about their role in the firm. Influential local executives do not resent their Japanese 'shadows', but actively seek out the very best they can get to work with them. 'To be successful here', commented one such local senior executive, 'you need an effective "shadow", someone who can deliver for you, someone who has the respect of the Japanese organization.'

It has often been said that the dominance of Japanese staff in the decision-making process is caused by the relative 'youth' of Japanese multinationals in contrast with their more mature Western counterparts. However, neither the survey data nor the interviews provide much support for this hypothesis. To the contrary, in many firms the frequency of top-down decision making dominated by the Japanese was reported to have increased, rather than decreased, over time. A changing role of the Japanese expatriate staff was often the issue.

An American executive remarked in a candid interview:

> In the past three years, there has been a major change in the approach to the American market by Japanese firms in my business. Previously, American management was in the forefront and was strongly involved in establishing goals, strategy and tactics. The Japanese operated as controllers, auditors and communicators between the Japanese HQ and the US subsidiary. Today, Japanese managers – the new breed – believe that they are smarter than Americans and can be in 'line' positions.

According to observations made by the headquarters staff in Japan, the shift in the mode of control was mainly due to the increased strategic value of the local investment. The term 'globalization' to this Japanese firm, as well as to many other firms with a similar philosophy of overseas expansion, means mainly an ability to manage globally with a core Japanese management staff. When globalization implies getting by without the locals, it is no surprise that there is no love lost.

IMPLICATIONS FOR THE FUTURE

The data from the survey and the interviews show that market share continues to be an important strategic objective of Japanese subsidiaries. At least in manufacturing, market share in conjunction with continuous cost reduction programmes is expected to translate into increased margins and profits. High margins without the benefit of market share protection are seen as vulnerable to attacks from determined competitors. This business logic served Japanese firms well in the past, and the current rhetoric on 'kyosei' notwithstanding, it is doubtful that they can shift gears in the near future.

However, as pointed out earlier, the pressures for higher profits are real and are not likely to diminish in future. It is doubtful that Japanese overseas subsidiaries, and in particular those in the USA, can cope with the harsh environment without making sure that their local managers and executives become true partners in the global decision making. As shown repeatedly in the analysis presented here, this is not a matter of 'good citizenship'. Empowering local management is, first of all, 'good business', essential for success in a global competition.

In addition, without opportunities for meaningful local input into corporate-level decision making, Japanese firms will not even be able to retain for long the management talent they desperately need. No one is immune from competition for capable people, as was recently demonstrated by the defection of the top local executives at Honda, a company aspiring to become the first true Japanese 'transnational'.

However, more is involved in restoring profitability to overseas subsidiaries than just avoiding local executive turnover. Many American managers working for the Japanese see strategies to increase profitability as futile, as subsidiary profits are regularly transferred to Japan. This is not so much an issue of tax avoidance (although at present the US tax authorities are reviewing closely the tax returns of most major Japanese firms), it is more a matter of accepted corporate policy that profits are to be channelled to the home office or home division, often with the blessing of the local tax code. This does not make much difference to the fortunes of the expatriate Japanese, but it has a considerable demotivating effect on the local managerial staff.

In this situation, it is only natural that local executives, when left with a choice, prefer to invest in building the market, rather than concentrating on making the market profitable, or else they simply stop being concerned with profitability at all. When plans come from above, and it is virtually impossible to attain high profitability for a local operation, why try at all? Thus, any serious attempt to increase profitability on a global basis must first deal with restructuring the 'who and where' in terms of decisions on strategic objectives, to be able to draw on resources and capabilities worldwide.

In order to support integrated decision making, the reward and recognition system for local managers and executives will have to be aligned with global objectives. Paradoxically, for Japanese firms to move in this direction, they need first to become more 'Japanese'. They need to learn to manage their local staff with the same care and determination that they show at home. This must start at the entry level, with more efforts dedicated to attracting qualified management candidates. In order to do so, Japanese companies need to offer careers, not just jobs – just like they do in Japan.

Because at least some experience in the parent firm is essential for a successful career with most Japanese companies (just like in any multinational firm), the availability of meaningful career opportunities for local executives at the head office in Japan is the benchmark of a company's commitment to true globalization. To prepare managers to take advantage of these opportunities then requires a substantial increase in investment for training and development. Only then is the full integration of local managers into the global network possible.

There is no doubt that the severity of global competition will force many Japanese multinationals to rethink their policies with respect to local management, in particular in the developed economies of the USA and Europe. They have no choice if they want to survive. However, this will not happen automatically as companies mature, but only through committed effort, continuous experimentation and trial and error.

The strength of excellent global companies is in their ability to capitalize on internal diversity. It is this diversity that promotes the flexibility and innovation needed to compete globally. Developing people who can manage effectively in a heterogeneous environment is not easy, and to maintain a steady course toward real globalization will be the ultimate test of corporate leadership. This is what the top Japanese industrialists should be concerned about.

REFERENCES

Bartlett, C.A. and Ghoshal, S. (1989) *Managing Across Borders*, Cambridge, MA: Harvard Business School Press.

Bartlett, C.A. and Yoshihara, H. (1988) 'New challenges for Japanese multinationals', *Human Resource Management*, 27 (1): 19–43.

DeNero, H. (1990) 'Creating the "hyphenated" corporation', *The McKinsey Quarterly*, 4: 153–74.

EPA (Economic Planning Agency) (1991) *Keizai Hakusho* (White paper on the Japanese economy), Tokyo: Okura-sho.

Evans, P. (1992) 'Management development as glue technology', *Human Resource Planning*, 15 (1): 85–106.

Kobrin, S.J. (1992) 'Multinational strategy and international human resource management policy', Working Paper, The Wharton School, University of Pennsylvania.

Kreinin, M.P. (1989) 'How closed is Japan's market? Additional evidence', *The World Economy*, 11 (4): 42–52.

MITI (Ministry of International Trade and Industry) (1991) *Kaigai Jigyo Katsudo Doko Chosa no Gaiyo* (*The Survey on Activities of Japanese Overseas Subsidiaries*), Tokyo: Okura-sho.

Morita, A. (1992) 'Nihon-gata Keiei ga Abunai'('Crisis of Japanese corporate management'), *Bungei Shunju*, 2.

Pucik, V. (1991) 'Japanese managers, foreign bosses', *Journal of Japanese Trade and Industry*, 1: 43–5.

Pucik, V. (1992) 'Globalization and human resource management', in V. Pucik, N.M. Tichy and C.K. Barnett (eds) *Globalizing Management*, New York: Wiley, pp. 61–81.

Pucik, V., Hanada, M. and Fifield, G. (1989) *Management Culture and the Effectiveness of Local Executives in Japanese-owned U.S. Corporations*, New York: Egon Zehnder International.

Pucik, V. and Katz,J.H. (1986) 'Information, control and human resource management in multinational firms', *Human Resource Management*, 25 (1): 121–32.

Thorton, E. (1992) 'How Japan got burned in the U.S.A.', *Fortune*, 15 June: 114–16.

Yamada, M. (1992) 'Survive, relocate or withdraw', *Tokyo Business Today*, 60 (6): 18–21.

Chapter 14

Compensation system and practice at a Japanese owned and managed sales subsidiary in the USA

Noriya Sumihara

ABSTRACT

This paper examines the salary and bonus systems of a Japanese company operating in the USA and the interactions of Japanese and American co-workers. The data are based upon my 13 months' participant observation and interviews from 1988 to 1989 in a suburb of New York City.

In analysing Japanese corporations operating in the Western world, some analysts propose a 'duality' in organization: the Japanese and the host cultures exist side by side in conflict within an organization, without either side yielding to the other. I suggest, however, that the cross-cultural interaction significantly influences each group, and thereby modifies the original management model. This modified aspect of management practices can be seen as a 'third culture'. While the idea of a 'third culture' comes from Anthony King, my major theoretical approach is based upon Anthony Giddens's theory of 'structuration'. Although Giddens assumed a monoculture setting, I have applied his theory to a bicultural society.

INTRODUCTION

Japanese multinationals operate in societies and cultures where national traditions of business and commercial laws differ from their home country. Moreover, they must hire workers with different cultural backgrounds to work for them. A major question is how they manage to remain Japanese in their management practices while operating in such a different business environment. Some analysts, especially Kidahashi (1987), say the answer is 'dual organization': the Japanese and the host cultures always exist side by side within an organization, without either side yielding to the other, and the result is conflict or mutual distrust between the Japanese and American employees. It may be, however, that the result of the day-to-day cross-cultural encounter is not that simple. This study shows how an aspect of Japanese management, the system and practices of compensation, is dynamically formed by a variety of interrelated factors: cultural and practical factors, interaction between Japanese and Americans' knowledge about salary and bonus and even an aspect of 'racial' consciousness. As a result of the dynamism, a 'third culture' develops within the bicultural workplace which does not duplicate either the original Japanese practices or those of the host society. This notion is borrowed from Anthony King, who argues that 'the important factor . . . is that the product of cultural contact is not simply "a combination of institutional elements from those cultures" but a completely new cultural phenomenon . . .' (1976: 58).

Drawing on Giddens's (1979) theory of structuration, it is assumed that the Japanese management of the Japanese multinational is produced and reproduced in social interactions within the company. By structuration, Giddens means the conditions governing the continuity or transformation of structures, and therefore the reproduction of systems. 'To study the structuration of a social system', he says, 'is to study the ways in which that system, via the application of generative rules and resources, and in the context of unintended outcomes, is produced and reproduced in interaction' (1979: 66). Our data suggest that Japanese management is, indeed, produced and reproduced through interaction.

This study focuses on the compensation system and practice of the New York sales subsidiary of a large Japanese multinational corporation. The data are based upon 13 months' participant observation and interview research during 1988 and 1989. By compensation is meant the totality of salary, bonus and benefits programme, but due to space limitation, discussion of the benefits programme is omitted. The basic assumptions are (a) personnel management is localized or Americanized, but (b) although much of the compensation system has been Americanized as formal rules, in actual practice the rules are not always operated in an American way.

THE SALARY SYSTEM

Salary is paid bi-weekly. Many years ago the subsidiary surveyed many American companies to find out how frequently they should pay salary. According to the survey, the majority of companies paid bi-weekly, so the subsidiary followed suit. The monetary salary that each worker receives every other week is called base salary. The base salary is determined by (a) the worker's grade level, (b) performance and (c) job. It is important to note that length of service, widely known as *nenko* in Japan, is not one of the elements.

The subsidiary has a grade system starting from 1 as the lowest level to 33, the highest. Every regular worker including the president is assigned a grade number as well as a job title, such as sales representative, assistant manager, manager, deputy general manager and so forth. The grade number directly corresponds to pay. Within each grade number, there are four different levels of pay, known as *quartiles*. As a worker goes from a low quartile to a higher one within the same grade number, he gets paid more; this is a *merit increase*. However, if he goes from one grade number to a higher one, he gets a *promotion*.

Second, each worker's performance is reviewed once a year and, based on this, the general manager of the division determines the percentage of salary hike for each worker. The percentage is also affected by the company's general performance. Third, the salary also reflects the nature of the worker's job. A worker with financial responsibility is slightly better paid than one with personnel responsibility at the same grade level, because salaries in the field of finance are higher in the USA. Therefore, the correspondence between actual pay and grade number is different between divisions according to market salary levels. However, the most important difference from a typical Japanese pay system is that *nenko*, the length of service, is not an integral part of the base pay of the subsidiary. In short, as American employees of the subsidiary notice, the pay system is American in style.

Of great significance concerning the company's definition of base pay in each division, however, is that the labour price line the subsidiary actually uses is slightly higher than the market levels provided by a consultant firm. This is partly because, according to a high-ranking Japanese manager, the company wants to attract able Americans by competitive pay. More important, he said that the company, as a 'Japanese-owned' company, had to compensate for a *jinshu jo no mondai*, a racial issue, by means of good pay. Many Japanese in the company were, to varying degrees, conscious of *hakujin shijo shugi*, attitudes of white superiority, which the Japanese believe is shared by white Americans.

The Japanese still firmly believe that in the West white superiority over non-whites is a dominant feeling, and that the Japanese have been discriminated against in the USA because they are not part of the Western world. The Japanese workers know that Japanese immigrants were openly discriminated against in the past, culminating in the forced relocation of Japanese-Americans during the Second World War by the

American government. The Japanese employees also feel that the Second World War experience symbolized by Pearl Harbor still lingers in the minds of Americans, and that the war memory provides Americans with an excuse for hating the Japanese.

At one lunch time in the company dining room, a Japanese employee of the company was overheard speaking to Japanese co-workers about a newspaper article he had recently read in which a non-Japanese Asian, whose nationality the Japanese have long been prejudiced against, built a factory near Tokyo and employed many local Japanese. The Japanese employee said that perhaps his company's Americans felt the same as the Japanese employees of the factory in Japan felt. This was interpreted to mean the feeling of working for those who are racially lower ranked.

On the other hand, the Japanese employees of the subsidiary in America also feel superior to many individual white American workers, including the subsidiary's local employees whom they define as *niryu* (second class) or *sanryu* (third class) workers based upon their observation. In short, the Japanese of the subsidiary do not respect individual whites, while feeling powerless against a 'dominant prejudice' that they believe Americans generally have.

The 'inflated' labour price line is thus at least in part a reflection of the Japanese perception of the 'dominant' feeling, as the Japanese understand it, that white Americans have about the Japanese. American employees of the subsidiary in both non-managerial and managerial posts say that base pay is competitive with or higher than the market. One American junior manager honestly said that every once in a while employment agencies, known as *head hunters*, called him to offer a job opportunity, but so far none of them had offered a better base salary for a similar responsibility than he currently received from the company. Thus, the competitive pay helps to retain workers.

THE CHRISTMAS BONUS SCHEME

As of the summer of 1989, the company had two kinds of bonus programmes. One, the Christmas bonus cheque, is issued to all American employees with non-sales responsibilities, such as administrative and clerical workers. The other is an incentive bonus, or commission, for people with sales responsibilities. All the Japanese staff are excluded from both bonus programmes, because their bonuses, not discussed here, come from the parent company.

To American employees of the company, the Christmas bonus cheque is 'strange' because it is given to everybody regardless of rank or of the business condition of the company for the past year. It also has very little to do with individual performance, but is primarily related to seniority and the length of each worker's service, *nenko*. An employee with less than one-year seniority receives between $200 and $400, depending upon the length of service and the level of rank. A worker with one to two years of service at any rank gets about 60 per cent of his two-week pay, a person with two to three years of service gets about 80 per cent and a person with three years and above of service receives almost the full equivalent of his two-week pay.

Theoretically, a high performer gets a higher Christmas bonus than a lower performer of the same rank and length of service. However, Japanese managers are reluctant to make big differences between high and low performers in terms of the bonus. As a consequence, the bonus programme barely reflects differences in performance. (The American employees regard this as 'unfair' egalitarianism. This is too big an issue to discuss in detail here. For details, see Sumihara 1992.)

Another important point is that the bonus programme lacks the idea of short-term profit sharing, with which American employees tend to associate such a programme. That is, in a good business year, a company ought to share the profits with its employees, whereas in a bad year, the company has no responsibility to do so. To Americans, it is natural for company business to fluctuate year by year.

By contrast, the subsidiary, based upon its long-term stabilized growth plan, also aims to secure the stable growth of each employee's annual income. The Christmas bonus programme seems to follow this basic guideline. At the end of 1988, there was no dramatic increase in the bonus, despite a highly successful year for the company. When some American employees expressed complaints, a high ranking Japanese explained by saying,

> You may be feeling you are not getting enough bonus this year, but even in bad years, the company gave bonus constantly . . . In this way, the company tries to guarantee the living of each employee, regardless of fluctuating national and world economy.

The Japanese manager said this was based on the belief that the management ought also to be responsible for each employee's personal life. Another Japanese senior manager said, 'Parents do not give children all they have. They have to look after children by saving for a rainy day.'

The parent–child metaphor may have appeal in Japan because of the 'lifetime employment' principle and also the fringe benefits programmes provided for all employees and their families. Seen from a wider viewpoint, the parent–child metaphor may have deeper ramifications. By keeping control of income sharing, the company seeks to achieve the goal of long-term steady growth. If the company proves reliable to stockholders and financial organizations by showing its steady growth, it becomes easier to get financial support, which in turn helps the company to grow steadily. In this way the company guarantees the steady growth of each employee's income, and much more easily secures his job. Thus, the company's planned control of income sharing is both a cause and a result of this relationship between the company, the financial organizations and the company's employees.

The management of the sales subsidiary seems to try to follow the example of the parent company, but its environmental conditions are far from being the same. Above all the most crucial difference is that in the USA, none of the American employees intend to stay with the company 'permanently'. To many of them, the company is no more than a 'current' employer, even if they are not 'job hoppers'. Whenever there is a better job opportunity, they are ready to quit. To them, their private life is their own business, having nothing to do with the employer. They want to control their own income, and they do not feel grateful to the company even if it is saving for 'a rainy day'. They know that the company's long-term income-sharing plan may benefit everybody in the long run, but only if everybody stays with the company 'permanently'. Some American employees said that the company's long-term plan may appeal to some 'conservative' or 'mediocre' Americans who have no desire to seek better jobs. They also said that to them, a short-term income-sharing plan based upon performance was more appealing. Thus, the Christmas bonus cheque reflects the Japanese, but not the American, assumption about a bonus.

MANAGER'S BONUS

However, the subsidiary's bonus programme for administrative division employees has undergone some change benefiting the American setting. Up to 1990, there was no incentive bonus programme for managers with non-sales responsibilities. A new bonus programme was introduced in the fall of 1990, aimed at all levels of managers with non-sales responsibilities throughout the company. This is one example of American influence on the Japanese management of the company. We will see below, first, how and why the new programme came into being, and then we will review its content and implication.

According to an American personnel manager in charge of the new bonus programme, the historical development of the company spurred the management to offer a new bonus programme:

in the past, the company has evolved from a trading company where you had many senior levels of expatriates from Japan, and many lower levels of Americans. So, you didn't need to attract or retain high powered or aggressive Americans. Whereas, today, more and more we're hiring highly competent executives and asking them to join our company . . . We looked at other plans that are very prominent in the USA, plans such as stock options, supplemental retirement plans, supplemental life insurance, company cars, and other types of perks. The management incentive program is the number one priority right now.

The new programme thus had two purposes, to attract able administrative executives from outside and to retain high-powered managers in the company.

In addition to the increasing necessity, the personnel manager stressed the merits of the programme in terms of personnel cost:

Many companies are very concerned with their fixed or permanent costs. For instance, if I receive a 5 per cent salary raise, that raise is with me for the rest of my career in the company. Whereas, a bonus of 10 per cent is only paid one time and may not be paid again next year.

He also said that the company's current payroll, as of 1990, was $55 million of which $50 million was fixed cost and only $5 million, including the bonus, was variable. By contrast, according to the same American manager, a certain Japanese company operating in the USA in a similar industry has an annual $100 million payroll of which $60 million was base payroll and the rest incentive bonus. The American manager said, 'Theoretically, in case of a bad business year, they can shrink payroll by 40 million dollars, whereas our company has very little flexibility.'

The company's newly introduced incentive bonus programme is applied only to those in managerial positions who will no longer receive the Christmas cheque, whether or not they get an incentive bonus. Non-managerial American employees would continue to get only a Christmas bonus cheque. However, in early 1992, there was a high possibility that the new incentive bonus programme would be extended to the non-managerial employees in the near future.

The new bonus programme is tied to corporate and divisional results. If the business of the company as a whole or within a division is very bad in a certain year, the company may not give bonuses to the executives.

This is a big difference from the old programme, but an even bigger difference is that the new programme is intended to be linked to 'management by objective', i.e. each individual executive's performance.

The procedure of the programme is that before a bonus period begins, 'an MBO (management by objective) evaluation form' for each administrative manager is completed. The form is to contain three or four concrete goals for the coming six months, because the company has a bi-annual fiscal period, known as *kami* and *shimo*, upper and lower. The goals, which are called 'hurdles' by American employees, are decided upon between each manager and his supervisor. A committee has been established to review and approve each form sheet before each period begins. The committee coaches and counsels supervisors on how to improve goal descriptions, and also checks whether a goal is too low and whether it is quantifiable or not. The committee is also careful to see that each goal is in harmony with overall divisional or company goals.

After the goals of each manager are set up, the value of each goal is 'weighted' by the supervisor. A relatively easy goal is of low weight. The total of the weighted scale is 100.

Towards the end of a bonus period, i.e. every six months, the supervisor 'rates' the achievement of each goal. The rating scale is from 1 to 5, lowest to the highest, and the final score is decided by a simple calculation, the rating times the weight. Each middle level manager from grade 18 to 22 is eligible for 0–15 per cent of his annual salary. Each senior manager of grade 23 and above is eligible for 0–22.5 per cent of his annual salary (see Sumihara (1992: 153–6) for a detailed account of how bonus is calculated).

SALES INCENTIVE BONUS

In the sales divisions of the subsidiary, the incentive bonus is also known as commission. The recipients of the bonus are necessarily American sales people, and no American administrators of sales divisions are beneficiaries.

According to the company's sales commission programme, the maximum commission rate is 34 per cent of a recipient's annual salary. At most sales divisions, each sales person receives an average of 20–30 per cent of his or her annual salary. At one division, the average rate is less than 20 per cent. The bonus is given every six months in accordance with the company's *kami–shimo*, upper–lower, fiscal periods.

At most sales divisions, the breakdown of a sales person's total yearly income is from 85 per cent as base salary and 15 per cent as bonus at the lowest, to 75 per cent as base salary and 25 per cent as bonus at the highest. To some American sales people, the company's commission rate is very low when compared with other American companies in the same industry.

One Japanese manager said that the American way of giving exceedingly high commissions was not '*rinriteki ni*', ethically, acceptable to him, since that would end up driving a sales person to work just for money, which is itself unethical because, he said, the person's greediness for money is openly expressed. In general the Japanese hesitate to associate work directly with money, even though they take it for granted that basically they are working for their living.

Besides 'ethical' reasons, there seem to be practical reasons why the company management keeps the commission rate relatively low. The company is merely a subsidiary of the parent company. Most products come from Japan, and although the subsidiary has some local plants in the USA, these are under the direct control of the parent company. For the parent company, the USA is only one of its worldwide markets, although not a minor one. Therefore, it would not be easy for the manufacturing section of the parent company to meet only the US demand, if the American sales people took orders excessively. Slow but steady growth of demand is desirable for the parent company. A high commission rate is more likely to undermine a good balance of production and sales.

According to a senior Japanese manager of a sales division, American sales people tend to rush to get orders by offering the product at very low prices to their customers so as to achieve high sales quickly. This may be beneficial to the sales people as individuals, but the company would have to meet the orders at a low level of profit. The parent company also has a strong commitment to the 'lifetime employment' of its blue-collar workers, and so the management does not let fluctuations of orders cause lay-offs and re-employment of the workers.

The management of the company, by keeping the commission rate low, seeks to control the sales people's pursuit of individual achievement. Moreover, the way in which the commission rate is determined also helps achieve that aim. In determining the commission rate, three factors are taken into consideration, (a) the division's budget, (b) the division's profit growth, and (c) MBO, or the individual sales person's quota. These three areas are almost equally weighted, but obviously the first two areas are associated with the division's overall financial situation and performance, and only the last is a direct reflection of an individual's achievement. Thus, it would be safe to say that the division's or the company's stability is given precedence over an individual's short-term reward.

As a result of the conservative nature of the commission programme, an American senior sales manager said explicitly,

[At the company] basic salary tends to be higher than the average US market, but the incentive is very small. So, a salesman doesn't have to sell a great amount, because he knows, even if he sells a great amount, he won't get a lot of commission. So, good sales people do not come to this company. The current program attracts mediocre sales people who want a safe salary. Actually, we do have good sales people, but they ask, 'Why should we give over 100 per cent, if we don't get any more for it?' If you want a good horse, you put carrots in front of it to keep it going forward. In sales, the same way. If you give a good salesman the opportunity to earn a lot of money, he'll go sell. If you don't put out money for him, he's not gonna work for you. Now, for a fair salesman, if you give him a high salary, he may feel comfortable, but it doesn't make any difference if he sells anything or not, because he is gonna make about the same amount of money.

However, no matter how strongly the American manager proposes that the division should employ a higher bonus plan, at the present stage of the company's position and development, the current commission seems satisfactory to the Japanese management.

CONCLUSION

The base salary of the company was already Americanized when this research started. As for bonus, the *nenko*-based (i.e. based on length of service) Christmas bonus cheque was drastically changed into a performance-based incentive bonus during and after the research. Thus, there was a strong tendency toward Americanization of the compensation system at least in its formal rules. However, close examination revealed that in actual practice, within the framework of the rules, the Japanese management keeps workers' behaviour in line so that the company may promote the long-term employment policy and keep pace with the parent company. That is to say, on the one hand, due to a relatively higher-than-market base salary, American employees find it difficult to find a better paid job. In the incentive bonus programme, on the other hand, sales people are not motivated to sell more than a certain level.

These adjustments were made largely because the subsidiary had to operate in a foreign country while at the same time keeping in close contact with the parent company. However, such practical necessities are not the only reason for the arrangements; at least to some extent, Japanese cultural values, ethics and even their racial consciousness also affect the direction of their policies and action.

Of significance is the fact that as a result of the local adjustments, the practices of the compensation system are not exactly either American or Japanese style, but have generated a 'third culture'.

ACKNOWLEDGEMENT

This research was made possible partly by the sponsorship of the David B. Dreiser Fellowship in Urban Anthropology at New York University. I want to express special thanks to the fellowship programme. Equally special thanks should go to Professor Owen Lynch for having given me plenty of valuable advice during and after the research, although the responsibility for all the content of this paper is mine.

REFERENCES

Giddens, A. (1979) *Central Problems in Social Theory: Action, Structure and Contradiction in Social Analysis*, Berkeley, CA: University of California Press.

Kidahashi, Miwako (1987) 'Dual organization: a study of a Japanese-owned firm in the USA', Ph.D. thesis, Columbia University.

King, A. (1976) *Colonial Urban Development: Culture, Social Power and Environment*, London: Routledge.

Sumihara, N. (1992) 'A case study of structuration in a bicultural work organization: a study in a Japanese-owned and managed corporation in the U.S.A.', Ph.D. thesis, New York University.

Chapter 15

Organizational development in Japanese overseas subsidiaries

Daniel Dirks

ABSTRACT

The rapid internationalization of Japanese companies and their accompanying investments abroad has brought to the forefront the issue of successfully organizing and managing these local subsidiaries. Assuming basic differences in management styles, work attitudes and business perceptions between Japanese expatriates and local staff, it is hypothesized that a focus on both the theory and practice of organizational development will substantially increase our understanding of the success (or failure) of Japanese multinationals abroad. Complex local environments necessitate adequate learning strategies incorporated into a wider concept of 'multinational management'. A framework for future research as well as a practical guidance for practitioners is proposed.

INTRODUCTION

Japanese foreign direct investment (FDI) has undergone some major shifts in the last 15 years, both geographically and strategically. Geographically, Europe – and here, some countries more than others – has profited considerably both from these shifts and from a dramatic rise of investment activity.[1]

Accompanying the internationalization process of Japanese companies, the number of foreign subsidiaries and, naturally, the number of local employees, both 'white-collar' and 'blue-collar', has risen continuously. The latest survey by JETRO (1991b) on the European operations of Japanese companies in the manufacturing sector reports not only a considerable management autonomy for Japanese subsidiaries *vis-à-vis* their parent companies (termed 'localization', p. 3) but also a 'progress in localizing management' (p. 8), whereby almost one-third of the companies surveyed are now headed by European presidents. Locals also comprise about one-third of 'other officers' of these firms. On the workers' side, of course, the employees are mainly locals.

Assuming basic differences in management styles, work attitudes and business perceptions between Japanese expatriates and their local colleagues, we attempt to explore what actually happens after an investment decision has been made and a subsidiary has been established. In other words, we will discuss how, within the same organization, people with different backgrounds, influenced by diverse norms, values and practices as well as their own distinct perspectives and expectations, can profitably relate to each other, co-operate and form what is usually referred to as a 'business unit'.

Hayashi (1988) lists several complaints voiced by local managers of Japanese plants in North America and Asia regarding their relationship with Japanese expatriates. Among them he reports the following:

- goals are not made clear,
- contributions by locals are ignored while all major decisions are made by the Japanese,
- irrespective of position or status, the Japanese employees can and do interfere with local management's decisions and activities,
- Japanese-style life-long employment systems, an atmosphere of being one family, or adequate opportunities for promotion are not discernible,
- Japanese managers do not trust local employees, function in systems of their own and are unable to manage conflicts,
- the underlying logic of the Japanese way of doing things is unintelligible,
- locals are not accepted into the management and consensus-building processes and evaluation methods or compensation and promotion rules are unclear.

It has been pointed out by Yoshihara (1989) that Japanese management culture, with its tendency towards ambiguity and egalitarianism, violates existing privileges of Western managers and, at the same time, leaves them with a feeling of insecurity and ambivalence which is strongly resented by local employees.

If Japanese companies are prone to be confronted by such fundamental obstacles in their affiliates overseas, then the focus of attention, strongly oriented towards how to achieve a 'strategic fit' between an organization's structure and strategy and environmental variables, must instead adopt a broader perspective to incorporate such questions as to how foreign affiliates in general, and Japanese subsidiaries in particular, devise and implement strategies, how they adapt to their environment and, perhaps most important, how they organize themselves. Hence, the basic thesis to be developed here is that

> The success or failure of Japanese companies abroad must be analyzed in terms of their capability for organizational development, and the concept of 'organizational learning' should be placed, both theoretically as well as in practice, at the center of attention.

The discussion is structured into nine subsequent sections, starting with a brief discussion of the relevant theory and its shortcomings in the following section. The third section proposes a perspective which espouses more action- and learning-oriented concepts. As this is basically a consequence of the growing complexity international managers are faced with, the most important dimensions of this complexity will be recalled in the fourth section. A conceptual framework for 'culture' and its role as an important ingredient in managerial relations is introduced in the fifth section, followed in the sixth section by a critical assessment of an 'interface' approach to reconcile or bridge cultural differences.

As an alternative path, a multi-faceted concept of organizational learning is presented in the seventh section and its practical translation into action is reviewed in the eighth section. The first results of this model, which has been tested on a preliminary basis, are presented in the penultimate section. The concluding section proposes an organizational development framework for further research and for practical guidance to international managers.

JAPANESE FOREIGN DIRECT INVESTMENT AND THE THEORY OF INTERNATIONAL PRODUCTION

If the statement by Rugman *et al.* (1985: 7) that 'international production is the essence of multinationality' is true, then Japanese companies are not only late but also rather 'reluctant multinationals' (Trevor 1983; Abo 1989, 1991). The typical Japanese-style production system being difficult to transfer, it seems only 'natural for many Japanese manufacturing firms to be reluctant to produce abroad' (Abo 1991: 2). And, despite the dramatic rise in the number and value of Japanese production sites abroad, there is still some way to go to any fully fledged localization.[2]

The theory of international investment, production and management (IM theory)[3] has made slow progress since Hymer's (1976) seminal work of the 1960s, and it seems fair to state that theory has yet to advance to a point where it can actually explain, let alone predict, why a particular firm should succeed in a foreign environment while other ostensibly similar firms should fail or perform less well.

One reason for this theoretical inadequacy may lie in the fact that the process of internationalization inevitably leads to a growing complexity, confronting management with a new, often distant and rather hetero-geneous environment, major informational shortcomings and, generally, a growing number of strategic options (Pausenberger 1989: 386).The theoretical Hymerian approach, which claims that a foreign company must hold some kind of unique advantage to offset its fundamental disadvantage of being 'foreign' *vis-à-vis* its local competitors and which is based on the 'supremacy of strategic fit – optimally configuring resources to coalign the firm with its environment' (Sullivan and Bauerschmidt 1991: 119), faces major difficulties in adequately addressing this new complexity.

Complex situations as in the case of international management are fundamentally and decisively determined by change. Hence, any theory explaining and critically assessing managerial practice in an international environment must incorporate this element, essentially in a way that analyses how managers deal with change. It is maintained here that this approach will have to test how they learn to adapt to and actively influence change.

Two strands within IM theory have so far attempted to address this notion of change. One has been the learning-curve theory which, however, is essentially a macroeconomic approach within the wider body of the Heckscher–Ohlin–Samuelson model of international trade and production, and thus will not be considered here.

The other, more microeconomic in focus, concentrates on the process of a firm's internationalization, claiming that this process unfolds through distinct stages (Johanson and Mattsson 1986). This seems to imply a process of learning, incorporated in the evolution from one stage to the next. This approach has been challenged mainly for empirical reasons (Turnbull 1987), although neither its proponents nor its challengers have actually considered its potential for dealing with the change element.

Instead, the arguments concentrate on the parent company's involve-ment in the internationalization process rather than telling us anything about the subsidiaries' development. They do concede, however, that the 'success of internationalization in any company depends heavily on the type of people both initiating and carrying through the various steps in the process' (Welch and Luostarinen 1988: 41), and that the 'actual paths [in the process of internationalization] taken are often irregular' and their outcome 'tends to be derived from a mixture of deliberate and emergent strategies' (p. 47).

Hence, notwithstanding the necessity to achieve strategic fit, the practice and reality of international management seems to be much more influenced by learning through action, rather than rational choice. Unless IM theory gains a clearer insight into these processes, a 'comprehensive, satisfying concept of international management, which is still lacking' (Pausenberger 1989: 392), will not be found.

MANAGING THE FOREIGN AFFILIATE

Organizational and management theories have dealt with the problem of managing companies abroad not much different from the way they have perceived managing a firm at home. There has been a continuous search for effective and efficient structures, either irrespective of the given situation (administrative science approach) or situationally adjusted (behavioural or contingency approaches), allowing strategy to perceive of organizational structure as a tool with which to achieve a fit with the organization's environment.

Mintzberg (1990) has pointed out that the corresponding model for the formation of strategy (the 'design school model'), present in most of these theories, rests on some fundamental premises (p. 175ff.):

- that strategy formation is a controlled, conscious process of thought devoid of intuition or evolution ('emergent strategies');
- that responsibility for that control and consciousness must rest with the CEO, who is the strategist;
- that strategies are tailored to a specific situation and build on distinctive competence, emerging from the design process fully formulated;
- that strategies can be implemented through a structure presumed to have no bearing on the new strategy (i.e. 'structure follows strategy').

Rational thought is thus detached from action and learning. Assuming no data loss in the process of analysing past and current phenomena and future scenarios, strategies are conceived, whereby in reality, as Mintzberg further notes, assessed strengths and weaknesses may be unreliable, 'all bound up with aspiration, biases, and hopes', concluding that 'strengths generally turn out to be far narrower than expected and weaknesses, consequently, far broader' (p. 182).

A major difficulty of this approach exists in making a clear-cut distinction between strategy formulation and its implementation. In fact, strategy and structure are interdependent elements of the same unit, the organization. As Mintzberg stresses,

> by overemphasizing strategy, and the ability of the strategist to act rather freely, the design school slights, not just the environment, but also the organization itself. Structure may be malleable, but it cannot be altered at will just because a leader has conceived a new strategy. Many organizations have come to grief over just such a belief.
>
> (p. 183)

Reinventing action as an important aspect of theoretical – and practical – consideration inevitably leads to the role learning plays in the process of strategy formation, its implementation, its reformulation and so on, and – we may add – in the management and organization processes in general. Learning is thus a response to the inadequate reduction of complexity advocated by the design school.

DIMENSIONS OF COMPLEXITY

The contextual complexity an international manager (or group thereof) is faced with makes it highly improbable that information and knowledge can be centrally collected, assessed and translated into a coherent strategy suitable for the situation at hand, without constantly adjusting to the shifting demands of the organization's environment or its intra-organizational reality. Thus, the local environment, the headquarter–subsidiary relationship and the intra-organizational situation at the affiliate may be distinguished for analytical reasons as three dimensions, although in reality, of course, they are interrelated.

Environment

On the one hand, the local environment is assumed to be predominantly 'foreign' and thus largely unknown to the subsidiary. Recalling the reluctance with which Japanese multinationals have proceeded to become what they are today, this foreignness of local environments is not just a matter of information that needs to be explored and extracted. Rather, in the Japanese case, it seems to be difficult to create a willingness and, alongside this, an ability to penetrate the European local communities beyond the steady build-up of market shares, as has over and over again been found, and only recently confirmed (JETRO 1991b: 65f.).

This reluctance to 'localize' has been criticized ever since the advent of Japanese FDI, and any attempt to learn how to become a 'good citizen' will most likely also lead to an improved understanding of local networks, customs and legal traditions.

Headquarter–subsidiary relationships

Welge (1990) has argued that in order for a strategy of global rationalization to succeed, an efficient and productive organizational structure is required. Referring primarily to the vertical relationships between head offices, regional and local affiliates, we may argue that a combination of centralization (the lack of subsidiary autonomy in decision making), formalization (the systematic use of rules and procedures) and integration (decision making based on common values and consensus orientation), defines the ground on which this relationship takes place (Ghoshal and Nohria 1989: 323).

In practice, however, increased environmental complexities, strategic shifts and a constant flux between orientations towards greater independence by the subsidiary versus a need for interdependence among corporate units poses a continuous source of possible conflict.

It thus comes as no surprise that Kumar and Steinmann (1986) have extracted a series of complaints voiced by Japanese expatriates concerning their relationship with head office, in a survey conducted among Japanese affiliates in Germany. Generally speaking, these complaints express the desire for the parent company to acknowledge the particularities of the local environment (p. 505). Although the inquiry featured some inconsistent results, since 65 per cent of those surveyed also said that they felt they had ample scope for own activities (p. 505), Günther and von der Osten (1991) have only recently confirmed in an empirical study of Japanese companies based in Germany that autonomy has not increased since an earlier survey in 1984–5 (p. 49). Thus, as more and more management positions have been filled with local employees, while at the same time the authority for major decisions has been retained within the parent company, we find that the relationship between Japanese parent companies and their local subsidiaries has been relatively stagnant and inflexible, leaving in doubt whether the complexities of the internationalization process have been adequately responded to.

Intra-organizational

Finally, the subsidiary's intra-organizational structure and processes are influenced by the need to manage a growing number of tasks and functions that are being transferred from the headquarters, and by an increase in the number of people employed coming from very diverse cultural backgrounds.

Kumar and Steinmann's survey also concluded that Japanese managers perceived their most important problem to be cultural adaptation, while task-related difficulties were seen as relatively minor (p. 496). This may partly be attributable to the fact that only 43 per cent of those surveyed recalled some kind of preparation prior to being sent abroad (p. 500). Thus, these managers were faced with mainly culturally related difficulties they were not accustomed to. However, since the norms, values, assumptions and perceptions of organizational members are of primary importance to most of what happens in a company, the intricacies and complexities of this intercultural confrontation, and any changes that arise for members out of this encounter, must be analysed, understood and, as a matter of prime practical importance, supported and positively influenced.[4]

Before proceeding to aspects of organizational learning and development that can, it is argued, lead to an increased 'closeness' to the situation by understanding the underlying factors influencing the behaviour of organizational members, a word about 'culture' and its role in this context.

MULTICULTURAL MANAGEMENT – AN EVOLVING CONCEPT

Scrutinizing the elements which make up the managerial process of leading and organizing the international conglomerate, including the overseas affiliates, Fayerweather (1982) notes three systems: the decision-making system, the control system and the communications system (p. 498ff.), all of which are affected and influenced by the fourth factor of the management process, the 'behavioural dynamics' (p. 506). Different cultural spheres, in turn, affect this behaviour: the national culture, the organization's culture and various environmental 'cultures'.

National culture

The behaviour of host nationals *vis-à-vis* their expatriate superiors and peers (usually from the parent company) is 'notably affected by the differences in culture and nationality' (p. 507) and is assumed to bear definite, though sometimes less conspicuous, consequences on managerial action. Furthermore, the 'cultural gap' (p. 439) between these different nationalities is of greater importance than any locational and/or informational gaps between headquarters and their subsidiaries, which may be bridged more easily by the expatriate(s) delegated to assume local managerial responsibility.

The debate on culture has played a prominent role in the business field for quite some time, so there is no need to delve too far into the specifics. Here, it should only be recalled that when we talk about culture and its consequences for management, we are addressing questions and problems arising from the fact that people originating from different cultural backgrounds interact, and that differences in their values, norms, perceptions and attitudes have a bearing, via the multitude of interactions within an organization, on the overall management process.

Hofstede's notion that culture is a 'collective programming of the mind' (1980: 13) leads to the following eight elements that characterize 'culture' (von Keller 1982: 114ff.):

1 culture is man-made
2 culture is a social phenomenon
3 culture is acquired through learning
4 culture is transmitted and expresses itself through symbols
5 culture influences action
6 cultures strive for internal coherence
7 culture is an instrument with which individuals, groups and societies adapt to their environment
8 culture itself possesses adaptive capabilities.

This programming of the mind is generally assumed to occur on a very broad, general level, guiding the individual in terms of fundamental relationships with regard to, for example, other people, nature, time, space or concepts of work.

Organizational culture

At the organizational level, however, culture describes yet another set of phenomena than does the national culture[5] with its emphasis on norms and values. 'Organizational culture' denotes differences in workplace practices, learned through socialization at the workplace (Hofstede *et al.* 1990: 312). Perceived common practices within an organization (or an organizational unit therein) are expressed through symbols, heroes and rituals, each carrying their own specific meaning within that organization or unit.

These practices, rules and standards influence the way information is gathered, perceived and interpreted by the organization and its sub-units.

This, in turn, has an influence on such managerial processes as the formulation of strategies (Schneider 1989) and their implementation, as well as the structuring and development of the internal organization.

As the term 'national culture' has been shown to be too broad to qualify for explaining behaviour in individual organizations, the notion of 'the' organizational culture may yet be too broad. 'There cannot be culture unless there is a group that "owns" it. Culture is embedded in groups, hence the creating group must always be identified' (Schein 1984: 5). Defining a group as a set of people with a shared history, having had the opportunity to commonly face and solve significant problems, we can agree with Schein's assertion that a 'corporation will have multiple cultures within it' (p. 7).

Environmental cultures

If groups can thus be understood as cultures, we may also regard the organization's environment as a cluster of groups, alias cultures. These groups, according to their own specific 'practices', rules etc., and, most important, their different expectations, place demands and claims on the subsidiary's management. Hence, a profound understanding of the environment and its influencing factors will be necessary lest the affiliate be severely limited in its strategic options.

Although environmental groups' goals, aspirations or claims against the foreign subsidiary are usually not dealt with in the debate on culture and its economic implications, these (strategic) considerations should be incorporated in a culturally oriented framework.

Managing a foreign subsidiary can in consequence be understood as a 'multicultural management', sitting at the crossroads between various external and internal cultures, i.e. groups, which function according to their own historically evolved practices, standards and rules (Figure 15.1). The environment and its diverse groupings, the parent company and other members of the conglomerate, as well as the organizational members, influenced by different national and organizational/group cultures, all demand respect and attention which the international, i.e. 'multicultural', manager must recognize and incorporate in his decisions and actions.

AN INTERMEDIATE SOLUTION – THE INTERFACE

It has been argued that any type of division of labour involving people from different cultural backgrounds will have, through the cultural gaps arising in the processes of perception, communication, decision making

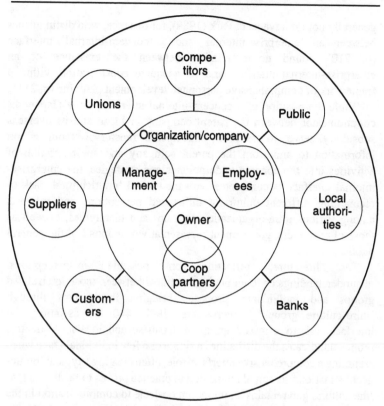

Figure 15.1 Crossroads of multicultural management
Source: Dülfer 1991: 203

etc., an effect on the firm's behaviour and development. We may perceive the intersecting points, where these culturally diverging people and groups meet, as 'interface situations' and the immediate actors involved as 'interfaces' (Hayashi 1985, 1988). In the case of Japanese affiliates overseas, these interfaces act as a liaison between the Japanese top management and the local employees.

Almost always Japanese, these interfaces interpret, explain and pass on directives, opinions and decisions of higher echelons down the line and, at the same time, communicate 'bottom-up' those concerns, ideas and suggestions voiced by local employees.

Though obviously a function of great importance, reference to this interface role is relatively scarce in the literature. This may partly reflect the fact that in practice this 'tool' remains unmanaged, unplanned and generally not far advanced. Park (1989), for instance, who distinguishes between an 'enterprise-internal' and a 'concern-internal' interface (p. 210), found no correlation between the existence of an enterprise-internal interface and its adequate consideration within a framework of comprehensive personnel development planning (p. 211).

While the position of a concern-internal interface, i.e. a (Japanese) communicator between the parent company in Japan and its overseas subsidiary, serves to assure an unhampered transfer of resources and information to and from the parent company and an integration of activities into the concern-wide policies and strategies, the enterprise-internal interface is confronted with the crucial 'multicultural' task of reconciling different culturally influenced perceptions and interests among various intra-organizational groups and hierarchies, as well as those of customers, government representatives, unions and the general public.

The literature, reflecting on possible misperceptions, misunderstandings or 'communication traps' between those interrelated groups and individuals, proposes bridging those gaps through 'third-culture groups' (Fayerweather 1982: 440) by assigning the interface task to a mixed group of Japanese and locals. While this proposal indicates the difficulties a single or a few individuals face when assuming a comprehensive interface-role, often creating a typical 'bottle-neck' situation,[6] its actual realization in practice proves to be difficult, as 'the cultural gap remains an important obstacle to communication in the MNC (multinational corporation)' (ibid.).

Instead, via a preliminary interface stage, a more promising road to success seems to be the involvement of as many employees as possible in the acculturation process. As Sera (1992) reports, various methods are actually being employed and tested, such as an increased usage of intercultural small-group activities (quality circles, environmental protection committees, cost-reduction committees etc.) and a transfer of local employees to Japan for up to two years. Evidently, a proper theoretical (and practical) treatment of the interface concept must be to consider the reasons for their employment and, at the same time, analyse new limitations and problems they create through their very existence.

It appears that the interface solution to a multicultural management can only be an intermediate one, calling for a much broader and more comprehensive concept of organizational learning and development.

ORGANIZATIONAL LEARNING – THE CORE OF THE CONCEPT

Learning through implementing ideas is not confined to the strategic spheres alone, as the widely reflected debate on the transferability of Japanese management (techniques) has shown. Anecdotal evidence (Merz 1991; Fayerweather 1982) suggests that a gradual transfer and adjustment of what may be labelled Japanese management has resulted in a smoother and more successful acceptance by local managers, willing to integrate into the Japanese company.

Learning involves finding the 'right blend' (Thurow 1986: 6) between economic incentives and restraints on the one hand and cultural requirements on the other. We may, for analytical reasons, consider learning to take place on different levels:

- in the organization as an entity on its own
- at the management level and
- by the individual within the organization.

(Wolff 1982)

Organization learning

Organizational learning involves adjustment processes by which organizations react to changes in the environment as well as processes whereby the organization actively improves the fits between the organization and its environment (Hedberg 1981: 3). It has been debated whether organizations learn by themselves or whether this learning occurs through individuals. However, as Hedberg (1981: 3) points out,

> it would be a mistake to conclude that organizational learning is nothing but the cumulative result of their members' learning. Organizations do not have brains, but they have cognitive systems and memories. As individuals develop their personalities, personal habits, and beliefs over time, organizations develop world views and ideologies. Members come and go, and leadership changes, but organizations' memories preserve certain behaviours, mental maps, norms, and values over time.

Standard operating procedures, customs, symbols, myths and organizational sagas all contribute to what we typically refer to as the managerial and organizational culture discussed above. Changes within this culture through development processes induced by organizational learning, i.e. learning, unlearning and relearning of maps about the environment and using these maps to alter this environment, have an influence on the learning of individuals and groups within the organization. Organizational theories about (international) organizations must therefore attempt to study the factors influencing or inhibiting such learning and change, envisaging the ideal of a learning, flexible organization capable of balancing the needs for corporate change and stability, reconciling cumulated experiences with new visions, adjusting between long- and short-term goals, strategies of globalization and localization or tight and loose control mechanisms (Wolff 1982).

Managerial and individual learning

It is useful to consider the management/individual employee dichotomy when considering aspects of learning insofar as at the management level we are confronted with problems such as strategy formulation, the integration into the overall corporate activities, leadership styles etc. In other words, it is the 'overall picture' and its change that is to be constantly adjusted to or influenced (i.e. learned).

At the level of the individual, however, we are confronted with such questions as individuals' perceptions and definitions of roles and tasks, their performance and their (group-related) behaviour at the workplace.

Both managerial and individual learning are crucial elements for successfully managing the foreign subsidiary. This requires, as a first step, that Japanese and local employees learn about each others' perceptions and motivations. This will lead to the creation of trust and mutual understanding, strengthening the ability to co-operate and, eventually, to act and react flexibly and successfully in local environments.

THE PRACTICE OF LEARNING

Any attempt to improve interpersonal, intercultural relations should ideally pursue a step-by-step approach, fostering the ability to learn to solve problems within groups, as workplace situations are typically group oriented.

Learning and, more specifically, learning to learn, however, is more than simply searching for alternative solutions to less-than-satisfactory results.

People tend to be far more solution-minded than problem-oriented. Perhaps the major benefit for a problem-solving framework . . . is that it forces people to concentrate on defining the problem and considering a variety of alternatives before jumping to solutions. Diagnosis is a critical step in this process, because a full understanding of the problem and its various elements is necessary for the development of good solution alternatives.

(Morris and Sashkin 1976a: 123)

Learning how to learn thus involves three categories:

- the knowledge or conceptual understanding of the situation or problem at hand,
- the skills necessary for reacting to or actively transforming the problem,
- an attitudinal response, i.e. an open-mindedness congenial to the complexity of real problem situations.

A framework for learning

Incorporating these categories or conditions into an 'integrated problem solving' (IPS) framework, Morris and Sashkin have presented a course of action whereby diagnostic and action-oriented skills and procedures are acquired (Table 15.1)

Phase I, the problem definition phase, deals with the explanation and identification of the general problem area. Information is obtained and provided by all people involved in the problem situation. Furthermore, a consensus about the goals to be reached is developed. The problem-solution generation (phase II) usually employs a brainstorming method, attempting to generate solution ideas, refining them into alternatives and listing a variety of these alternatives.

Table 15.1 The phases of integrated problem solving

The task phases		The interaction phases	
Phase I:	Problem definition	Phase I:	Sharing information
Phase II:	Problem solution generation	Phase II:	Working as a group
Phase III:	Ideas to action	Phase III:	Developing consensus
Phase IV:	Solution action planning	Phase IV:	Making action commitment
Phase V:	Solution evaluation planning	Phase V:	Making evaluation commitments
Phase VI:	Solution evaluation	Phase VI:	Problem-solving process evaluation

Source: Morris and Sashkin 1976b: 5

Ideas generated for possible action are evaluated, modified and combined in phase III. A trial alternative is selected through a solution consensus. Phases IV and V are concerned with planning the solution action and evaluating it. Possible action steps and evaluative measures are listed, including their timing and the resources needed, and action responsibilities are determined. All group members are to be involved, possible resistance must be dealt with openly and commitments for action and evaluation are to be developed. Finally, in phase VI, outcomes are compared with objectives, new problems created within the foregoing process are analysed, and further necessary actions are determined. Also, the process of learning and the group behaviour, i.e. its members' interactions, are evaluated.

Through learning concepts such as the IPS method, it is hypothesized that, by individuals' learning to solve problems better in groups, the groups, and consequently the whole organization, will become more adaptable and more effective (Morris and Sashkin 1976a: 9).

LEARNING IN JAPANESE AFFILIATES

Arguing for the need to foster organizational learning within Japanese subsidiaries overseas in order to cope with the complex problems of, among others, culturally related differences within their workforce, we have tested the IPS method with Japanese and local employees of Japanese affiliates in the manufacturing and service sector. Within the framework of such a workshop, it was only possible to reach stage IV of the IPS process, mainly due to the fact that participants were not from the same company, rendering any action initiative almost impossible. However, in terms of analytical progress, important insights, including interesting theoretical insights into the organizational situation of these affiliates, may be gained by commonly working through the first four stages.

The appendix presents an overview of the results and inputs derived from the participants. Here, we make a few specific observations.

Contrary to expectations, Japanese expatriates were highly interested in participating, thus confirming the hypothesis that there is a perceived need on the management side for some careful and in-depth analysis of the intercultural issues within these organizations.

Problems of communication reach beyond the language issue. Different perceptions and misunderstandings are related to (culturally) diverging conceptions and emotionally charged opinions about such issues as work, interpersonal relations, responsibility and commitment.

These differences of values, norms, perceptions or intentions do not completely evade careful scrutiny, but they can instead be commonly made explicit, thus making them available for analysis and change.

The process of reconciling cultural differences does not necessarily have to be confined to one person or role (interface), but this approach can and should instead involve as many persons as possible, thereby facilitating subsequent implementation processes of organizational change.

In the long run, this type of planned and guided organizational learning may, by enhancing trust and commitment among organizational members through a joint process of improving communication, be the economically more viable solution.

CONCLUSION: ORGANIZATIONAL DEVELOPMENT – A BROADENED PERSPECTIVE

Apart from the practical application of learning models such as the IPS model, employing this concept as a tool to enhance organizational effectiveness in Japanese affiliates overseas, bridging communication gaps and improving the flexibility of actions in a volatile and highly competitive environment that is increasingly conditioned by political manoeuvres directed against international trade and investment, the idea of learning in and by organizations must be embedded in a broader concept of organizational development (OD).

An innovative and future-oriented OD as a systematic approach strives to create a structural climate that does not fruitlessly search for an optimal organizational setting, but instead treats change as a natural and necessary occurrence in the life of an organization. 'Organizational changes are often a clear statement of commitment to the objectives of international involvement' (Welch and Luostarinen 1988: 42), and an organizational culture positively affected by OD mechanisms will support and guide members to actively search for factors (norms, values, structural obstacles etc.) impeding this process of internationalization.

Concerning the individual Japanese affiliate overseas, the development of a multicultural management will thus include (at least) the following elements (Harvey and Brown 1976: 48):

1 an emphasis, although not exclusively so, on group and organizational processes,
2 an emphasis on the work team as the key unit for learning more effective modes of organizational behaviour,
3 an emphasis on the collaborative management of work team culture,

4   an emphasis on the management of the culture of the total system and
    total system ramifications,
5   the use of the action research model.

The interface currently used to facilitate communication may act as a
'change agent' to initiate OD efforts. It will be theory's task to critically
assess and accompany these processes in search of a modern, comprehensive and practical theory of international management. Here, once
again, Japanese experiences may be a valuable case in point.

APPENDIX: CO-OPERATION BETWEEN JAPANESE AND GERMAN EMPLOYEES IN JAPANESE SUBSIDIARIES – A WORKSHOP APPROACH TO ORGANIZATIONAL LEARNING

Participants

Japanese and German employees of Japanese subsidiaries in Germany
from the manufacturing and service industry.

Goals

• to identify typical problem situations of effective co-operation
• to analyse obstacles negatively influencing intercultural, effective
  co-operation
• to generate possible solutions and evaluate them in terms of their
  feasibility

Design

1   After an introductory session, participants are asked to answer
    spontaneously the question: 'How do you assess the co-operation
    between Japanese and German employees?' All answers are visibly
    recorded and the entire group evaluates them using a four-point scale
    (good, satisfactory, need to improve, strong need to improve)
2   Participants are then separated into a Japanese and a German group,
    supervised and guided by native moderators. Two questions are
    assigned to each group:

    'Which major difficulties do you perceive in co-operating with
    your Japanese (German) colleagues?'
    'Where do you see the greatest need for improvement?'

Answers are visibly recorded, assorted into clusters by the whole group and evaluated in terms of the second question. Perceived needs are ranked according to the scores attributed to them by each participant, representing their importance.

In a second round, participants are asked to consider two additional questions in a similar way:

> 'Which solutions to the perceived problems do you propose?'
> 'Which of these proposals can be best realized?'

3 The two groups are reunited, each group presenting its results and the process of achieving these results to the other. Results and proposals are discussed and evaluated.

Results

- The following are the results of a workshop attended by six Japanese and six German participants. Answers are ranked according to their evaluation by participants. High scores are equivalent to a high perceived need for improvement and the possibility of realization, respectively.

German group:

> 'Which major difficulties do you perceive in co-operating with your Japanese colleagues?'
> 'Where do you see the greatest need for improvement?'

- No clear 'no' or critical comments/feedback (7 points)
- Different solution methods – written contract-orientation (German) versus oral communication (Japanese) (6)
- General language problems/misunderstandings in communication processes (5)
- No access to information (4)
- Japanese managers are too strongly oriented on the parent company (2)
- German employees do not identify with the company (0)
- Japanese-style decision processes are not perceived as decision oriented (0)

> 'Which solutions to the perceived problems do you propose?'
> 'Which of these proposals can be best realized?'

- Mediation for co-ordination through an interface (6)
- Joint Japanese–German top management (3)

- Independent European headquarters with European managers in top positions (2)
- Intercultural training on Japanese-style non-verbal communication (2)
- Preparation for Japanese managers prior to coming to Germany

Japanese group:

> 'Which major difficulties do you perceive in co-operating with your German colleagues?'
> 'Where do you see the greatest need for improvement?'

- Germans shirk responsibility, do not excuse themselves and hide their weakness (6)
- Language and communications problems, partly due to shortened work hours on the German side (5)
- High egoism and selfishness, low flexibility (3)
- Inadequate team orientation (2)
- 'Different mentality' used as excuse, Germans do not enjoy work (1)

> 'Which solutions to the perceived problems do you propose?'
> 'Which of these proposals can be best realized?'

- Japanese must learn to become more assertive (5)
- Japanese companies must adapt to German working hours (2)
- Job descriptions need to be more detailed to avoid conflicts (2)
- Differences of perception and expression of thoughts must be mutually learned (2)
- Japanese should teach their colleagues that an excuse can have positive connotations/effects (1)

It must be pointed out that these results are only a very cursory summary of the workshop, since the problem identification and analysis and the solution generation and evaluation processes are of major importance. However, the list does give an impression of the discussion's content and direction.

NOTES

1 In Germany, for example, 42.2 per cent of all Japanese subsidiaries have been established in the last decade (Heidrick and Struggles 1990). For a data overview, see also JETRO (1991a).
2 Hirata (1991: 343), for example, points out a survey conducted by Toyo Keiza Shinposha, according to which by far the two most important goals for investment were 'increase of sales' and the 'collection of information' in the

host country, two reasons for which a simple sales office would suffice, were it not for protectionist pressures to move abroad.

3 As several labels for this strand of theory exist, we shall henceforward simply refer to it as IM theory (international management theory).

4 We are careful to avoid the word 'planning', as these processes can at best be influenced but probably never fully 'handled'.

5 National culture here is, as a matter of simplicity, understood to be synonymous with 'ethnoculture', although of course a more careful distinction is called for.

6 Anecdotal evidence found by the author as well as reported by, for example, Merz (1991), reveals that an interface, intentionally or not, acts as an informational filter, sometimes leaving doubt about who actually manages the affiliate.

REFERENCES

Abo, T. (1989) 'The emergence of Japanese multinational enterprise and the theory of foreign direct investment', in K. Shibagaki, M. Trevor and T. Abo (eds) *Japanese and European Management*, Tokyo: Univ. of Tokyo Press, pp. 3–17.

Abo, T. (1991) 'Sanyo's overseas production activities: seven large plants in US, Mexico, Germany, Spain, UK and China', in *Proceedings of the 1991 Symposium of the Euro-Asia Management Studies Association*, Euro-Asia Centre INSEAD.

Dülfer, E. (1991) *Internationales Management*, München: Oldenbourg.

Fayerweather, J. (1982) *International Business Strategy and Administration*, 2nd edn, Cambridge, MA: Ballinger.

Ghoshal, S. and Nohria, N. (1989) 'Internal differentiation within multinational corporations', *Strategic Management Journal*, 10: 323–37.

Günther, D. and von der Osten, B. (1991) 'Japanisches Management in der Bundesrepublik', in S.-J. Park (ed.) *Japanisches Management in der Bundesrepublik*, Frankfurt: Campus, pp. 11–69.

Harvey, D. and Brown, D. (1976) *An Experiential Approach to Organization Development*, Englewood Cliffs, NJ: Prentice-Hall.

Hayashi, K. (1985) *Ibunka Intafeisu Kanri*, Tokyo: Yuikaku.

Hayashi, K. (1988) 'Kaigai Kogaisha no Genchikeiei', in H. Yoshihara, K. Hayashi and K. Yasumuro (eds) *Nihon Kigyo no Gurobaru Keiei*, Tokyo: Toyo Keizai. pp. 143–170.

Hedberg, B. (1981) 'How organizations learn and unlearn', in P. Nystrom and W. Starbuck (eds) *Handbook of Organizational Design*, vol. 1, Oxford: Oxford University Press.

Heidrick and Struggles (1990) *Japanische Unternehmen in der Bundesrepublik Deutschland und ihre Personalsituation*, Düsseldorf: Heidrick and Struggles International.

Hirata, M. (1991) 'Die Reaktion japanischer Unternehmen auf den europäischen Binnenmarkt', *Die Betriebswirtschaft*, 51 (3): 341–53.

Hofstede, G. (1980) *Culture's Consequences*, Beverly Hills, CA: Sage.

Hofstede, G., Neuijen, B., Ohayv, D. and Sanders, G. (1990) 'Measuring organizational cultures: a qualitative and quantitative study across twenty cases', *Administrative Science Quarterly*, 35: 286–316.

Hymer, S. (1976) *The International Operations of National Firms: A Study of Direct Investment*, Cambridge, MA: MIT Press.

JETRO (1991a) *1991 JETRO White Paper on Foreign Direct Investment*, JETRO Special Report, Summary, Tokyo: JETRO.

JETRO (1991b) *7th Survey of European Operations of Japanese Companies in the Manufacturing Sector*, Tokyo: JETRO.

Johanson, J. and Mattsson, L.G. (1986) 'International marketing and internationalization processes – a network approach', in P. Turnbull and S. Paliwoda (eds) *Research in International Marketing*, London: Croom Helm, pp. 234–265.

von Keller, E. (1982) *Management in fremden Kulturen*, Bern: P. Haupt.

Kidd, J.B. (1991) 'Globalisation through localisation: reflections on the Japanese production subsidiaries in the United Kingdom', in *Proceedings of the 1991 Symposium of the Euro-Asia Management Studies Association*, Euro-Asia Centre INSEAD.

Kumar, B. and Steinmann, H. (1986) 'Japanische Führungskräfte in Deutschland', *Zeitschrift für betriebswirtschaftliche Forschung*, 38 (6): 493–516.

Merz, H.-P. (1991) 'Sand im Getriebe. Aus dem Alltag der Arbeitsbeziehungen in japanischen Auslandsniederlassungen', in S.-J. Park (ed.) *Japanisches Management in der Bundesrepublik*, Frankfurt: Campus, pp. 111–46.

Mintzberg, H. (1990) 'The design school: reconsidering the basic premises of strategic management', *Strategic Management Journal*, 11: 171–95.

Morris, W. and Sashkin, M. (1976a) *Organization Behaviour in Action*, St Paul, MN: West Publishing.

Morris, W. and Sashkin, M. (1976b) *Organization Behaviour in Action. Instructor's Manual*, St Paul, MN: West Publishing.

Park, S.-J. (1989) 'Personnel management of Japanese subsidiaries in West Germany', in K. Shibagaki, M. Trevor and T. Abo (eds) *Japanese and European Management*, Tokyo: University of Tokyo Press, pp. 206–13.

Pausenberger, E. (1989) 'Plädoyer für eine 'Internationale Betriebswirtschaftslehre', in W. Kirsch and A. Picot (eds) *Die Betriebswirtschaftslehre im Spannungsfeld zwischen Generalisierung und Spezialisierung*, Wiesbaden: Gabler, pp. 382–96.

Rugman, A., Lecraw, D. and Booth, L. (1985) *International Business. Firm and Environment*, New York: McGraw-Hill.

Schein, E. (1984) 'Coming to a new awareness of organizational culture', *Sloan Management Review*, 25 (2), Winter: 3–16.

Schneider, S. (1989) 'Strategy formulation: the impact of national culture', *Organization Studies*, 10 (2): 149–68.

Sera, M. (1992) 'Rolle des Interface bei der Kommunikation im multinationalen Unternehmen', in D. Dirks and I. Yamaguchi (eds) *Unternehmens- kultur japanischer Unternehmen in Deutschland: Proceedings of a Symposium held at Witten/Herdecke University*, November 1991, Witten/ Germany: Witten/Herdecke University.

Sullivan, D. and Bauerschmit, A. (1991) 'The "basic concepts" of international business strategy: a review and reconsideration', *Management International*

Review, Special Issue, 31: 111–24.

Thurow, L. (1986) 'Introduction', in L. Thurow (ed.) *The Management Challenge. Japanese Views*, Cambridge, MA: MIT Press, pp. 1–17.

Trevor, M. (1983) *Japan's Reluctant Multinationals*, London: Frances Pinter.

Turnbull, P. (1987) 'A challenge to the stages theory of the internationalization process', in P. Rosson and S. Reid (eds) *Managing Export Entry and Expansion*, New York: Praeger, pp. 21–40.

Welch, L. and Luostarinen, R. (1988) 'Internationalization: evolution of a concept', *Journal of General Management*, 14 (2): 34–55.

Welge, M. (1990) 'Globales Management', in M. Welge (ed.) *Globales Management. Erfolgreiche Strategien für den Weltmarkt*, Stuttgart: C.E. Poeschel, pp. 1–16.

Wolff, R. (1982) *Der Prozess des Organisierens*, Spardorf: Wilfer.

Yoshihara, H. (1989) 'The bright and the dark sides of Japanese management overseas', in K. Shibagaki, M. Trevor and T. Abo (eds) *Japanese and European Management*, Tokyo: University of Tokyo Press, pp. 18–30.

Chapter 16

Supplier relations in the Japanese auto industry
An empirical comparison with the US industry

M. Bensaou

ABSTRACT

This chapter presents and comments on the differences in buyer–supplier co-ordination practice between US and Japanese automobile manufacturers. Based upon the empirical findings from a cross-sectional study of supplier relationships in the two national settings, we examine for a wide range of different components and companies (a) the characteristics of the environment within which a relationship operates (i.e. characteristics of the supply market, economic and climate characteristics of the relationship and task characteristics of boundary spanners), and (b) the co-ordination mechanisms in terms of structures, processes and technologies put in place for the effective co-ordination between the assembler and its supplier.

We discuss the existence of two internally consistent yet inherently different co-ordination practices in the USA and Japan. We conclude that US practice is changing, but that the piecemeal adoption of Japanese practice, which has so far been achieved, is only a partial solution.

INTRODUCTION

In response to the new strategic challenges of global competition many firms are undergoing profound organizational transformations. They are streamlining their operations, typically moving away from traditional vertical integration towards more external contracting of activities. These emerging inter-organizational arrangements imply much higher levels of interdependence between a focal firm and its growing network of business partners. The input of any member firm (e.g. its product design, quality or cost structure) significantly and directly affects the value-adding process as well as the performance of the focal firm (e.g. time to market, price structure, design and manufacturing quality, delivery and inventory constraints).

Despite the importance of these changes, managers and researchers alike still have little understanding of the new organizational, managerial and technological skills necessary for the effective co-ordination of these changing interfirm relationships. In particular, we need to develop a better understanding of how different relationships are co-ordinated differently and why. In this chapter we offer to examine these two questions in the specific context of buyer–supplier relationships in the US and Japanese automobile industries, which have been described as typical of the organizational transformations reshaping many other industries.

To define and describe how two firms co-ordinate across their organizational boundaries we distinguish between the (i) structural, (ii) process and (iii) technological characteristics of the relationship. Structure represents the use of various organizational mechanisms for information exchange such as contracts, pre-defined rules and procedures, liaison personnel, task forces or teams. Technological characteristics represent the use of information technology and telecommunications applications, such as electronic data interchange (EDI), to exchange data across firm boundaries. Process characteristics represent the socio-political reality of the relationship and can be described by conflict and its resolution, joint action or interfirm co-operation and mutual commitment. Under the same structure and using the same technology co-ordination capabilities will tend to decrease in a negative, conflictual and non-cooperative climate.

To understand the differences in co-ordination between one relationship and another we identify three contextual dimensions: (i) the characteristics of the supply market for the given part or component (e.g. concentration, stability of the market), (ii) the economic and climate characteristics of the relationship (e.g. interdependence, mutual trust) and (iii) the characteristics of the boundary roles in the relationship, such as purchasing and engineering (e.g. routineness, structuredness of the tasks).

The following discussions and conclusions are based upon the findings from the research conducted by the author as part of the Massachusetts Institute of Technology (MIT) International Motor Vehicle Programme (IMVP). The results derive from industry interviews and questionnaire data for a representative sample of 447 buyer–supplier relationships in the US and Japanese auto industries. The question- naires, collected during the summer of 1991, were used to capture the six dimensions described above. The objective of this chapter is then to present and discuss the differences in co-ordination practices across the two countries, and draw some implications for the US industry.

MANUFACTURER–SUPPLIER CO-ORDINATION IN THE US/JAPANESE AUTO INDUSTRIES

Supplier relations in the US auto industry have been described as undergoing major changes, indicating far-reaching transformations in the way automobile production and automobile companies themselves are organized (Helper 1987; Lamming 1989; Nishiguchi 1989; Womack *et al.* 1990). Traditionally, auto makers designed the car, manufactured nearly all the necessary core components and co-ordinated final production. The trend, however, is towards a car company becoming the co-ordinator of an increasingly intricate production network, typically purchasing many core components, thus reducing its level of vertical integration and increasing the number and relative importance of relations with suppliers.

At the same time, the climate and governance of supplier relations seem to be changing, moving away from the traditional model where a large number of suppliers were competing for short-term contracts on the primary basis of price. The trend is for the assembler to establish longer-term contracts and work more closely with suppliers to ensure that problems of financing, design, quality, delivery and cost are tackled at the earliest opportunity and resolved co-operatively. The process involves a smaller number of suppliers capable of providing a greater share of the value of the product and competing on quality, delivery and engineering capabilities as well as price.

To examine empirically the extent and nature of this trend, questionnaires (in English and Japanese) were administered to a large and representative sample of managers from all auto firms in the USA and Japan. Two central boundary roles, i.e. purchasing managers and engineers, from the manufacturer side were asked to provide information about the relationship with a single supplier for only one component. Thus results were derived from 447 independent observations of manufacturer–supplier relationships in the two national settings (see Table 16.1 for response pattern across firms). The questionnaire used and the detailed results will be found in Bensaou (1992).

We first discuss below differences in the underlying assumptions and conditions under which supplier relations currently operate in the two countries. For each relationship we have data about (a) the characteristics

Table 16.1 Number of responses from purchasing and engineering managers

	Purchasing	Engineering	Total
US auto firms			
in the USA			
A	32	24	56
B	10	10	20
C	22	22	44
D	20	–	20
Total	84	56	140
Japanese firms			
E	14	–	14
F	26	24	50
G	9	16	25
H	1	1	2
I	2	2	4
J	24	24	48
K	25	25	50
L	22	23	45
M	10	10	20
N	12	13	25
O	24	–	24
Total	169	138	307
All	253	194	447

of the supply market, (b) the economic and climate characteristics of the relationship and (c) the characteristics of the respondents' job.

The characteristics of the supply market

The characteristics of the supply market for components, as shown in Figure 16.1, dramatically differ across the US and Japanese auto industries. US component markets exhibit greater market instability and lower market concentration. This seems to indicate that the US supply market still operates under traditional market mechanisms, where manufacturers spread their business among many potential suppliers (Table 16.2). In contrast, there is little change in the number and composition of competitors for the supply of a component in the Japanese supply industry (i.e. higher market stability). Mostly, the same few suppliers have been and are still competing in the same market segments and deliver a much broader range of parts to the manufacturer (i.e. lower average number of distinct parts sourced from one supplier). Also, in spite of their larger number of suppliers (and purchasing staff), US manufacturers are still producing internally a greater proportion of a component's total volume (i.e. greater internal sourcing and lower external sourcing). Interviews with US suppliers revealed that the big three still want to keep their suppliers in competition with their internal divisions.

In contrast, Japanese manufacturers design and manufacture fewer components, and on average outsource a greater proportion of the total volume for a component. They maintain only a few potential suppliers (i.e. greater market concentration), who typically have the design and manufacturing skills and capabilities to produce a wide range of related components. According to Asanuma (1989), Japanese auto makers rarely practice sole sourcing, and usually share the business for a given component among two or three suppliers who compete in areas of technology development, improvement in process, product, quality and cost.

Japanese manufacturers' strategy is to concentrate on their core competencies, keeping in-house the design and manufacture of the key components, technologies and systems that distinguish them from their competitors, but they rely heavily on an elaborate multi-tier structure of suppliers for other components (Mitsubishi Research Institute 1987). First-tier firms, generally larger ones, assemble and deliver large integrated systems, and together carry much of the burden and responsibility for the co-ordination of second- and third-tier suppliers. This pyramid structure permits

> a form of vertical coordination within the industry that simultaneously provides the manufacturer benefits that are traditionally associated with high levels of vertical integration, such as control of the production process, profit opportunity, and protection of their technical core, and those associated with low degrees of vertical integration, such as low cost and a high degree of independence.
>
> (Flynn and Andrea 1989: 2)

Table 16.2 Automotive purchasing in the 1980s

	Number of suppliers	Number of purchasing staff	Vehicles built (millions)
GM in USA	2,500	4,000	5.1
Ford in USA	1,800	2,200	3.6
Toyota in Japan	340	185	4.2
Nissan in Japan	310	250	2.4

Source: Lamming 1990; IMVP Research and estimates

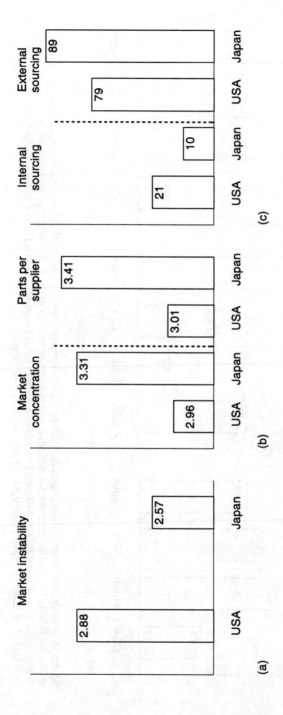

Figure 16.1 Characteristics of the supply market: (a) $t = 2.12$, $p < 0.05$, 1–7 scale; (b) market concentration, $t = -4.17$, $p < 0.001$, 1–7 scale; parts per supplier, $t = -3.01$, $p < 0.005$, 0–5 scale; (c) internal sourcing, $t = 2.95$, $p < 0.005$, 0–100 scale; external sourcing, $t = -2.73$, $p < 0.01$, 0–100 scale

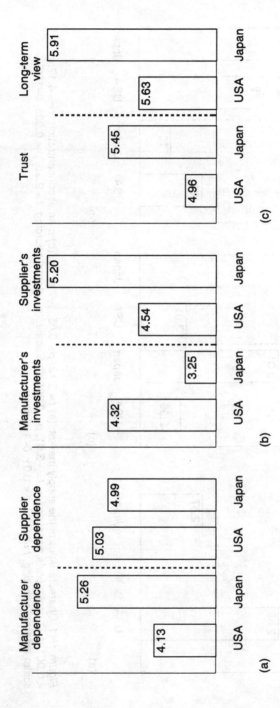

Figure 16.2 Economic and climate characteristics of the relationship with a supplier: (a) manufacturer dependence, $t = -6.76$, $p < 0.001$, 1–7 scale; supplier dependence, not significant at 0.05 level, 1–7 scale; (b) manufacturer's investments, $t = 8.41$, $p < 0.001$, 1–7 scale; supplier's investments, $t = -4.48$, $p < 0.001$, 1–7 scale; (c) trust, $t = -4.35$, $p < 0.001$, 1–7 scale; long-term view, $t = -2.29$, $p < 0.05$, 1–7 scale

Economic and climate characteristics of buyer–supplier relationships

The characteristics of the relationships reflect the differences in the market conditions discussed above. In their highly concentrated component markets, Japanese manufacturers have fewer viable alternative suppliers and thus perceive themselves to be more dependent on a specific supplier than are US firms (Figure 16.2). Indeed, faced with larger, more unstable and competitive component markets, US manufacturers can keep their switching costs and dependence on suppliers low. As for suppliers' dependence on manufacturers, the data show no significant difference across the two countries. In both cases component suppliers, generally smaller firms, are highly dependent on business with a single manufacturer.

US managers reported a higher score than Japanese managers when questioned on the extent to which they felt that they were making important investments specific to their relationship with a supplier. This may suggest that top management's vision for change is gradually diffusing within US organizations and affecting attitudes and behaviours. Another explanation for lower investments by Japanese manufacturers was offered by a Japanese manager: 'we have spent the last thirty years developing our relationship with our first-tier suppliers and we now let them do much of the design and development of the component . . . there is little we need to discover about each other any more . . . and we trust they will try hard to keep our business.' In other words, Japanese suppliers seem to be the ones in the relationship who are making the critical investments and efforts. US suppliers, in contrast, despite their high dependence on auto companies, seem to avoid tying their assets and investments to any one manufacturer, thus protecting their chance of contracts to supply any one of the big three or the Japanese transplants.

The high level of mutual interdependence in Japanese manufacturer–supplier relationships seems to foster higher mutual trust and a stronger predisposition to continue the relationship in the future (i.e. long-term view). We also found that Japanese supplier relations on average have a longer history (USA = 4.42, Japan = 4.90, $t = -4.03$, $p < 0.001$, 1–6 ordinal scale). Interviews with US suppliers revealed that relationships in the USA typically date back a long time but tend to be highly inconsistent and intermittent, with little assurance that long-term suppliers will get the contract the next time around.

Task characteristics of boundary roles

The task characteristics of purchasing and engineering also differ across the two countries, as shown in Figure 16.3. Task interdependence, i.e. the time purchasing managers and engineers spend working with a given supplier (e.g. in meetings, over the phone or on visits), is significantly higher in the US sample. A high turnover rate among suppliers may explain the need for more interaction just to keep track of a relationship. Japanese boundary roles, on the other hand, manage a larger portfolio of suppliers and components, thereby leveraging the synergy embedded in the multiple sharing of routines in co-ordination, communication, negotiation and joint production. We also find boundary roles in Japan to involve more structured, modularized and routine tasks than their US counterparts. Japanese managers attributed this difference to trust, a high level of information and knowledge exchange over the years and early involvement of the supplier in the design and development of the component. In contrast, US purchasing managers complained 'of too much time firefighting and bringing suppliers up to speed'.

In sum, supplier relations in the US and Japanese auto industry operate under very different sets of conditions. Markets for components are structured and regulated under different economic mechanisms, relationships reflect a different logic and different assumptions about effective governance, while the tasks that regulate the relationship are configured differently. Let us now turn to a discussion of the differences found across the two countries in their use of structure, process and information technology to increase effective co-ordination with suppliers.

Structural co-ordination mechanisms

This was measured along several dimensions, four of which exhibit interesting and significant differences: the frequency of visits to each other's location, the extent to which managers at the manufacturer work together with multiple functions from the supplier, managers' time allocation to different tasks that span the life cycle of the relationship, and the comparative use of different media (written mail, phone, fax, face-to-face) for co-ordination with external suppliers (see Figure 16.4).

US managers report more exchange of visits between them and their supplier, and Japanese managers report working together with a greater number of different functional areas in the supplier companies. The former finding seems to confirm and illustrate the efforts US

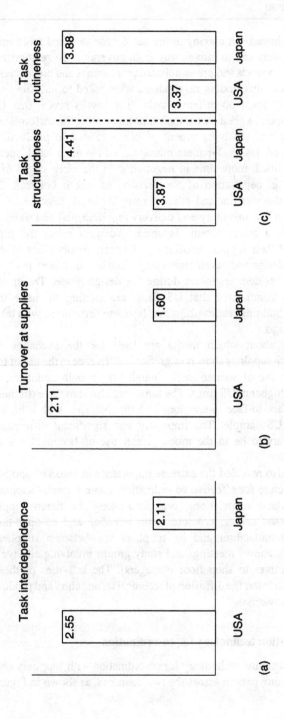

Figure 16.3 Task characteristics of boundary roles: (a) task interdependence, $t = 5.49$, $p < 0.001$, 1–7 scale; (b) turnover at suppliers, $t = 3.45$, $p < 0.001$, 1–5 scale; (c) task structuredness, $t = -6.64$, $p < 0.001$, 1–5 scale; task routineness, $t = -3.21$, $p < 0.005$, 1–7 scale

manufacturers have been making in the last decade to spend more time with their suppliers and to move away from governing the relationship simply through contracts and pre-established programmes and procedures.

To understand this finding respondents were asked to indicate how much time they spent on different tasks. The results reveal that US managers still spend a great part of their time monitoring the performance of the supplier and resolving urgent problems related to production, quality or delivery issues. Japanese managers, on the other hand, spend comparatively much more time in negotiation in the early stages of a relationship (e.g. negotiation of the division of labour between the manufacturer, the supplier and other players involved, negotiation of design, cost, quality, inventory and delivery requirements) and monitor the supplier to a lesser extent. Japanese managers relate the high performance of their supplier relations to the early involvement of the supplier in the design and development stages and the customary practice of exchanging resident engineers during the design phase. Transplant managers also commented that US firms are starting to make the investments in building relationships that Japanese firms made with their suppliers long ago.

The results about which media are used for the exchange of information with suppliers show no significant difference in the use of the telephone. The use of written mail, though low in both countries, is comparatively higher in US firms. The same data also show an extremely high level of face-to-face interactions in both countries, with a higher score for the US sample. The important and significant difference, however, appears to be in the much greater use of fax machines in Japanese firms.

Interviews also revealed the extreme importance in Japan of another distinctive structure for effective co-ordination, namely formal supplier associations. These associations, organized along the tiered supply pyramid discussed earlier, promote communication and co-operation between the manufacturer and its suppliers and between suppliers themselves (e.g. annual meetings and study groups involving all levels from top executives to shop floor managers). The activities of these associations also foster the diffusion of technical information and product and process innovations.

Use of information technology for co-ordination

The use of information technology for co-ordination with suppliers also offers a contrasting pattern across the two countries, as shown in Figure

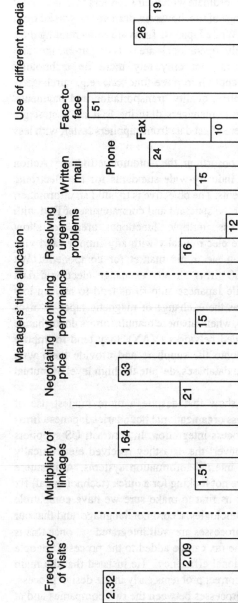

Figure 16.4 Structural co-ordination mechanisms, Japan versus USA: (a) frequency of visits, $t = 2.09$, $p < 0.05$, 0–3 scale; (b) negotiating price, $t = -2.06$, $p < 0.05$, 0–3 scale; monitoring performance, $t = 9.29$, $p < 0.001$, 0–100 scale; resolving urgent problems, $t = -8.10$, $p < 0.001$, 0–100 scale; (c) written mail, $t = 9.87$, $p < 0.001$; phone, not significant at 0.05 level; fax, $t = -8.23$, $p < 0.001$

16.5. First, Japanese manufacturers are making a greater use of information technology to co-ordinate with their suppliers than is usually expected. The pattern and scope of use, however, dramatically differ from US car companies' strategy. While Japanese firms are concentrating their investments in a few highly operational areas (i.e. purchasing and production control), US firms not only rely more on technology altogether, but also already apply it to more functions (e.g. purchasing, engineering, production control, quality, transportation and payment). Some US information systems managers describe EDI as 'a strategic weapon that should allow them to get data from suppliers faster, with less errors and at a lesser cost'.

US firms have created a consortium, the Automotive Industry Action Group (AIAG), to develop industry-wide standards for the electronic exchange of data and documents. The objective is to build an information technology infrastructure for the standard and common use of EDI with all potential suppliers across multiple functional areas to allow manufacturers to co-ordinate electronically with any supplier and vice versa, eventually creating an electronic market for components. We found, in particular, that US firms already exchange electronic data mainly over a network, while Japanese auto firms tend to rely on low technology solutions, such as the exchange of magnetic tapes or discs when not using the fax. Also, when Japanese manufacturers do exchange data over existing value-added networks (VAN), they tend to impose their proprietary standards onto the suppliers and provide them with restricted access to their own databases, despite the high level of mutual trust.

More importantly, data show that despite a more modest use of information technology across organizational boundaries Japanese firms achieve greater data and process integration. In contrast, US suppliers often need to re-enter or convert the data they received electronically before using them in their internal information systems. A Japanese manager commented, 'we are not looking for a quick (technological) fix . . . it is more important for us first to make sure we have compatible assessment methods and technologies, a common language, and that our scheduling and production processes are well integrated . . . once this is accomp- lished a tool like the fax can be added to the process if people think we can gain in operational efficiency'. He insisted that the main objectives are to detect and correct problems early in the design process, to integrate the production processes between the two companies and at the same time to ensure the perfect execution and co-ordination of these processes within each company.

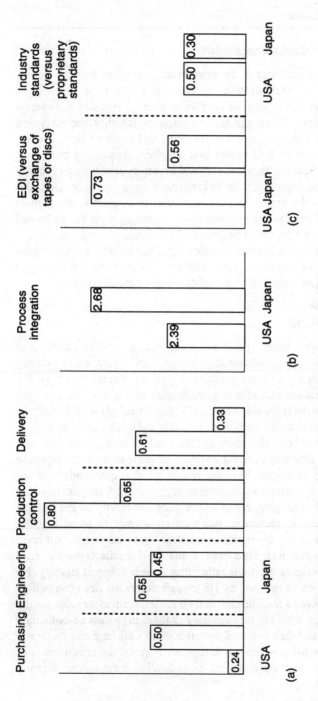

Figure 16.5 Use of information technology for co-ordination, Japan versus USA: (a) purchasing, $t = -5.37$, $p < 0.001$, 0–1 scale; engineering, not significant at 0.05 level; production control, $t = -4.78$, $p < 0.001$; (b) process integration, $t = -3.44$, $p < 0.001$, 0–3 scale; (c) EDI (versus exchange of tapes or discs), $t = 3.16$, $p < 0.005$, 0–1 scale; industry standards (versus proprietary standards), $t = 2.65$, $p < 0.01$, 0–1 scale

Process co-ordination mechanisms

The processes prevalent in the relationship can either foster or inhibit information exchange between manufacturer and supplier. Strikingly, a comparatively higher level of conflict or stress is revealed in Japanese supplier relations. This suggests a less harmonious reality than the typical image of Japanese management practices, and confirms that Japanese manufacturers exert their power over suppliers, demanding from them high levels of quality, tight delivery and inventory schedules and shorter lead times and expecting them to lower their costs over time. Data also show that, at the same time, the resolution of conflict is much more collaborative in Japanese relationships, contrasting with the traditional bargaining and adversarial practices of US firms. In addition, there is more co-operation in Japanese relationships, particularly in areas of joint design and development, together with more commitment (i.e. sharing of burden, risks and benefits) to the relationship by manufacturers.

CONCLUSIONS

The findings from the 447 independent observations of manufacturer–supplier relationships in the US and Japanese auto industry show two radically different models of buyer–supplier relationships. The fierce competition and virtual globalization of the auto industry has contributed to the recognition by the US 'Big Three' of the importance of their suppliers to their own bottom-line cost and quality performance, as shown in Figure 16.6. This has been followed by a variety of programmes to promote a new way of doing business adopting some of the Japanese co-ordination practices. Yet, the results of this quantitative survey corroborated by interview data seem to suggest that US supplier relations are effectively changing, but at a slow pace and mostly on the surface. These changes, in particular, represent an attempt to blend together elements of two internally consistent yet inherently different co-ordination practices. Their implementation also reflects more a series of reactive business decisions rather than a clear coherent strategy. No sustained action or measure by US manufacturers has been compelling enough to convey a realistic shift in their commitment to the relationship. Little attention is paid to the necessary changes in process co-ordination mechanisms and their potential contribution to a closer, more stable and trusting relationship which would together augment the effectiveness of the structural and technological co-ordination mechanisms recently implemented.

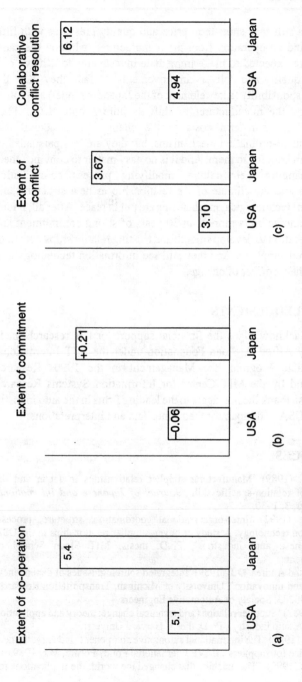

Figure 16.6 Process co-ordination mechanisms, Japan versus USA: (a) extent of co-operation, $t = 2.12$, $p < 0.05$, -3 to $+3$ scale; (b) extent of commitment, $t = 2.12$, $p < 0.05$, -3 to $+3$ scale; (c) extent of conflict, $t = -5.97$, $p < 0.001$, 1–7 scale; collaborative conflict resolution, $t = -8.54$, $p < 0.001$, 0–7 scale

Suppliers still face short-term price and quality pressures with little assistance and co-operation from the manufacturer, while at the same time they are expected to make immediate investments to achieve cost reductions, quality and delivery improvements. In fact, they view the increased responsibility (a key element of the Japanese model) as another way used by the manufacturer to shift its burden onto them. They understand the short-term costs of the changes in structural and technological co-ordination mechanisms, but they are less persuaded of the long-term benefits to them. And it is no easy matter to convince them without changing their culture, modifying process co-ordination mechanisms and the climate of the relationship as new structural and (information) technological mechanisms are put in place. After all, it took Japanese manufacturers more than 30 years of strong commitment and close co-operation to develop smooth and trusting relationships with their now preferred suppliers. And they still see information technology as a tool rather than a driver of change.

ACKNOWLEDGEMENTS

The author acknowledges the financial support for this research made available by Alfred P. Sloan Foundation under the MIT International Motor Vehicle Program, the Management in the 1990s Research Program, and by the MIT Center for Information Systems Research (CISR). I also thank the managers in the leading firms in the auto industry both in the USA and Japan for their time, data and interpretations.

REFERENCES

Asanuma, B. (1989) 'Manufacturer–supplier relationships in Japan and the concept of relation-specific skill', *Journal of Japanese and International Economies*, 3: 1–30.

Bensaou, M. (1992) 'Inter-organizational coordination: structure, process, information technology. A study of buyer–supplier relationships in the USA and Japanese auto industries', Ph.D. thesis, MIT Sloan School of Management.

Flynn, M.S. and Andrea, D.J. (1989) 'Integrated sourcing: issues of dependency, reliance, and innovation', University of Michigan, Transportation Research, Paper #890233, Society of Automotive Engineers.

Helper, S. (1987) 'Supplier relations and technical change: theory and application to the USA auto industry', Ph.D. thesis, Harvard University.

Lamming, R. (1989) 'The international automotive components industry: the next best practice for suppliers', IMVP International Policy Forum, May 1989.

Lamming, R. (1990). 'The machine that changed the world: the implications for component suppliers', Motor and Equipment Manufacturers Association Presentation, IMVP, September 1990.

Mitsubishi Research Institute, Inc. (1987) 'The relationship between Japanese auto and parts makers', 6 February.

Nishiguchi, T. (1989) 'Strategic dualism: an alternative in industrial societies', Ph.D. thesis, University of Oxford.

Womack, J.P., Jones, D.T. and Roos, D. (1990) *The Machine That Changed The World*, New York, Rawson Associates.

Index